Concise Dictionary of New Testament Words

E. Richard Pigeon, Ph.D.
with Gretchen S. Lebrun

Chattanooga, TN

Concise Dictionary of New Testament Words

Published by AMG Publishers
6615 Standifer Gap Rd.
Chattanooga, TN 37421

Based on and adapted from the *AMG's Comprehensive Dictionary of New Testament Words* (2014) and the *Dictionnaire du Nouveau Testament* (2008).

ISBN: 978-1-61715-630-4
E-book: 978-1-61715-631-1

Cover design by Amanda Jenkins, AMG Publishers.
Text Design and layout by PerfecType, Nashville, TN.

Printed in the United States of America

Abbreviations and Sign

Old Testament Books

Gen.	→	Genesis
Ex.	→	Exodus
Lev.	→	Leviticus
Num.	→	Numbers
Deut.	→	Deuteronomy
Josh.	→	Joshua
Judg.	→	Judges
Ruth	→	Ruth
1 Sam.	→	1 Samuel
2 Sam.	→	2 Samuel
1 Kgs.	→	1 Kings
2 Kgs.	→	2 Kings
1 Chr.	→	1 Chronicles
2 Chr.	→	2 Chronicles
Ezra	→	Ezra
Neh.	→	Nehemiah
Esther	→	Esther
Job	→	Job
Ps.	→	Psalms
Prov.	→	Proverbs
Eccl.	→	Ecclesiastes
Song	→	Song of Solomon
Is.	→	Isaiah
Jer.	→	Jeremiah
Lam.	→	Lamentations
Ezek.	→	Ezekiel
Dan.	→	Daniel
Hos.	→	Hosea
Joel	→	Joel
Amos	→	Amos
Obad.	→	Obadiah
Jon.	→	Jonah
Mic.	→	Micah
Nah.	→	Nahum
Hab.	→	Habakkuk
Zeph.	→	Zephaniah
Hag.	→	Haggai
Zech.	→	Zechariah
Mal.	→	Malachi

New Testament Books

Matt.	→	Matthew	1 Tim.	→	1 Timothy
Mark	→	Mark	2 Tim.	→	2 Timothy
Luke	→	Luke	Titus	→	Titus
John	→	John	Phm.	→	Philemon
Acts	→	Acts	Heb.	→	Hebrews
Rom.	→	Romans	Jas.	→	James
1 Cor.	→	1 Corinthians	1 Pet.	→	1 Peter
2 Cor.	→	2 Corinthians	2 Pet.	→	2 Peter
Gal.	→	Galatians	1 John	→	1 John
Eph.	→	Ephesians	2 John	→	2 John
Phil.	→	Philippians	3 John	→	3 John
Col.	→	Colossians	Jude	→	Jude
1 Thes.	→	1 Thessalonians	Rev.	→	Revelation
2 Thes.	→	2 Thessalonians			

The sign ¶ at the end of an entry indicates that all N.T. references have been provided for this word.

Other Abbreviations

adj. (adjective, adjectival)
adv. (adverb, adverbial, adverbially)
approx. (approximately)
Aram. (Aramaic)
art. (article)
B.C. (before Christ)
cf. (compare, comparison)
comp. (compare)
compar. (comparative)
defin. (definition)
dimin. (diminutive)
Engl. (English)
etc. (*et cetera*: and so forth)
expr. (expression, expressions)

e.g. (*exempli gratia*: for example)
et al. (*et alii:* and others)
fem. (feminine)
figur. (figuratively)
Heb. (Hebrew, Hebraic)
i.e. (*id est*: that is)
incl. (including)
indef. (indefinite)
intens. (intensive)
KJV (King James Version)
Lat. (Latin)
lit. (literal, literally)
masc. (masculine)
mss. (manuscripts)
neg. (negative)
num. (number, numeral)
N.T. (New Testament)
O.T. (Old Testament)
pass. (passive)
plur. (plural)
poss. (possibly)
prep. (preposition, prepositional)
pres. (present)
prob. (probably)
pron. (pronoun, pronominal)
(in) re (in the matter of, about, concerning)
ref. (reference)
refs. (references)
sing. (singular)
syn. (synonym)
transl. (translated, translations)
v. (verse)
vs. (*versus*: as opposed to, against)
vv. (verses)

Preface

The entries of this *Concise Dictionary of New Testament Words* have been borrowed and adapted from the *AMG's Comprehensive Dictionary of New Testament Words* (2014) and the *Dictionnaire du Nouveau Testament* (2008). It includes all the names of people and places as well as more theologically significant common words found in the New Testament. Overall, there are more than 1,350 definitions in this Dictionary.

In this *Concise Dictionary*, we have often indicated all the Biblical references for the entries of the terms listed, thus allowing the work to serve also as a concordance. For each entry or sub-entry defining a term, the reader will find the English transliteration of the Greek word, the etymology of the word where applicable, a definition of the common word or the meaning of the proper name, paraphrased verses enabling the understanding of the context in which the term is used, and other N.T. references.

We trust that you will find this tool helpful in your reading and study of God's Word, as well as in your service for the Lord.

Thank you for your interest!

Richard Pigeon
October 2024

A

AARON (*Aarōn*) **Older brother of Moses.** He was an ancestor of Elizabeth (Luke 1:5). He made a golden calf (Acts 7:40). He represents Christ as high priest (Heb. 5:4). His staff had budded (Heb. 9:4). ¶

ABADDON (*Abaddōn*: destruction) **Hebrew term found in the O.T.** This name is given to the king of the locusts (Rev. 9:11; see Job 26:6; 28:22; 31:12). ¶

ABBA (*Abba*: Father) **Aram. term of affection meaning "father".** The expr. "Abba, Father" is used by Jesus at Gethsemane (Mark 14:36), Christian believers (Rom. 8:15), and the Spirit in them (Gal. 4:6). ¶

ABEL (*Abel*: vapor, vanity, in Heb.) **Second son of Adam and Eve.** He was called "righteous" (Matt. 23:35). He was killed by his brother Cain (Matt. 23:35; Luke 11:51; see Gen. 4:3-6). He offered to God a more excellent sacrifice (Heb. 11:4). See also Heb. 12:24. ¶

ABIA (*Abia*: the Lord is my father, in Heb.) **a. King of Judah, grandson of Solomon.** He is mentioned in the genealogy of Jesus Christ (Matt. 1:7). **b. Family of priests.** Zacharias is a member of it (Luke 1:5). ¶

ABIATHAR (*Abiathar*: the great one is father, in Heb.) **A priest in Israel.** He is mentioned by Jesus (Mark 2:26). ¶

ABIHUD (*Abioud*: father of renown, in Heb.) **Son of Zorobabel.** He is mentioned in the genealogy of Jesus Christ (Matt. 1:13). ¶

ABILENE (*Abilēnē*) **Region in the north of Israel (in Syria, northwest of Damascus).** Lysanias was its tetrarch (Luke 3:1). ¶

ABOMINATION (*bdelugma*; from *bdelussō*: to abhor, to detest) **A detestable, repulsive object in the eyes of God and Christians; it takes the place of God.** In Matt. 24:15 and Mark 13:14, mention is made of the abomination of desolation. Other refs.: Luke 16:15; Rev. 17:4, 5; 21:27. ¶

ABRAHAM (*Abraam*: father of a multitude, in Heb.) **Patriarch from whom the Israelites originate.** He believed God (Rom. 4:3). His faith was made perfect (Jas. 2:21, 23; see v. 22). He is the father of those who walk in faith (Rom. 4:12). He is called a friend of God (Jas. 2:23) and named as a man of faith (Heb. 11:8, 17). Abraham is mentioned in the genealogy of Jesus Christ (Matt. 1:1, 2; Luke 3:34).

ACCUSER (*katēgoros*; from *katēgoreō*: to speak against, to accuse) **One who charges another with an offence, who declares him guilty.** Accusers opposed Paul (Acts 23:30, 35; 24:8; 25:16, 18). Satan is the accuser of the brothers before God (Rev. 12:10). Other ref.: John 8:10 in some mss. ¶

ACELDAMA (*Hakeldama*: field of blood) **Place known as the "potter's field".** It was bought as a burial place for strangers (Acts 1:19; see Matt. 27:1–10). ¶

ACHAIA (*Achaia*: trouble) **Region of Ancient Greece in which Corinth was the capital.** Paul visited it (Acts 18:12, 27; 19:21). Christians from there made some contribution for the poor (Rom. 15:26). Stephanas was most likely one of the first converts there (1 Cor. 16:15). Other refs.: Rom. 16:5; 2 Cor. 1:1; 9:2; 11:10; 1 Thes. 1:7, 8. ¶

ACHAICUS (*Achaikos*: belonging to Achaia) **Christian who came to Corinth to visit Paul.** Paul rejoiced at his coming (1 Cor. 16:17). ¶

ACHIM (*Achim*: the Lord will establish, in Heb.) **Man in the O.T.** Achim is mentioned in the genealogy of Jesus Christ (Matt. 1:14). ¶

ADAM (*Adam*: ruddy, in Heb.) **Name of the first man.** By his disobedience, sin entered the world (1 Cor. 15:22). Jesus Christ is the "last Adam" (1 Cor. 15:45; see Rom. 5:14–21). Adam was created from dust (see 1 Cor. 15:47). Other refs.: Luke 3:38; 1 Tim. 2:13, 14; Jude 14. ¶

ADDI (*Addi*) **Man in the O.T.** He is mentioned in the genealogy of Jesus (Luke 3:28). ¶

ADJURE 1. (*horkizō*; from *horkos*: pledge, oath) **a. To solemnly entreat, to request earnestly.** A man with an evil spirit adjured Jesus not to torment him (Mark 5:7). Paul adjured the Thessalonians to have his letter read (1 Thes. 5:27). **b. To command.** Some exorcists were adjuring (trying to exorcise) evil spirits (Acts 19:13). ¶ **2.** (*exorkizō*; from *ek*: intens., and *horkizō*: to adjure) **To ask someone to testify, to order.** The high priest adjured Jesus to say if He was the Son of God (Matt. 26:63). ¶

ADMINISTRATION 1. (*diakonia*; from *diakonos*: servant, deacon) **What a servant must do, ministry.** The Corinthians had an administration of a service (2 Cor. 9:12). **2.** (*kubernēsis*; from *kubernaō*: to govern, to direct) **Spiritual gift that relates to the direction given to a local church**. Administration was given by God (1 Cor. 12:28). ¶

ADOPTION (*huiothesia*; from *huios*: son, and *tithēmi*: to place, to designate; lit.: sonship) **Act of taking legally as a son into one's family.** The Spirit of adoption is received by Christians (Rom. 8:15). They are waiting for it

(Rom. 8:23). It also belongs to the Israelites (Rom. 9:4). It has been made possible by the redemption accomplished by the Son of God (Gal. 4:5). Christians are predestined for it (Eph. 1:5). ¶

ADRAMYTTIUM (OF) (*Adramuttēnos*) **Port of Asia Minor on the Aegean Sea.** Paul boarded a ship returning to its home port of Adramyttium (Acts 27:2). ¶

ADRIATIC SEA (*Adrias*) **Part of the Mediterranean Sea between Italy and the Balkan Peninsula.** Paul faced a fierce storm on the Adriatic (Acts 27:27). ¶

ADULTERY 1. (*moicheia*; from *moicheuō*: to commit adultery) **Sexual intercourse outside marriage of which a married person is guilty.** It comes forth out of the heart (Matt. 15:19; Mark 7:21 or 22). It is a work of the flesh (Gal. 5:19). A woman caught in adultery was brought to Jesus (John 8:3). ¶ **2.** (to commit adultery: *moichaō* or *moicheuō*; from *moichos*: adulterer) **To have sexual intercourse outside marriage.** One can commit it in one's heart (Matt. 5:28). Other refs.: Matt. 5:27, 32; 19:9, 18; Jas. 2:11; Rev. 2:22.

ADVOCATE (*Paraklētos*; from *parakaleō*: to encourage) **One who defends the cause of someone else, who intercedes on his behalf; this includes the notions of helping, comforting, and encouraging.** It is a title of Jesus Christ the righteous (1 John 2:1). It also designates the Holy Spirit (John 14:16, 26; 15:26; 16:7). ¶

AENEAS (*Aineas*) **Paralyzed man of Lydda.** Peter healed him (Acts 9:33, 34). ¶

AENON (*Ainōn*) **Place in Israel near Salim.** John was baptizing there (John 3:23). ¶

AGABUS (*Hagabos*) **Christian prophet, poss. from Judea.** He foretold a great famine by the Holy Spirit (Acts 11:28). He also predicted that Paul would be made prisoner (Acts 21:10; see v. 11). ¶

AGE 1. (*aiōn*) **Period of time of undetermined duration; also transl.: world.** The word has this meaning, e.g., in Matt. 12:32; Luke 16:8. It is used in various expr.: **a.** "Before the ages of time": before creation (2 Tim. 1:9; Titus 1:2). It has the same meaning in the expr. "before the ages" (1 Cor. 2:7), "throughout the ages" (Eph. 3:9), "from ages" (Col. 1:26), and "from before the whole age" (Jude 25). **b.** "The ages" (Heb. 9:26) are those times prior to the first coming of the Lord. **c.** "The present age" began with the rejection of the Son of God (1 Tim. 6:17). Its characteristics are evil (Gal. 1:4), vanity, corruption, alienation from God (Matt. 13:39, 40; Rom. 12:2; 1 Cor. 1:20; 2:6, 8; 3:18; 2 Cor. 4:4; 2 Tim. 4:10; Titus 2:12). During this period, the Lord preserves His own (Matt. 28:20). **d.** "The coming age" then follows; it is characterized by the full power and dominion of the Lord Jesus (Mark 10:30; Luke 18:30; 20:35; Eph. 1:21; 2:7; Heb. 6:5). **e.** "The ages of ages" correspond to eternity, beyond time (Gal. 1:5; Eph. 3:21; Phil. 4:20; 1 Tim. 1:17; 2 Tim. 4:18). **2.** (*hēlikia*; from *hēlikos*: how great or from *hēlix*: comrade, of the same age) **a. Maturity, state of full development.** The word is used re a man born blind (John 9:21, 23), Sarah (Heb. 11:11). **b. Stature.** The word is used re Zaccheus (Luke 19:3). Other refs.: Luke 2:52; Eph. 4:13. ¶ **3.** (*hēmera*) **Day.** Anna was of a great age (Luke 2:36). **4.** (who has passed the flower of age: *huperakmos*; from *huper*: beyond, and *akmē*: point, tip) **Who has passed their prime.** Paul uses this word re an older person who is not married (1 Cor. 7:36). ¶

AGRIPPA (*Agrippas*) **This name refers to Herod Agrippa II, great-grandson of Herod the Great.** Paul made his defense before him. Refs.: Acts 25:13, 22–26; 26:1, 2, 7, 19, 27–32. ¶

AHAZ (*Achaz*: possessor, in Heb.) **King of Judah.** He is mentioned in the genealogy of Jesus Christ (Matt. 1:9). ¶

ALABASTER BOX (*alabastron*) **Alabaster is a variety of gypsum once commonly used to make boxes or flasks.** Such a box contained a very precious ointment poured out on the head of Jesus (Matt. 26:7; Mark 14:3). It contained myrrh used to anoint the feet of Jesus (Luke 7:37, 38). ¶

ALEXANDER (*Alexandros*: defender of men; from *alexō*: to defend, to protect, and *anēr*: man) **a. Son of Simon of Cyrene.** His father was compelled to carry the cross of Jesus (Mark 15:21). **b. Name of a priest.** He served in the Sanhedrin (Acts 4:6). **c. Jew from Ephesus.** He was intending to make a defense to the people (Acts 19:33). **d. Worker in copper.** He had done many evil things against Paul (2 Tim. 4:14). Maybe he is the same as the one in 1 Tim. 1:20. ¶

ALEXANDRIAN 1. (*Alexandreus*; from the name Alexander) **Native or resident of Alexandria, a port city in Egypt.** Apollos was one by birth (Acts 18:24). Other ref.: Acts 6:9. ¶ **2.** (*Alexandrinos*; from the name Alexander) **Belonging to Alexandria.** Paul boarded an Alexandrian ship sailing to Italy (Acts 27:6; 28:11). ¶

ALLEGORY 1. (*paroimia*; from *para*: beside, and *oimē*: story, poem) **Briefer account than a parable, but also setting forth a spiritual teaching.** Jesus used an allegory regarding a shepherd (John 10:1–6). Other refs.: John 16:25–29; 2 Pet. 2:22. ¶ **2.** (to be an allegory: *allēgoreō*; from *allos*: another, and *agoreuō*: to speak in a public place) **To use a concrete reality to illustrate an abstract principle.** Paul uses the two sons of Abraham in an allegory describing two covenants (Gal. 4:24). ¶

ALLELUIA (*hallēlouia*) **Heb. term which signifies "Praise Jah" (the Lord).** This word of praise is used both in heaven and on earth (Rev. 19:1, 3, 4, 6). ¶

ALOES (*aloē*) **Very aromatic, resinous plant with bitter juice.** Aloes was used to embalm the body of Jesus (John 19:39). ¶

ALPHA (*alpha*) **First letter of the Greek alphabet written "α".** It is used with the letter "omega" in the expr. "the Alpha and the Omega": a name of God and of Christ (Rev. 1:8; 21:6; 22:13); it underlines their eternal existence. ¶

ALPHAEUS (*Halphaios*) **a. Father of James, an apostle of the Lord.** Refs.: Matt. 10:3; Mark 3:18; Luke 6:15; Acts 1:13. **b. Father of Levi, also called Matthew.** Ref.: Mark 2:14. ¶

ALTAR 1. (*bōmos*; from *bainō*: to go, to step) **Idolatrous table on which to offer sacrifices.** Paul found an altar to the unknown God in Athens (Acts 17:23). ¶ **2.** (*thusiastērion*; from *thusiazō*: to sacrifice) **Structure made according to divine instructions on which were offered sacrifices or incense to God.** Refs.: Matt. 5:23, 24; 23:18-20, 35. In Heb. 13:10, the altar symbolizes Jesus Christ (see vv. 8–10).

AMBASSADOR (BE) (*presbeuō*; from *presbus*: older person, ambassador) **To be a person with experience chosen to represent the interests of another person or a country.** Christians are ambassadors for Christ (2 Cor. 5:20). Paul was an ambassador in chains (Eph. 6:20). ¶

AMEN 1. (*Amēn*: verily, surely, in Heb.) **Name of Christ.** Ref.: Rev. 3:14. **2.** (*amēn*; word borrowed from the Heb.) **In truth, verily, may it be so!** This word refers to what is sure and worthy of trust (2 Cor. 1:20; Rev. 1:7). It is a name of Christ (Rev. 3:14). It indicates our agreement, e.g., when giving thanks (1 Cor. 14:16). It is used with blessings (Rom. 1:25; 9:5), glory to God and Jesus Christ (Rom. 11:36; 16:27; Rev. 1:6; 7:12), honor and strength to God (1 Tim. 6:16), praises (wishes or greetings) (Rom. 15:33; 16:24; 1 Cor. 16:24; Gal. 6:18; Phil. 4:23; Heb. 13:25, Rev. 5:14; 19:4), the Lord's promise of return (Rev. 22:20).

AMETHYST (*amethustos*) **Variety of quartz, a precious stone of purple or violet color.** It adorns a foundation of the wall of the heavenly Jerusalem (Rev. 21:20). ❡

AMMINADAB (*Aminadab*: people of liberality) **Man in the O.T.** He is mentioned in the genealogy of Jesus Christ (Matt. 1:4; Luke 3:33). ❡

AMON (*Amōn*) **King of Judah.** He is mentioned in the genealogy of Jesus Christ (Matt. 1:10). ❡

AMOS (*Amōs*: strong, in Heb.) **Man in the O.T.** He is mentioned in the genealogy of Jesus (Luke 3:25). ❡

AMPHIPOLIS (*Amphipolis*: city surrounded) **City of Macedonia, founded by the Greeks during the 5th century B.C.** Paul travelled through it (Acts 17:1). ❡

AMPLIATUS (*Amplias*; from *amplus,* in Lat.: enlarged, distinguished) **Christian from Rome.** Paul greets him as his beloved in the Lord (Rom. 16:8). ❡

ANANIAS (*Hananias*: Jehovah has dealt graciously) **a. Christian of Jerusalem.** He was married to Sapphira (Acts 5:1); he lied to the Holy Spirit (v. 3). Both died (Acts 5:5; see vv. 5–10). **b. Disciple of Damascus.** He was sent so that Paul might recover his sight (Acts 9:10, 12, 13, 17); he was a devout man, having a good witness (22:12). **c. High priest.** He commanded to strike Paul (Acts 23:2). See Acts 24:1. ❡

ANCHOR (*ankura*; from *ankōn*: curvature, act or result of bending) **Iron instrument, with a curved shape, used to keep a vessel from drifting.** Four anchors were dropped from the stern of the ship that Paul had boarded (Acts 27:29, 30, 40). The Christian hope is compared to an anchor of the soul (Heb. 6:19). ❡

ANDREW (*Andreas*; from *anēr*: man) **One of the twelve apostles of the Lord Jesus.** He was the brother of Simon Peter (Matt. 4:18; 10:2; Mark 1:16; 3:18; Luke 6:14); he led Peter to the Lord (John 1:40; see v. 42). He was a fisherman (Matt. 4:18) from Bethsaida (John 1:44) and a disciple of John the Baptist (see John 1:35–42). According to tradition, he suffered martyrdom and was crucified on an X-shaped cross. Other refs.: Mark 1:29; 13:3; John 6:8; 12:22; Acts 1:13. ¶

ANDRONICUS (*Andronikos*: man of victory; from *anēr*: man, and *nikos*: victory) **Christian, Paul's kinsman and fellow prisoner.** Paul saluted him (Rom. 16:7). ¶

ANGEL 1. (*angelos*) **Celestial being created by God.** Angels are spirits created by God to praise Him (e.g., Ps. 148:2) and His Son (e.g., Heb. 1:6), and to serve Him (e.g., Ps. 91:11). They can take a human form (e.g., Luke 1:19; John 20:12). Some angels have sinned (2 Pet. 2:4) and have not kept their first estate (Jude 6). Angels are sent out to serve for those inheriting salvation (Heb. 1:14). **2.** (equal unto angels, like angels: *isangelos*; from *isos*: equal, and *angelos*: angel) **Similar to angels, the celestial beings created by God.** Those who are resurrected from the dead are such (Luke 20:36). ¶

ANISE (*anēthon*) **Plant with fragrant seeds used as a condiment.** The Pharisees were paying tithes of it (Matt. 23:23). Other ref.: Luke 11:42 in some mss. ¶

ANNA (*Hanna*: grace, in Heb.) **A prophetess far advanced in age who served God in the temple.** She is mentioned when Jesus was presented there (Luke 2:36). ¶

ANNAS (*Hannas*: grace, in Heb.) **Father-in-law to Caiaphas.** During the high priesthood of Annas and Caiaphas, the word of God came to John (Luke

3:2). Jesus was led away to him (John 18:13). He inquired of Peter and John after their arrest (Acts 4:6). ¶

ANOINT 1. (*aleiphō*; akin to *lipos*: oil) **a. To cover a part of the body with a liquid substance, in general a perfumed oil.** Jesus said to anoint one's head when fasting (Matt. 6:17). Many infirm people were anointed by the disciples (Mark 6:13). A woman anointed the feet of Jesus (Luke 7:38, 46). Other refs.: John 11:2; 12:3; Jas. 5:14. **b. To rub a dead body with ointment.** The body of Jesus was anointed (Mark 16:1). ¶ **2.** (*murizō*; from *muron*: ointment) **To anoint for burial.** The body of Jesus had been anointed beforehand for His burial (Mark 14:8). ¶ **3.** (*chriō*; similar to *chrainō*: to touch lightly, and later: to anoint) **To consecrate, or set apart, for God and His service.** Jesus was anointed by God to preach the gospel (Luke 4:18; see also Acts 4:27; 10. 38; Heb. 1:9). God has also anointed Christians (2 Cor. 1:21). ¶ **4.** (*enchriō*; from *en*: in, and *chriō*: to anoint, to consecrate) **To apply a substance.** The angel of Laodicea is advised to anoint his eyes with an eye salve (Rev. 3:18). ¶ **5.** (*epichriō*; from *epi*: upon, and *chriō*: to anoint, to consecrate) **To apply a substance, to smear it over.** Jesus anointed the eyes of a blind man (John 9:6, 11). ¶

ANTICHRIST (*antichristos*; lit.: who is against Christ, who is instead of Christ) **a. One who opposes Christ, His adversary.** He is coming and his spirit is already in the world (1 John 2:18; 4:3). Read Dan. 11:36–39; 2 Thes. 2:1–12; Rev. 13:11–18; 19:19–21. **b. Another person who opposes Christ, who is His adversary.** Many antichrists went out from among the Christians (1 John 2:18, 22; 2 John 7). ¶

ANTIOCH 1. (*Antiocheia*; from Antiochus, a Syrian king) **a. Capital of Syria founded around 300 B.C. by a general of Alexander the Great.** The disciples of the Lord Jesus were first called Christians there (Acts 11:26). Paul visited it (Acts 11:26; 13:1; 14:26; 15:30, 35; 18:22). **b. Roman colony of Pisidia in Asia Minor.** Paul preached the gospel there (Acts 13:14). Other refs.: Acts

14:19, 21; 2 Tim. 3:11. **2.** (from Antioch: *Antiocheus*) **Native of Antioch.** Nicolas, a proselyte, was one (Acts 6:5). ¶

ANTIPAS (*Antipas*: against all, or: like his father) **Christian who suffered martyrdom at Pergamum.** He was a faithful witness (Rev. 2:13). ¶

ANTIPATRIS (*Antipatris*: like his father) **City northeast of Jerusalem.** Paul was brought there, on his way to Caesarea (Acts 23:31). ¶

APELLES (*Apellēs*) **Christian of Rome.** Paul considered him as "approved in Christ" (Rom. 16:10). ¶

APOLLONIA (*Apollōnia*: belonging to Apollo, a god of the Greek mythology) **City of Macedonia.** Paul passed through it (Acts 17:1). ¶

APOLLOS (*Apollōs*: prob. from Apollo, the god of light) **A Jew from Alexandria; he became a Christian and served the Lord.** He was an eloquent man and mighty in the Scriptures (Acts 18:24). He had worked in Corinth (Acts 19:1; 1 Cor. 1:12; 3:4–6, 22; 4:6); he would return later there (1 Cor. 16:12). Other ref.: Titus 3:13. ¶

APOLLYON (*Apolluōn*: Destroyer; from *apollumi*: to destroy, to corrupt) **A name given to Abaddon.** Ref.: Rev. 9:11; see **ABADDON.** ¶

APOSTASY (*apostasia*; from *aphistēmi*: to go away) **Giving up of the truth, leaving of the faith.** Paul was accused of teaching it (Acts 21:21). There will be an apostasy first before the day of Christ (2 Thes. 2:3). ¶

APOSTLE (*apostolos*; from *apostellō*: to send away) **One who is sent on a mission, delegate; also transl.: messenger.** Apostles were chosen by Jesus (Luke 6:13), to be with Him during His ministry on earth (see Mark 3:14). They were eyewitnesses of the events of His ministry (see 2 Pet. 1:16). They were given power against unclean spirits and to heal all kinds of sickness and disease (see Matt. 10:1). Jesus ate the Passover with them before suffering (Luke 22:14; see v. 15) and instituted the Lord's Supper on this occasion (see vv. 19, 20). They witnessed the resurrection of the Lord (see Acts 1:22). Paul was also one, having seen the Lord in glory (1 Cor. 9:1). This term is also used to designate other servants (Acts 14:4, 14; 1 Cor. 15:7). Christ Jesus is called the "Apostle and High Priest of our confession" (Heb. 3:1).

APPEARING 1. (*epiphaneia*; from *epi*: upon, and *phōs*: light) **Manifestation of Jesus Christ to the world when He will come to establish His reign of glory.** This word is found in 1 Tim. 6:14 and 2 Tim. 4:1, 8. It is used re the second coming of the Lord Jesus (2 Thes. 2:8) as well as His first coming (2 Tim. 1:10). Other ref.: Titus 2:13. ¶ **2.** See **REVELATION**.

APPHIA (*Apphia*) **Christian woman from Colossae.** She was prob. the wife of Philemon (Phm. 2). ¶

APPII FORUM → MARKET OF APPIUS

AQUILA (*Akulas*; from Lat. *aquila*: eagle) **Christian of Jewish origin.** He came from Italy with his wife Priscilla (Acts 18:2). He accompanied Paul to Ephesus (Acts 18:18). He unfolded to Apollos the Christian doctrine (Acts 18:26). He and his wife were Paul's fellow workers (Rom. 16:3; 2 Tim. 4:19). A church gathered in their house (1 Cor. 16:19). ¶

ARAB (*Araps*) **Person from Arabia.** On the Day of Pentecost, Arabs heard the gospel in their own tongue (Acts 2:11). ¶

ARABIA (*Arabia*: sterility, dry country, in Heb.) **Region located east and south of Israel.** Paul went there (Gal. 1:17). Mount Sinai is located there (Gal. 4:25). ¶

ARAM (*Aram*: elevated, in Heb.) **Man in the O.T.** He is mentioned in the genealogy of Jesus Christ (Matt. 1:3, 4; Luke 3:33). ❡

ARCHANGEL (*archangelos*; from *archō*: to lead, to command, and *angelos*: messenger, angel) **Angel of a superior rank.** The voice of the archangel will be heard at the rapture (1 Thes. 4:16). Michael is the only one named (Jude 9). ❡

ARCHELAUS (*Archelaos*: leader of the people; from *archō*: to rule, and *laos*: people) **King of the Jews, son of Herod the Great.** He reigned in Judea (Matt. 2:22). ❡

ARCHIPPUS (*Archippos*: master of the horse; from *archē*: rule, and *hippos*: horse) **Christian from Colossae.** He had received a ministry in the Lord (Col. 4:17). He was Paul's fellow soldier (Phm. 2). ❡

AREOPAGITE (*Areopagitēs*: from Ares, the god of war among the Greeks) **Judge serving as a member of the court of the Areopagus.** Dionysius was one (Acts 17:34). ❡

AREOPAGUS (*Areios Pagos*: rocky height of Ares; from *Ares*: the Greek god of war, and *pagos*: what is fixed) **Hill situated to the west of the Acropolis, the citadel of Athens.** Paul was brought there (Acts 17:19, 22). ❡

ARETAS (*Aretas*: a name common to kings of Arabia) **King of Arabian descent.** His governor wanted to seize Paul (2 Cor. 11:32). ❡

ARIMATHEA (*Arimathaia*: heights, in Heb.) **Native town of Joseph, the disciple who took upon himself the burial of Jesus.** This town is mentioned in Matt. 27:57; Mark 15:43; Luke 23:51; John 19:38. It was a city of the Jews (see Luke 23:51). ❡

ARISTARCHUS (*Aristarchos*: best ruler; from *aristos*: best, and *archō*: to rule) **Macedonian Christian from Thessalonica.** He was a travelling companion of Paul (Acts 19:29; 20:4; 27:2). Other refs.: Col. 4:10; Phm. 24. ¶

ARISTOBULUS (*Aristoboulos*: best counsellor; from *aristos*: best, and *boulē*: advice) **Christian of Rome.** Paul saluted those of his household (Rom. 16:10). ¶

ARK (*kibōtos*; lit.: coffer, chest) **a. Huge floating vessel built by Noah with God's specifications.** It was prepared by faith (Heb. 11:7; 1 Pet. 3:20). Noah entered it with his family and the animals before the flood (Matt. 24:38; Luke 17:27). See Gen. 6:14–16. **b. Principal object in the holy place of the tabernacle.** The ark of the covenant (Heb. 9:4) was in the tabernacle when Israel was in the desert. It appears in Rev. 11:19. ¶

ARMAGEDDON (*Harmaged(d)ōn*: mountain of appointment in Heb.) **Plain in Israel, north of Jerusalem, which is about 35 kilometers in length by 25 kilometers in width.** Many armies will be gathered there (Rev. 16:16); see Rev. 19:11–21. ¶

ARMOR (armor, whole armor, panoply: *panoplia*; from *pas*: all, and *hoplon*: weapon, armor) **Combination of protective parts worn by a warrior.** Satan is like a strong man confiding in his armor (Luke 11:22). The armor of God corresponds to resources available to the Christian (Eph. 6:11, 13; see 10–20). ¶

ARPHAXAD (*Arphaxad*) **Man in the O.T.** Arphaxad is mentioned in the genealogy of Jesus (Luke 3:36). ¶

ARTEMAS (*Artemas*; poss. from Artemis, goddess of hunting) **Companion of Paul.** Paul speaks of sending him to Titus (Titus 3:12). ¶

ASA (*Asa*: physician, in Heb.) **King of Judah.** He is mentioned in the genealogy of Jesus Christ (Matt. 1:7, 8). ¶

ASCENSION — Term describing the elevation of Christ into heaven from the midst of His own disciples. Some use the expression "receiving up" (Luke 9:51). The ascension is related in the Gospels and the Acts (see Mark 16:19; Luke 24:51; Acts 1:9).

ASH 1. (*spodos*) **What is left from the combustion of some organic matter.** "Sitting in sackcloth and ashes" is an expression of sorrow, humiliation, and repentance (Matt. 11:21; Luke 10:13). The ashes of a red heifer were used for the purification of the Israelites (Heb. 9:13). ¶ **2.** (to reduce, to burn to ashes: *tephroō*; from *tephra*: ashes) **To consume by fire.** Sodom and Gomorrah were reduced to ashes (2 Pet. 2:6). ¶

ASHER (*Asēr*: blessed, in Heb.) **Son of Jacob as well as one of the twelve tribes named after him.** Anna was from that tribe (Luke 2:36). Twelve thousand from it will be sealed (Rev. 7:6). ¶

ASIA (*Asia*) **In the N.T., a name indicating Asia Minor (present-day Turkey), corresponding roughly to the Roman province bearing the same name; situated to the east of Europe and north of the Mediterranean.** Paul visited Asia and founded many Christian churches there (Acts 19:10, 22, 26; 20:4, 16, 18; 1 Cor. 16:19; 2 Cor. 1:8). The seven churches of Revelation 3 and 4 are situated in Asia Minor (Rev. 1:4; see v. 11). The first letter of Peter was sent to the Christians of Asia (1 Pet. 1:1). Other refs.: Acts 2:9; 6:9; 16:6; 19:27; 21:27; 24:18; 27:2; Rom. 16:5; 2 Tim. 1:15. ¶

ASIARCH (*Asiarchēs*; from *Asia*: Asia, and *archē*: rule) **An elected ruler in the Roman province of Asia.** Paul had friends who were Asiarchs (Acts 19:31). ¶

ASSEMBLING (*episunagōgē*; from *episunagō*: to bring together) **a. Gathering of believers in the Lord Jesus in heaven at His coming.** There will be an assembling of believers with the Lord Jesus at His coming (2 Thes. 2:1). **b. Gathering of Christian believers during the time of the church on the**

earth, particularly for the meetings of the local church. Hebrew Christians are exhorted not to forsake their assembling (Heb. 10:25). ¶

ASSEMBLY 1. (*panēguris;* from *pas*: all, and *agora*: place of meeting) **Gathering of all the Greek people to celebrate a religious ceremony or games.** Some apply the term to the church of the Firstborn in Heb. 12:23. ¶ **2.** See **CHURCH**.

ASSOS (*Assos*) **City of Mysia in Asia Minor and port of the Aegean Sea.** Paul sailed to this city (Acts 20:13, 14). ¶

ASYNCRITUS (*Asunkritos*: incomparable) **A Christian in Rome.** Paul salutes him (Rom. 16:14). ¶

ATHENIAN (*Athēnaios*: from Athena, goddess of wisdom) **Resident of the city of Athens.** They spent their time telling or hearing something new (Acts 17:21). Paul preached the gospel to them (v. 22). ¶

ATHENS (*Athēnai*: name given in honor of Athena, the goddess of wisdom who, according to mythology, founded the city) **The capital of Greece in the plain of Attica, which became the metropolis of culture and arts in antiquity; it fell to the Romans in 86 B.C.** Paul preached there (Acts 17:15, 16). He was left alone there (1 Thes. 3:1), from whence he departed for Corinth (Acts 18:1). ¶

ATONEMENT → MERCY SEAT, PROPITIATION

ATONEMENT COVER → MERCY SEAT

ATTALIA (*Attaleia*; from Attalos, a king of Pergamum) **Seaport in Pamphylia.** Paul passed through it (Acts 14:25). ¶

AUGUSTUS 1. (*Augoustos*: venerable) **Title given to the Roman emperors.** The first emperor of Rome was Octavius, great-nephew of Gaius Julius Caesar; he was the first one to take up this title, having himself called Caesar Augustus (Luke 2:1). ¶ **2.** (*Sebastos*; from *sebazomai*: to venerate) **Title of Roman emperors.** Nero was called Augustus (venerable, in Lat.) (Acts 25:21, 25). A company was named after Augustus (or Augustan cohort) (Acts 27:1). ¶

AZOR (*Azōr*: helper, in Heb.) **Man in the O.T.** Azor is mentioned in the genealogy of Jesus Christ (Matt. 1:13, 14). ¶

AZOTUS (*Azōtos*: ravager, in Heb.) **City located between Gaza and Joppa, a few kilometers from the Mediterranean.** Philip was found there (Acts 8:40). ¶

B

BAAL (*Baal*: lord, owner, in Heb.) **Main deity of the Phoenicians and the Canaanites.** He was worshipped by many Israelites (Rom. 11:4). ¶

BABYLON (*Babulōn*; from Babel: confusion, in Heb.; see Gen. 11:1–9) **a. Capital of Babylonia (or Chaldea), country of western Asia, east of Israel. The Jews were deported to Babylon by Nebuchadnezzar in 606 B.C.** A remnant of them came back to Jerusalem (Matt. 1:11, 12, 17; Acts 7:43). **b. City where a church might have existed.** A Christian sister of Babylon sent her greetings to the Christians of the dispersion (1 Pet. 5:13). **c. Mystical name of heathen Rome.** It will be destroyed by the Beast (Rev. 14:8; 16:19; 17:5; 18:2, 10, 21). ¶

BALAAM (*Balaam*: not of the people, i.e., foreigner, in Heb.) **A soothsayer in the O.T.** His doctrine is associated with sexual immorality (Rev. 2:14). He was killed by the Israelites (see Josh. 13:22). Other refs.: 2 Pet. 2:15; Jude 11. ¶

BALAC, BALAK (*Balak*: spoiler, devastator, in Heb.) **King of Moab.** He convinced Balaam to curse Israel (Rev. 2:14; see Num. 22:5, 6). ¶

BAPTISM 1. (baptism: *baptisma*; to baptize: *baptizō*; from *baptō*: to dip, to immerse) **a. Christians who have been baptized with Christ Jesus have been baptized for His death; they have been buried with Him through baptism into death to walk in newness of life.** Read Rom. 6:4; Gal. 3:27; Col. 2:12. Baptism is in the name of the Father and of the Son and of the Holy Spirit (Matt. 28:19; Mark 16:16). Refs. to the baptism of Christians: Acts 8:12,

13, 16, 36, 38; Rom. 6:3; 1 Cor. 1:13–15; Eph. 4:5). **b. Baptism of fire.** Jesus would baptize with the Holy Spirit and with fire (Matt. 3:11). **c. Baptism of John.** This baptism was with water in the Jordan (Matt. 3:6; Mark 1:4; Luke 3:3; John 1:26, 31; Acts 13:24). This baptism was to prepare the Jews to receive a living Christ and be introduced in His kingdom (Acts 19:4). Other refs.: Matt. 21:25; Acts 1:5, 22; 10:37; 11:16; 18:25; 19:3. **d. Baptism of the death of Jesus.** This baptism is an aspect of the sufferings and death of the Lord Jesus in which His disciples could also have part (Mark 10:38, 39; Luke 12:50). **e. Baptism of the Holy Spirit.** This baptism happened at Pentecost (see Acts 2:1–4). Refs.: Matt. 3:11; Mark 1:8; Luke 3:16; John 1:33; Acts 1:5; 11:16. **f. Baptism for the dead.** This expression is found in 1 Cor. 15:29. **g. Baptism for Moses.** This baptism refers to the sons of Israel crossing the Red Sea (1 Cor. 10:2). **2.** (*baptismos*) **The action of washing in relation to Judaic rites of purification.** This baptism is found in Heb. 6:2; 9:10.

BAR-JESUS (*Bariēsous*: son of Jesus, or Joshua, in Aram.) **Magician and Jewish false prophet.** He sought to turn away Sergius Paulus from the faith (Acts 13:6). ¶

BARABBAS (*Barabbas*: son of the father, in Aram.) **A man imprisoned for murder in the days of the Lord.** He was chosen to be released instead of Jesus (Matt. 27:16, 17, 20, 21, 26; Mark 15:7, 11, 15; Luke 23:18; John 18:40). He was a robber (John 18:40); he had been imprisoned for murder (see Acts 3:14). ¶

BARACHIAS (*Barachias*: blessing of Jehovah, in Heb.) **Father of Zechariah, a priest.** His son Zechariah was put to death (Matt. 23:35). ¶

BARAK (*Barak*: lightning, lightning flash, in Heb.) **A man in the O.T.** He was a man of faith (Heb. 11:32). See Judg. 4. ¶

BARBARIAN (*barbaros*) **a. Stranger to the Greek and Roman cultures.** Refs.: Acts 28:2, 4; Rom. 1:14; Col. 3:11. **b. Person speaking a language not understood.** Ref.: 1 Cor. 14:11. ¶

BARLEY (adj.) (*krithinos*; from *krithē*: barley) **Made of barley.** Five loaves of barley were multiplied to feed a crowd (John 6:9; also v. 13). ¶

BARLEY (noun) (*krithē*) **Cereal used to make bread.** Three measures will be worth a denarius during the apocalyptic judgments (Rev. 6:6). ¶

BARNABAS (*Barnabas*: son of prophet or son of consolation, in Aram.) **Jewish Christian from Cyprus whose name was Joseph (or Joses).** This name was given to a certain Joseph (Acts 4:36). He sold some land and brought the money to the apostles (see Acts 4:37). He led Saul to the apostles (Acts 9:27). He taught the Christians (Acts 11:22). He accompanied Paul during a missionary journey (see Acts 13, 14). He had a contention with Paul regarding Mark (Acts 15:37, 39). Other ref.: Gal. 2:13.

BARSABBAS (*Barsabbas*: son of Saba, i.e., son of rest, in Aram.) **a. Another name for Joseph, one of the two men proposed to replace Judas Iscariot.** He was surnamed Justus (Acts 1:23). **b. Surname of a man, Judas, who accompanied Paul and Barnabas to Antioch.** He was a leading man among the brothers (Acts 15:22). ¶

BARTHOLOMEW (*Bartholomaios*: son of Tolmai, meaning ridged) **One of the apostles.** Bartholomew is mentioned in Acts 1:13. He is associated with Philip (Matt. 10:3; Mark 3:18; Luke 6:14). ¶

BARTIMAEUS (*Bartimaios*: son of the honorable) **Blind beggar.** He was healed by Jesus and followed him (Mark 10:46, 52). ¶

BASKET 1. (*kophinos*) **Hamper smaller than the next one.** This word is used re bread that remained after the miracle of Jesus (Matt. 14:20; 16:9; Mark 6:43; 8:19; Luke 9:17; John 6:13). ¶ **2.** (*spuris*; from *speira*: something that is coiled) **Container for food, relatively big and circular, made of intertwined reeds or straw.** This word is used re the fragments of loaves and fish that were left after the miracle of Jesus (Matt. 15:37; 16:10; Mark 8:8, 20). A basket was used to allow Paul to escape (Acts 9:25; see 2 Cor. 11:32, 33). ¶ **3.** (*sarganē*; from a Heb. word meaning: to intertwine) **Hamper prob. made of ropes.** Ref.: 2 Cor. 11:33. ¶

BEAST 1. (*zōon*; from *zōos*: alive) **a. Living being; also transl.: living creature.** John saw beasts, i.e., symbolical creatures, standing before the throne of God (Rev. 4:6–9; 5:6, 8, 11, 14; 6:1, 3, 5–7; 7:11; 14:3; 15:7; 19:4). **b. Animal creature.** They were offered in sacrifice (Heb. 13:11). Those walking according to the flesh are like brute and irrational beasts (2 Pet. 2:12; Jude 10). ¶ **2.** (beast, wild beast: *thērion*; dimin. of *ther*: wild animal) **a. Wild animal.** Refs.: Mark 1:13; Acts 11:6; 28:4, 5; Heb. 12:20; Jas. 3:7; Rev. 6:8. **b. Term used figur. to describe people.** The Cretans had been described as evil beasts (Titus 1:12). **c. Term used figur. to describe the antichrist.** Refs.: Rev. 11:7; 13:1–4, 11, 12, 14, 15, 17, 18; 14:9, 11; 15:2; 16:2, 10, 13; 17:3, 7, 8, 11–13, 16, 17; 18:2 in some mss.; 19:19, 20; 20:4, 10). ¶ **3.** (*ktēnos*; from *ktaomai*: to acquire, to possess) **Animal used to carry heavy loads; animal in general.** The Samaritan put the wounded man on his own beast (Luke 10:34). The word designates a quadruped animal in 1 Cor. 15:39. Other refs.: Acts 23:24; Rev. 18:13. ¶ **4.** (slain beast: *sphagion*; from *sphazō*: to slay, to sacrifice) **Victim for a sacrifice, slaughtered offering.** Beasts were offered to God (Acts 7:42). ¶ **5.** (to fight with beasts, to fight wild beasts: *thēriomacheō*; from *thērion*: beast, and *machomai*: to fight) **To struggle with wild animals.** Paul had fought with beasts at Ephesus (prob. in a figur. sense) (1 Cor. 15:32). ¶

BEAUTIFUL 1. (*asteios*; from *astu*: city; lit.: from the city, of good taste) **Agreeable, gracious.** Moses was a beautiful child (Acts 7:20; Heb. 11:23). ¶ **2.** (*kalos*) **Good, nice; worthy, precious.** This word is used re pearls (Matt. 13:45), stones (Luke 21:5). **3.** (*hōraios*; from *hōra*: time, season; lit.: which is of the season) **Good-looking, nice.** This word is used re whitewashed tombs (Matt. 23:27), a gate of the temple (Acts 3:2, 10), the feet of those who preach the gospel of peace (Rom. 10:15). ¶

BEELZEBUL (*Beelzeboul*: lord of the flies, in Heb.) **Name given to Satan, the chief of the demons.** Ref.: Matt. 10:25. Jesus was accused of casting out demons by him (Matt. 12:24, 27; Mark 3:22; Luke 11:15, 18, 19). ¶

BEGINNING (*archē*) **Start, commencement.** Mark 10:6 and Heb. 1:10 refer to the beginning of the creation. John 1:1 indicates before the course of time; it attests to the eternal existence of the Son of God (John 1:2). Having no beginning, Melchizedek typifies the Son of God (Heb. 7:3). It is a name given to the Son of God (Col. 1:18; Rev. 3:14; 21:6; 22:13).

BELIAL (*Belial* or *Beliar*: worthless, wickedness, in Heb.) **O.T. name symbolizing evil, wickedness (e.g., see Prov. 6:12).** It applies to Satan (2 Cor. 6:15). It symbolizes iniquity, wickedness (e.g., Deut. 13:13; Judg. 19:22; 1 Kgs. 21:10). ¶

BENJAMIN (*Beniamin*: son of the right hand, in Heb.) **Youngest of Jacob's twelve sons and name of a tribe descended from him.** King Saul (Acts 13:21) and the apostle Paul (Rom. 11:1; Phil. 3:5) are from that tribe. Twelve thousand from that tribe will be sealed (Rev. 7:8). ¶

BEREA 1. (*Beroia*) **City of Macedonia, near Thessalonica, which Paul visited during his second missionary journey.** Many Jews in Berea believed, as well as Greek women and a great number of men (Acts 17:10, 13). ¶ **2.** (of Berea: *Beroiaios*) **Inhabitant of the city of Berea.** Sopater was from Berea (Acts 20:4). ¶

BERNICE (*Bernikē*: victorious) **Sister of King Agrippa II.** She and Agrippa heard Paul's defense (Acts 25:13, 23; 26:30). ¶

BERYL (*bērullos*) **Precious stone of a green or blue color.** This stone adorns a foundation of the heavenly Jerusalem (Rev. 21:20). ¶

BETHANY 1. (*Bēthania*: house of depression or misery, in Heb.) **a. Village of Israel.** It was visited by Jesus (Matt. 21:17; 26:6; Mark 11:11; 14:3; John 11:1; 12:1); it was near Jerusalem (Mark 11:1; Luke 19:29; John 11:18). Jesus cursed a fig tree there (Mark 11:12). Jesus' ascension took place there (Luke 24:50). **b. Name of a place beyond the Jordan.** John baptized there (John 1:28). ¶ **2.** (*Bēthabara*: house of the crossing, in Heb.) Some mss. have this name in John 1:28. ¶

BETHESDA (*Bēthesda*: house of mercy, in Heb.) **Pool in Jerusalem.** Sick people were laid there, hoping to be healed (John 5:2; see vv. 3, 5–9). ¶

BETHLEHEM (*Bēthleem*: house of bread, in Heb.) **Small city of Judea.** It is mentioned re Jesus' birth (Matt. 2:1, 5, 6; Luke 2:4; John 7:42), shepherds rendering homage to Him (Luke 2:15), wise men bringing Him offerings (see Matt. 21. 1, 2), children's death by Herod (Matt. 2:8, 16). ¶

BETHPHAGE (*Bēthphagē*: house of figs, in Heb.) **Village near the Mount of Olives in Jerusalem.** Disciples were sent there to look for a colt (Matt. 21:1; Mark 11:1; Luke 19:29). ¶

BETHSAIDA (*Bēthsaida*: house of fishing or hunting, in Heb.) **City north of the Sea of Galilee near Capernaum.** It was visited by Jesus (Mark 6:45; Luke 9:10). He rebuked it for its unbelief (Matt. 11:21; Luke 10:13). Philip, Andrew, and Peter were from there (John 1:44; 12:21). Jesus healed a blind man there (Mark 8:22; see vv. 22–26). ¶

BIER (*soros*) **Portable funeral bed.** Jesus touched the bier of the only son of a mother (Luke 7:14). ¶

BISHOP → OVERSEER

BITHYNIA (*Bithunia*) **Mountainous Roman province in northern Asia Minor.** Paul was not allowed by the Spirit to go there (Acts 16:7), but the gospel was preached there later (1 Pet. 1:1). ¶

BLASPHEME (*blasphēmeō*; poss. from *blaptō*: to harm, and *phēmē*: reputation) **To speak slanderously, in a defaming way, more specifically against God; to curse.** Jesus was accused of blaspheming (Matt. 9:3; 26:65; Mark 2:7; John 10:36). He speaks of the sons of men blaspheming (Mark 3:28). The word of God must not be blasphemed because of the conduct of older Christians (Titus 2:5). There are rich men who blaspheme the name of Jesus (Jas. 2:7). The beast, as well as men, will blaspheme God's name (Rev. 13:6; 16:9, 11, 21).

BLASTUS (*Blastos*: sprout, what germinates) **Chamberlain of King Herod Agrippa I; as such, he was responsible for the service of the sovereign's chamber.** People of Tyre and Sidon gained his support (Acts 12:20). ¶

BOANERGES (*Boanērges*: sons of thunder, in Aram.) **Surname of James and John.** Ref.: Mark 3:17; comp. Luke 9:54. ¶

BOAZ (*Booz*: in him is strength, in Heb.) **Man of Bethlehem, husband of Ruth the Moabitess.** He used his right as kinsman-redeemer to marry Ruth (see Ruth 4:13). He is mentioned in the genealogy of Jesus (Matt. 1:5; Luke 3:32). ¶

BOOK 1. (*biblos*; whence Bible, the Book by excellence) **Volume, scroll, roll.** A lengthy written work that forms a whole. This word is used re the Gospel of Matthew (Matt. 1:1), the Gospel of John (John 20:30), the book of Moses (Mark 12:26), the Psalms (Luke 20:42; Acts 1:20), the prophets (Acts 7:42), Isaiah (Luke 3:4), the book of Revelation (Rev. 22:19). The book of life (Phil. 4:3; Rev. 3:5; 20:15) contains the names of all those who have eternal life (comp. Ex. 32:32; Luke 10:20; Heb. 12:23); it corresponds to the book of life of the Lamb (Rev. 13:8). The books burned in Acts 19:19 were most likely books of magic. **2.** (*biblion*; dimin. of *biblos*) **Small volume; also transl.: scroll.** The book of the prophet Isaiah was read by Jesus (Luke 4:17, 20). Many miracles of Jesus are not written in the book, i.e., the Gospel of John (John 20:30; also 21:25). **3.** (little book: *biblaridion*; dimin. of *biblos*) **Small volume, booklet.** John ate the little book taken from the angel (Rev. 10:2, 8–10). ¶

BORN AGAIN (BE) 1. (to be born: *gennaō*; from *genna*: birth, race; again, from above: *anōthen*) **To receive by the Holy Spirit a new nature which comes from above, i.e., from God.** One must be born again to enter the kingdom of God (John 3:3, 7). Such a one is born of water and of the Spirit (see John 3:5; 1 John 3:9). **2.** (*anagennaō*; from *ana*: again, and *gennaō*: to be born) **To cause to be born anew.** Believers have been born again into a living hope (1 Pet. 1:3), by the word of God (v. 23). See **REGENERATION**. ¶

BOSOM (*kolpos*; lit.: the front of the body between the arms) **a. The "bosom of the Father" speaks of eternal affections between the Father and the Son.** The Son, who is in the bosom of the Father, has made God known (John 1:18). **b. The "bosom of Jesus" speaks of proximity.** John was reclining on the bosom of Jesus (John 13:23). **c. The "bosom of Abraham" evokes the blessed place of Christians after death, like that of Abraham, while waiting for the resurrection.** Lazarus died and was carried away in the bosom of Abraham (Luke 16:22, 23). **d. Lap.** Ref.: Luke 6:38. Other ref.: Acts 27:39 (bay). ¶

BOTTOMLESS (abyss: *abussos*; from *a*: intens., and *buthos*: deep, bottom, bottom of the sea) **Profound depth, chasm; it symbolizes also the source of Satanic evil and misery; it is also transl. "abyss".** Demons did not want Jesus to send them into the abyss (Luke 8:31). A star fallen from heaven will open the abyss (Rev. 9:1, 2). Satan is the angel of the abyss (Rev. 9:11). The beast will ascend out of it (Rev. 11:7; 17:8). It is reserved for fallen angels (see Luke 8:31) and later for the devil (Rev. 20:1, 3). Other ref.: Rom. 10:7. ¶

BRASS 1. (*chalkos*) **Copper, an alloy of copper and zinc, or bronze (an alloy of copper and tin).** Money (Matt. 10:9), musical instruments (1 Cor. 13:1), and various articles (Rev. 18:12) were made of brass. Other refs.: Mark 6:8; 12:41. ¶ **2.** (of brass: *chalkeos*; from *chalkos*: brass) **Made of copper or brass.** Men will worship idols of brass (Rev. 9:20). ¶ **3.** (fine brass: *chalkolibanon*; from *chalkos*: brass, and *libanos*: frankincense-tree) **High quality brass.** The feet of the Son of Man were like fine brass (Rev. 1:15; 2:18).

BRIAR (*tribolos*; from *treis*: three, and *belos*: point, dart) **Prickly shrub, thistle.** Figs cannot be gathered on them (Matt. 7:16). The earth bearing thorns and briars is rejected (Heb. 6:8). ¶

BRIDE (*numphē*) **Woman recently united to a man by marriage.** The word has this usual meaning in Rev. 18:23. It designates the church of God, the bride of Christ: John 3:29; Rev. 21:2, 9; 22:17. It also means "daughter-in-law": Matt. 10:35; Luke 12:53. ¶

BRIDECHAMBER (*numphōn*; from *numphē*: bride) **Room in which was the nuptial bed; the sons of the bride chamber were the friends of the bridegroom and were providing what was required for the wedding.** The sons of the bridechamber cannot mourn (Matt. 9:15) or fast (Mark 2:19; Luke 5:34). ¶

BRIDEGROOM (*numphios*; from *numphē*: bride) **Man newly united to a woman by marriage.** The word has this usual meaning in John 2:9; Rev. 18:23. Jesus was like the bridegroom with the friends of the bridegroom (Matt. 9:15; Mark 2:19, 20; Luke 5:34, 35; John 3:29). This word also refers to Christ met by ten virgins in Matt. 25 (vv. 1, 5, 6, 10). ¶

BROTHER (*adelphos*; from *a*: particle of union, and *delphus*: womb; lit.: of the same womb) **Relative born of the same parent(s); in particular, a Christian believer.** This word may refer to a brother according to the flesh, e.g., Andrew was the brother of Peter (Matt. 4:18). It is also used regarding the Jews (e.g.,

Acts 3:17) and the Christians (e.g., Acts 10:23; Rom. 16:23). It may designate any man (Matt. 5:22; 7:3), in the sense of neighbor.

BURNT OFFERING (*holokautōma*; from *holos*: all, whole, and *kaiō*: to consume, to burn) **Sacrifice offered to God under the law, in virtue of which the worshipper was accepted.** It symbolizes the offering of Jesus Christ to God on the cross (see Lev. 1:1–17; 6:1–6). Loving God and one's neighbor is more than burnt offerings (Mark 12:33; see Hos. 6:6). God did not take pleasure in them (Heb. 10:6, 8). ¶

BUSHEL (*modios*; from the Lat. *modius*) **Unit of dry measure equivalent to approx. 9 liters; the word also means a container.** A lighted lamp is not put under the bushel (Matt. 5:15; Mark 4:21; Luke 11:33). ¶

BUSYBODY 1. (to be a busybody, to act like a busybody: *periergazomai*; from *peri*: around, about, and *ergazomai*: to work) **To be occupied with things that are without importance or to bustle about in the affairs of other people**. Some Thessalonians were busybodies (2 Thes. 3:11). ¶ **2.** (*periergos*; from *peri*: around (intens.), and *ergon*: work, business) **Occupying oneself with things of no importance or interfering in the affairs of others.** Young widows should not be busybodies (1 Tim. 5:13). Other ref.: Acts 19:19. ¶ **3.** (busybody in other people's matters: *allotriepiskopos*; from *allotrios*: which concerns others, and *episkopos*: overseer) **One who mixes in other people's affairs.** No one should act as a busybody (1 Pet. 4:15. ¶

BUY (*agorazō*; lit.: to go to the marketplace, the *agora*) **The verb usually means to obtain an object by paying for it; also transl.: to redeem, to purchase.** The Christian who was a slave of sin was bought with a price (1 Cor. 6:20; 7:23; Rev. 5:9). The 144,000 will have been bought from among men (Rev. 14:3, 4).

C

CAESAR (*Kaisar*) **Title held by several Roman emperors belonging to the family of Gaius Julius Caesar.** It was given to the emperors Augustus (Luke 2:1), Tiberius (Matt. 22:17), Caligula (Acts 17:7), Claudius (see Acts 18:2), Nero (Acts 25:8; Phil. 4:22), and Titus who besieged Jerusalem in A.D. 70. ¶

CAESAREA (*Kaisareia*; from the name of Tiberius Augustus, the Roman emperor) **Seaport of Israel, northwest of Jerusalem.** Philip preached the gospel from Azotus to Caesarea (Acts 8:40). Other refs.: Acts 9:30; 10:1, 24; 11:11; 12:19; 18:22; 21:8, 16; 23:23, 33. ¶

CAESAREA PHILIPPI (*Kaisareia tēs Philippou*; so named by Philip the tetrarch in honor of Tiberius Caesar and himself) **City in Northern Israel.** Jesus asked there: "Who do men say that I am?", "And you, who do you say that I am?" (Matt. 16:13; Mark 8:27). ¶

CAIAPHAS (*Kaiaphas*) **High priest in Israel.** During the high priesthood of Caiaphas and Annas, the word of God came to John (Luke 3:2); Annas was his father-in-law (John 18:13). Caiaphas was high priest during the year in which Christ was to die (John 11:49). He accused Jesus of blasphemy because He said that He was the "Messiah" and the "Son of God" (John 18:24, 28; see Matt. 26:63–65). He was willing to let Jesus die (John 18:14).

CAIN (*Kain*: acquisition, in Heb.) **First child of Adam and Eve.** He killed Abel (1 John 3:12; see Gen. 4:1–16). Other refs.: Heb. 11:4; Jude 11. ¶

CAINAN (*Kainan*: possession, in Heb.) **Name of two men of the O.T.** They are mentioned in the genealogy of Jesus, one time before and one time after the flood (Luke 3:36, 37). ¶

CALVARY → SKULL

CAMEL (*kamēlos*) **Large domesticated ruminant, most useful to carry people and burdens on great distances.** Reference is made to camel's hair (Matt. 3:4; Mark 1:6). Other refs.: Matt. 19:24; 23:24; Mark 10:25; Luke 18:25. ¶

CAMP (*parembolē*; from *paremballō*: to set alongside) **a. Organized encampment of the people of Israel.** The bodies of the beasts were burned outside the camp (Heb. 13:11). **b. Figur., the Judaic religious system and, in general, any religious system established by men.** We are to go forth to Jesus outside of the camp (Heb. 13:13). **c. Defensive gathering.** The camp of the saints will be surrounded by the nations (Rev. 20:9).

CANA (*Kana*: place of reeds, in Heb.) **City of Galilee.** Jesus performed His first miracle there during a wedding (John 2:1, 11). Other refs.: John 4:46; 21:2. ¶

CANAAN (*Chanaan*: humiliated, in Heb.) **Region occupied by Ham, Noah's son (see Gen. 9:20–25); it corresponds to Israel.** A famine that came upon Canaan prompted Jacob to seek food in Egypt (Acts 7:11). Seven of its nations were destroyed by the Israelites (Acts 13:19). ¶

CANAANITE (*Chananaios*; from *Chanaan*: Canaan) **Person descended from the lineage of Canaan, the people occupying the land before the Israelites.** The daughter of a Canaanite woman was healed by Jesus (Matt. 15:22). ¶

CANANITE (*Kananaios*: zealous, in Aram.) **Member of a Jewish national party.** Simon, a disciple of Jesus, was called a Cananite (Matt. 10:4; Mark 3:18). ¶

CANDACE (*Kandakē*; possibly a general designation for Ethiopian queens) **Queen of Ethiopia.** An important official under her (Acts 8:27) was converted and baptized (see 8:26–40). ¶

CAPERNAUM (*Kapernaoum*: comfortable village, village of consolation, in Heb.) **Village of Galilee, northwest of the Sea of Galilee.** Jesus stayed there (John 2:12; also Matt. 4:13). There He healed a centurion's servant (Matt. 8:5; Luke 7:1; John 4:46). He taught in its synagogue (John 6:59) and healed a man possessed by an unclean spirit (Mark 1:21; also vv. 23–26; Luke 4:31; also vv. 33–35). Other refs.: Matt. 11:23; 17:24; Mark 2:1; 9:33; Luke 4:23; 10:15; John 6:17, 24. ¶

CAPPADOCIA (*Kappadokia*) **Roman province in eastern Asia Minor.** Jews from there were present in Jerusalem at Pentecost (Acts 2:9). Other ref.: 1 Pet. 1:1. ¶

CAPTAIN 1. (*archēgos*; from *archē*: beginning, rule, and *agō*: to lead) **One who occupies a preeminent position, chief.** Jesus is the captain of the salvation of Christians (Heb. 2:10). **2.** (*stratēgos*; from *stratos*: army, and *agō*: to lead) **Chief of the guards, commanding officer.** A captain was guarding the temple (Luke 22:4, 52; Acts 4:1; 5:24, 26). Other refs.: Acts 16:20, 22, 35, 36, 38; see **MAGISTRATE.** ¶ **3.** (captain, chief captain, commander: *chiliarchos*; from *chilioi*: thousand, and *archē*: beginning, authority) **Tribune, i.e., a commanding officer in the Roman army, in charge of one thousand soldiers; any military commander.** Jesus was arrested by one (John 18:12). Lysias was one (Acts 24:7, 22). Captains will hide themselves from the wrath of the Lamb (Rev. 6:15). Other refs.: Mark 6:21; Acts 21:31–33, 37.

CARNAL 1. (*sarkikos*; from *sarx*: flesh) **Concerning the flesh; material, physical; also transl.: material, worldly.** This word is used re Christian (Rom. 7:14; 1 Cor. 3:1, 3; 1 Pet. 2:11), things (Rom. 15:27; 1 Cor. 9:11), a commandment (Heb. 7:16), and ordinances (9:10). The weapons of the Christian warfare

are not carnal (2 Cor. 10:4). Paul did not conduct himself with carnal wisdom (2 Cor. 1:12). ¶ **2.** (carnal things: *ta sarkikai*) **Matters which are temporal, material, of this world.** Paul was reaping the carnal things of the Corinthians (1 Cor. 9:11).

CARPUS (*Karpos*: fruit, profit) **Christian man of Troas.** Paul had left a cloak with him (2 Tim. 4:13). ¶

CENCHREA (*Kenchreai*: millet) **Port near Corinth on the Aegean Sea.** Paul shaved his head there (Acts 18:18). Phoebe was a servant of the church there (Rom. 16:1). ¶

CENSER 1. (*thumiatērion*; from *thumiaō*: to burn incense) **Article used for burning incense.** There was a golden censer in the holy place of the tabernacle (Heb. 9:4). ¶ **2.** (*libanōtos*; from *libanos*: incense, frankincense) **Container to burn incense or frankincense.** This censer will be filled from the fire of the altar and cast on the earth (Rev. 8:3, 5). ¶

CENSUS 1. (*apographē*; from *apographō*: to make a census) **Enrollment of individuals in a public register, enumeration of persons and property.** Refs.: Luke 2:2; Acts 5:37. ¶ **2.** (to make a census, to take a census: *apographō*; from *apo*: from, and *graphō*: to write) **To make the enumeration of property and persons during a census.** A census was made of all the inhabited earth (Luke 2:1, 3, 5). Other ref.: Heb. 12:23. ¶

CENTURION 1. (*hekatontarchēs* and *hekatontarchos*; from *hekaton*: one hundred, and *archō*: to command) **Commanding officer of a Roman century, i.e., a troop of 50 to 100 soldiers; a regiment (or band) was made of six centuries.** The servant of a centurion was healed by Jesus (Matt. 8:5, 8, 13; Luke 7:2, 6). A centurion said that Jesus was truly the Son of God and a righteous Man (Matt. 27:54; Luke 23:47). Cornelius was a centurion (Acts 10:1, 22), Julius also (Acts 27:1, 6, 11, 31, 43). Other refs.: Acts 21:32; 22:25, 26;

23:17, 23; 24:23. ¶ **2.** (*kenturiōn*; from the Lat. *centurio*, which is from *centum*: one hundred) **See defin. above.** A centurion said that Jesus was truly the Son of God (Mark 15:39, 44, 45). ¶

CEPHAS (*Kēphas*: rock, in Aram.) **Surname of the apostle Peter.** This name was given by Jesus to Simon (John 1:42). Peter (*Petros*) is the Greek equivalent of Cephas. Other refs.: 1 Cor. 1:12; 3:22; 9:5; 15:5; Gal. 1:18; 2:9, 11, 14. ¶

CHAFF (*achuron*) **Hay, stubble.** Chaff is the husk of cereal grain (Matt. 3:12; Luke 3:17. ¶

CHALCEDONY (*chalkēdōn*) **Precious stone found near an ancient city of the same name in Asia Minor.** This stone adorns the third foundation of the heavenly Jerusalem (Rev. 21:19). ¶

CHALDEAN (*Chaldaios*) **Inhabitant of Chaldea or Babylonia, lands of Western Asia.** Abraham was told to go out from their land (Acts 7:4). ¶

CHERUBIM (*cheroubim*) **Angels overseeing the administration of divine justice and judgment (e.g., Gen. 3:24; Ps. 80:1).** They are mentioned only once in the N.T. (Heb. 9:5) in relation to the mercy seat; see Ex. 25:18–20. ¶

CHILIARCH → **CAPTAIN**

CHIOS (*Chios*) **Island in the Aegean Sea, at the entrance of the Gulf of Smyrna.** Paul's ship passed near this island (Acts 20:15). ¶

CHLOE (*Chloē*: new verdure) **Christian woman of Corinth.** Ref.: 1 Cor. 1:11. ¶

CHORAZIN (*Chorazin*) **City of Galilee near Capernaum.** Jesus reproached this city for not having repented despite His miracles (Matt. 11:21; Luke 10:13). ¶

CHRIST (*Christos*: anointed, consecrated; from *chriō*: to anoint) **Originally one of the titles of the Lord Jesus; see Ps. 2:2, 6; later one of His names.** Christ is the Greek equivalent of the Hebrew name "Messiah," He whom the Jews were to expect and who would reign over them (John 4:25; see v. 42). Jesus was acknowledged by Peter as the Christ, the Son of the Living God (Matt. 16:16). False christs will arise before His return (Matt. 24:23, 24; Mark 13:22).

CHRISTIAN (*Christianos*; from *Christos*: Christ, which is from *chriō*: to anoint) **Name given to people belonging to Christ and following Him.** The disciples of Jesus Christ were first called Christians in Antioch (Acts 11:26). Agrippa was almost persuaded to become one (Acts 26:28). One suffering as a Christian should not be ashamed but glorify God (1 Pet. 4:16). ¶

CHRYSOLITE (*chrusolithos*; from *chrusos*: gold, and *lithos*: stone) **Precious stone of a golden color.** It adorns the seventh foundation of the heavenly Jerusalem (Rev. 21:20). ¶

CHRYSOPRASE (*chrusoprasos*; from *chrusos*: gold, and *prason*: leek) **Precious stone, variety of chalcedony of a golden green and translucent.** It adorns the tenth foundation of the heavenly Jerusalem (Rev. 21:20). ¶

CHURCH (*ekklēsia*; from *ekkaleō*: to call out) **a. The church (or assembly) of God is composed of all Christian believers redeemed by the blood of Christ, since the coming of the Holy Spirit at Pentecost until the return of the Lord.** Jesus is building His church (Matt. 16:18; see Eph. 2:20–22). The church is made of all the true believers in the Lord Jesus, known by God, who live at a certain time on earth (see 2 Tim. 2:19–21). Christ has loved the church and has given Himself for her (Eph. 5:25). Other refs.: Acts 2:47; 5:11; 8:1, 3; 1 Cor. 12:28. **b. The local church is made of all the true Christian believers living in a locality.** It is a gathering of Christians around the Lord in a given place (1 Cor. 11:16; 14:19, 34, 35). It is an expression of the universal church, the body of Christ (1 Cor. 1:2; 1 Thes. 1:1). Other refs.: Matt. 18:17; Acts 9:31.

c. Group of people gathered together. The Greek term is used for the assembly of Israel in the desert (Acts 7:38). It designates also an assembly of citizens in Ephesus (Acts 19:32, 41) and a lawful assembly (v. 39). ¶

CHUZA (*Chouzas*) **Herod's steward.** He was the husband of Joanna, a woman attending to Jesus out of her own means (Luke 8:3). ¶

CILICIA (*Kilikia*) **Province located in southern Asia Minor and northeast of the Mediterranean Sea.** Paul was originally from Tarsus, its capital (Acts 21:39; 22:3; 23:34). Men from Cilicia disputed with Stephen (Acts 6:9). Churches were found there (Acts 15:23, 41). Paul returned there after his conversion (Gal. 1:21). Other ref.: Acts 27:5. ¶

CIRCUMCISION (*peritomē*; from *peritemnō*: to circumcise, which is from *peri*: around, and *temnō*: to cut) **Cutting off the foreskin of a male, as a religious rite in Israel.** This rite was ordained by God to Abraham and his male descendants as a sign of a covenant and performed on the eighth day after birth (Acts 7:8). It was given to the Jews (John 7:22, 23). In the N.T., the Jews are those of the circumcision (Acts 10:45; 11:2; Gal. 2:12; Eph. 2:11; Col. 4:11; Titus 1:10); the Gentiles are uncircumcised men (see Acts 11:3). In the church, there is no difference between the Jews and the Gentiles, circumcision and uncircumcision (Col. 3:11). The "circumcision" of the Christian is of the heart, in spirit (Rom. 2:25, 26–29; Col. 2:11). The Christians are now figur. the circumcision (Phil. 3:3).

CITIZEN (*politēs*; from *polis*: city) **One who is an inhabitant of a city, a state, a district, and who is entitled to full civil rights.** This word is used re the prodigal son (Luke 15:15), a noble man (Luke 19:14), Paul (Acts 21:39). Other ref.: Heb. 8:11 (fellow citizen). ¶

CITIZENSHIP 1. (*politeia*; from *polis*: city) **Quality and right of a citizen.** A chiliarch bought his own citizenship (Acts 22:28). The Gentiles were aliens from the citizenship of Israel (Eph. 2:12). ¶ **2.** (*politeuma*; from *polis*: city)

Participation in the matters of the state; the term means both "citizenship" and "state". The citizenship of Christians is in heaven (Phil. 3:20). ❡

CLAUDA (*Klauda*) **Small island of the Mediterranean Sea, southwest of Crete.** Paul's ship was driven under the shelter of this island (Acts 27:16). ❡

CLAUDIA (*Klaudia*; perhaps from the Lat. *clauda*: lame) **Christian woman of Rome.** She sent greetings to Timothy (2 Tim. 4:21). ❡

CLAUDIUS (*Klaudios*; perhaps from the Lat. *claudus*: lame) **Roman emperor.** He banished the Jews from Rome (Acts 18:2). A great famine took place under his reign (Acts 11:28). ❡

CLEMENT (*Klēmēs*: mild-tempered, merciful) **Christian man of the city of Philippi.** He was a fellow worker of Paul (Phil. 4:3). Perhaps this is Clement of Rome, one of the Fathers of the church. ❡

CLEOPAS (*Kleopas*: very renowned) **Disciple of Jesus.** He was one of the two disciples to whom Jesus resurrected manifested Himself (Luke 24:18). He may be the same Clopas of John 19:25. ❡

CLOPAS → CLEOPAS

CNIDUS (*Knidos*) **Greek city located in southwest Asia Minor.** Paul's ship passed near there (Acts 27:7). ❡

COAL 1. (*anthrax*) **Piece of charred wood used as a fuel.** The expr. "to heap coals of fire on the head of an enemy" (Rom. 12:20; see Prov. 25:22) means that by doing good in response to evil, one may reach the conscience and the heart of his enemy. ❡ **2.** (fire of coals: *anthrakia*; from *anthrax*: coal) **Heap of burning coal lumps.** Servants and officers had made a fire of coals (John 18:18). The disciples saw a fire of coals and fish laid on it (John 21:9). ❡

COHORT (*speira*) **Body of infantry made of 500 to 600 men; ten cohorts made a legion.** The whole cohort was gathered against Jesus (Matt. 27:27; Mark 15:16). Julius was a centurion of the Augustan cohort (Acts 27:1). Cornelius was commanding the Italian cohort (Acts 10:1). Other refs.: John 18:3, 12; Acts 21:31. ¶

COIN (coin, silver coin: *drachmē*; from *drassomai*: to seize, to take) **Greek piece of money worth approx. one Roman denarius; it was the average pay for an average workday; also transl.: drachma.** A woman was searching for one which was lost (Luke 15:8, 9). ¶

COLLECTION (*logeia* or *logia*; from *legō*: to choose, to set aside) **Gift made by Christians, as money given during a church service.** Refs.: 1 Cor. 16:1, 2; see 1 Cor. 9:6–14; Heb. 13:15, 16. ¶

COLONY (*kolōnia*; similar to Lat. *colonia*: settlement) **District inhabited by Roman citizens (at first, veterans) and governed by Roman laws.** Philippi in Macedonia was a Roman colony (Acts 16:12). ¶

COLOSSAE (*Kolossai* or *Kolassai*: giant, colossal statue) **City of Phrygia in Asia Minor, not far from Laodicea and Hierapolis.** Paul wrote to the Christians of this city (Col. 1:2). He warns them against the deceptions of philosophy (see Col. 2:8), religious ordinances and worship of angels (see vv. 16–19). He reminds Christians that they are dead and risen with Christ and that they are to live accordingly (see Col. 2:20 to 3:4). In this letter, the supremacy of Christ (Col. 1:13–20) and the effectiveness of His work on the cross (2:13, 14) have an important place. ¶

COLOSSIAN (*Kolassaeus*) **Inhabitant of the city of Colossae, in Asia Minor.** This name is found only in the inscription to the letter to the Colossians. This letter is addressed to the believers of Colossae (see Col. 1:1, 2). ¶

CONFESSION 1. (*homologia*; from *homologeō*: to make confession) **Declaration, profession, public acknowledgment.** Jesus witnessed the good confession before Pontius Pilate (1 Tim. 6:13). Jesus is the high priest of the Christians' confession (Heb. 3:1); they are to hold fast their confession (Heb. 4:14) and the confession of their hope (10:23). **2.** (to make confession: *homologeō*; from *homologos*: assenting, of one mind) **To acknowledge, to openly declare the truth.** Confession is made to salvation by the mouth (Rom. 10:10).

CONSCIENCE (*suneidēsis*; from *sun*: together, and *oida*: to know, to perceive) **Faculty to discern right and wrong, given by God to the human race since the fall of Adam and Eve; it is more or less blinded in the natural man.** The conscience of the Christian is purified (Heb. 9:14; 10:2), but he must apply himself to have a conscience that is good (Acts 23:1; 1 Tim. 1:5, 19; Heb. 13:18; 1 Pet. 3:16, 21), pure (1 Tim. 3:9; 2 Tim. 1:3), and without offence toward God and men (Acts 24:16). Some are cauterized as to their conscience (1 Tim. 4:2).

CONVERSION (*epistrophē*; from *epistrephō*: to turn about) **Stopping on the way to eternal loss, changing direction, and turning to the Savior God.** Paul and Barnabas related the conversion of those among the Gentiles (Acts 15:3). ¶

COPY 1. (*antitupon*; from *anti*: in the place of, and *tupos*: figure, form) **What corresponds to a reality, representation.** The tabernacle's holy places are copies of the heavenly places (Heb. 9:24). Other ref.: 1 Pet. 3:21. ¶ **2.** (*hupodeigma*; from *hupo*: under, and *deiknumi*: to show) **Example set forth as an imitation, a pattern.** The sanctuary under the law was a copy and shadow of heavenly things (Heb. 8:5; 9:23).

CORBAN (*korban*) **Heb. or Aram. word meaning a gift, an offering to God.** Pharisees told men to declare corban what could have been used to assist parents. (Mark 7:11) ¶

CORINTH (*Korinthos*) **City of Greece located west of Athens; Corinth was the capital of Achaia.** Paul wrote two letters to the Christians of Corinth (1 Cor. 1:2; 2 Cor. 1:1). Paul stayed there for a year and a half, with Aquila and Priscilla (Acts 18:1); he discoursed in the synagogue there and persuaded Jews and Greeks (see v. 4). Apollos also stayed at Corinth (Acts 19:1). Paul wrote a second letter to the Corinthians to give a final warning to those who were dishonoring the Lord (2 Cor. 1:23). Erastus remained at Corinth (2 Tim. 4:20). ¶

CORINTHIAN (*Korinthios*) **Inhabitant of the city of Corinth, capital of the Roman province of Achaia in Greece.** Many Corinthians believed in the Lord Jesus and were baptized (Acts 18:8). Paul's heart was opened wide to them (2 Cor. 6:11). Two letters addressed by Paul to them are included in the N.T. Other ref.: Acts 18:27 in some mss. ¶

CORNELIUS (*Kornēlios*; Lat. name) **Roman centurion commanding a cohort stationed at Caesarea.** He was told to send for Peter. Jesus was preached to him as well as to his relatives and close friends. The Holy Spirit fell upon them. They were baptized in the name of the Lord. Refs.: Acts 10:1, 3, 7, 17, 21, 22, 24, 25, 30, 31. ¶

CORNER STONE 1. (head: *kephalē*; corner: *gōnia*; lit.: head of the corner) **Stone that plays a fundamental role in the stability of a construction; the word "head" emphasizes its importance.** Jesus Christ has become the corner stone (Matt. 21:42; Mark 12:10; Luke 20:17; Acts 4:11; 1 Pet. 2:7). **2.** (stone: *lithos*; corner: *akrogōniaios*; from *akron*: extreme, and *gonia*: corner; lit.: chief corner stone) **Stone that plays a fundamental role in the stability of a construction.** The corner stone has been laid in Zion (1 Pet. 2:6; see Is. 28:16). Jesus Christ Himself is the corner stone of the church (Eph. 2:20). ¶

COS (*Kōs*) **Island of the Mediterranean Sea located southwest of Asia Minor.** Paul's ship came there (Acts 21:1). ¶

COSAM (*Kōsam*: diviner, in Heb.) **Man of the O.T.** He is mentioned in the genealogy of Jesus (Luke 3:28). ¶

COUNSEL (*boulē*) **a. Plan, purpose of God.** Counsels are divine and eternal principles determining irrevocable decisions (Luke 7:30; Acts 2:23; 4:28; 13:36; 20:27; Eph. 1:11; Heb. 6:17). **b. Goal, plan, intention.** The counsel of the Jews was to kill Jesus (Luke 23:51). The Lord will manifest the counsels of the hearts (1 Cor. 4:5). **c. Advice, opinion after reflection.** The counsel of the soldiers was to kill the prisoners (Acts 27:42). Other refs.: Acts 5:38; 27:12 (in some mss.). ¶

COVENANT (*diathēkē*; from *diatithēmi*: to place in a particular order) **Alliance; also transl.: testament.** A covenant is a disposition without prior conditions on the part of God, e.g., toward the earth with Noah (see Gen. 9:8–17) or toward His people with Abraham (Luke 1:72; Acts 3:25; Rom. 9:4; Eph. 2:12; Heb. 8:9; 9:4, 15, 20). Signs of God's covenants are the rainbow (see Gen. 9:16), the circumcision (Acts 7:8), and the Sabbath (Ex. 31:12–17). No one can set it aside or add to it (Gal. 3:15, 17). Gal. 4:24 speaks of two covenants, the old and the new. The old covenant (2 Cor. 3:14) was concluded with Israel under the condition of their obedience. According to Heb. 8:8, a new covenant will be made; see Rom. 11:27; 2 Cor. 3:6; Heb. 7:22; 8:6, 10; 10:16, 29; 12:24. This new covenant is based on the value of the blood of Christ, the blood of the new covenant (Matt. 26:28; Mark 14:24; Luke 22:20). The church already benefits from the blessing of this new order of things to be introduced (Luke 22:20; 1 Cor. 11:25), because of this eternal covenant (Heb. 13:20). The ark of the covenant of God was seen in the temple (Rev. 11:19). Other refs. (testament): Heb. 9:16, 17. ¶

CROSS (*stauros*; from *histēmi*: to stand) **Vertical post, usually with a horizontal bar to which criminals were fastened to die.** The legs of the individuals on the cross were broken to accelerate their death (John 19:31). Jesus went out of Jerusalem bearing His cross (John 19:17); Simon of Cyrene was compelled to bear it (Matt. 27:32; Mark 15:21; Luke 23:26). A title was put on the cross: "Jesus of Nazareth, the King of the Jews" (John 19:19). Three women were standing by the cross of Jesus (John 19:25). Mockers challenged Jesus to descend from the cross (Matt. 27:40; Mark 15:30, 32). The disciple of Jesus must take up his cross and follow Him (Matt. 10:38; 16:24; Mark 8:34; 10:21 in some mss.; Luke 9:23; 14:27). Refs. to the cross of Christ: 1 Cor. 1:17, 18; Gal. 5:11; 6:12, 14; Eph. 2:16; Phil. 2:8; 3:18; Col. 1:20; 2:14; Heb. 12:2. ¶

CROWN (noun) **1.** (*diadēma*; from *diadeō*: to bind around) **Band worn around the head representing the power and the dignity of a monarch.** There are crowns on the heads of the dragon (Rev. 12:3), on the horns of the first beast (Rev. 13:1), and on the head of Him who sat on the white horse (Rev. 19:12). ¶ **2.** (*stephanos*; from *stephō*: to surround) **Ornament worn on the head which symbolizes kingship or victory.** A crown of thorns was put on the head of Jesus (Matt. 27:29; Mark 15:17; John 19:2, 5), but God has given Him a golden crown (Rev. 14:14; Ps. 21:3). This word is used re a corruptible crown and an incorruptible one (1 Cor. 9:25), the crown of righteousness (2 Tim. 4:8), the crown of glory (1 Pet. 5:4), the crown of life (Jas. 1:12; Rev. 2:10).

CROWN (verb) (*stephanoō*; from *stephanos*: crown) **To put a crown on the head of someone as a sign of victory or of honor.** This verb is used re one competing in the games (2 Tim. 2:5). Jesus has been crowned with glory and honor (Heb. 2:7, 9; Ps. 8:5). ¶

CUBIT (*pēchus*) **Measure of length of approx. 18 inches (45 centimeters); but some have transl. by "yard".** This word is used in Matt. 6:27 and Luke 12:25 (stature of a person); John 21:8 (distance from the land); Rev. 21:17 (wall of Jerusalem). ¶

CUP (*potērion*; from *poō*, which became *pinō*: to drink) **Container for drinking.** Jesus spoke of giving a cup of cold water (Matt. 10:42; Mark 9:41). The

Pharisees were cleaning the outside of the cup (Matt. 23:25, 26; Luke 11:39). The cup often speaks of the sufferings of the Lord (Matt. 20:22, 23; 26:39; Mark 10:38, 39; 14:36; Luke 22:42; John 18:11). The cup calls to mind the blood of the Lord Jesus to be shed at the cross (Matt. 26:27; Mark 14:23; Luke 22:20; 1 Cor. 11:25–28); it is also a cup of blessing (1 Cor. 10:16).

CURSE (noun) **1.** (*anathema*; from *anatithēmi*; *ana*: above, up (intens.), and *tithēmi*: to put, to place; lit.: to place up) **The word denotes the fact of being given over to God's condemnation.** Some Jews had bound themselves under a curse until they should have killed Paul (Acts 23:14). Paul could wish to be accursed from the Christ for his Jewish brothers (Rom. 9:3). No man speaking by the Spirit of God calls Jesus accursed (1 Cor. 12:3). Paul says that a curse be on any man not loving the Lord (1 Cor. 16:22) and to let any man preaching a different gospel than Paul's be under God's curse (Gal. 1:8, 9). ¶ **2.** (*katanathema*; from *kata*: against (intens.), and *anathema*: malediction) **Malediction.** There will be no more curse in eternity (Rev. 22:3). ¶ **3.** (*katara*; from *kata*: against, and *ara*: cursing) **Word invoking evil on someone, malediction.** Christ has become a curse for us at the cross (Gal. 3:10, 13). The earth bearing thorns and briars is near to being a curse (Heb. 6:8). Blessing and curse should not proceed out of the mouth (Jas. 3:10). Peter calls unjust people children of curse (2 Pet. 2:14). ¶ **4.** (to invoke, to put, to bind oneself under a curse, an oath: *anathematizō*; see the verb **CURSE**) **To invoke a malediction on oneself should one not accomplish what one had vowed.** The Jews had put themselves under a curse to kill Paul (Acts 23:12, 14, 21). Other ref.: Mark 14:71. ¶

CURSE (verb) **1.** (*anathematizō*; from *anatithēmi*: to put upon) **To invoke a malediction on oneself should one not accomplish what one had vowed.** Peter began cursing, saying he did not know Jesus (Mark 14:71). Other refs.: Acts 23:12, 14, 21. ¶ **2.** (*katathematizō*; from *kata*: intens., and *anathematizō*: to curse) **Stronger verb than the previous one.** Peter cursed, saying he did not know Jesus (Matt. 26:74). ¶ **3.** (*kakologeō*; from *kakos*: evil, and *legō*: to speak) **To speak evil against someone.** Under the Law, one who cursed father or mother was liable to be put to death (Matt. 15:4; Mark 7:10; see Ex. 21:17). Other refs.: Mark 9:39 and Acts 19:9. ¶ **4.** (*kataraomai*; from *kata*: against, and *katara*: imprecation, malediction) **To verbally wish evil upon a person or thing.** The Lord tells us to bless those who curse us (Matt. 5:44; Luke 6:28; Rom. 12:14). James warns us against using the tongue to curse men (Jas. 3:9). The fig tree cursed by Jesus had dried up (Mark 11:21). Other ref.: Matt. 25:41. ¶

CYPRIAN (*Kuprios*; from *Kupros*: Cyprus) **Inhabitant of the island of Cyprus; also transl.: of Cyprus.** Barnabas was one by birth (Acts 4:36), as was Mnason (21:16). Men of Cyprus were preaching the Lord Jesus (Acts 11:20). ¶

CYPRUS (*Kupros*: fairness) **Large island in the northeast of the Mediterranean Sea.** The gospel was preached there (Acts 11:19; 13:4). Barnabas and Mark sailed away to Cyprus (Acts 15:39). Paul passed near Cyprus (Acts 21:3; 27:4). ¶

CYRENE (*Kurēnē*) **City in northern Africa located southeast of the Island of Crete.** Libya is near Cyrene (Acts 2:10). ¶

CYRENIAN (*Kurēnaios*) **Inhabitant of Cyrene, city of a Greek colony in North Africa (Tripoli).** A certain Simon, Cyrenian, was constrained to carry the cross of Jesus (Matt. 27:32; Mark 15:21; Luke 23:26). Cyrenians rose up against Stephen and took part in stoning him (Acts 6:9; see chapter 7). Cyrenians announced the gospel of the Lord Jesus to the Greeks (Acts 11:20). Lucius was a Cyrenian (Acts 13:1). ¶

CYRENIUS → QUIRINIUS

D

DALMANUTHA (*Dalmanoutha*) **Place in Israel near the region of Magdala.** Jesus reproached the Pharisees there for asking of Him a sign from heaven (Mark 8:10; see vv. 11–13). ¶

DALMATIA (*Dalmatia*) **Region of Illyria in Europe on the eastern coast of the Adriatic Sea.** Titus had departed to Dalmatia (2 Tim. 4:10). ¶

DAMARIS (*Damaris*; perhaps: gentle) **Christian woman of Athens.** She believed the preaching of Paul and joined him (Acts 17:34). ¶

DAMASCENE (*Damaskēnos*) **Inhabitant of Damascus.** Paul was able to flee out of their city (2 Cor. 11:32; see v. 33). ¶

DAMASCUS (*Damaskos*) **Major city in southern Syria, near Israel.** On the road leading there, Paul saw the Lord in His glory and was converted; he preached the gospel first in this city, but he was obliged to flee (Acts 9:2, 3, 8, 10, 19, 22, 27). He would later recall this episode (Acts 22:5, 6, 10, 11; 26:12, 20; 2 Cor. 11:32) and his subsequent return to Damascus (Gal. 1:17). ¶

DANIEL (*Daniēl*: God is judge, in Heb.) **Prophet of the O.T.** His name appears in connection with the abomination of desolation (Matt. 24:15; Mark 13:14 in some mss.). ¶

DARKNESS 1. (*zophos*; related to *gnophos*: darkness, obscurity) **Blackness of the infernal regions.** This is where disobedient angels (see Gen. 6:2) are kept (2 Pet. 2:4; Jude 6). Other refs.: 2 Pet. 2:17; Jude 13; Heb. 12:18 in some mss. ¶ **2.** (*skotia, skotos*) **Obscurity, night.** Darkness is characterized by the absence of light (Matt. 10:27; 27:45; Mark 15:33; Luke 12:3). The word is used in the moral sense (Matt. 4:16; 6:23; Luke 1:79; 11:35; John 8:12; 12:35, 46; Rom. 2:19; 13:12; 1 Cor. 4:5). It symbolizes distance and separation from God who is light (John 1:5; 3:19; Acts 26:18; 1 John 1:5). It is the realm of man without God (Eph. 5:8; 1 Thes. 5:4, 5), subjected to Satan (Luke 22:53; Eph. 6:12; Col. 1:13). Outer darkness refers to the eternal dwelling place of wicked men, with Satan and demons (Matt. 8:12; 22:13; 25:30; 2 Pet. 2:17; Jude 13). Other refs.: John 6:17; 20:1. **3.** (full of darkness: *skoteinos*; from *skotos*: darkness) **Dark, full of blackness, in the lit. or moral sense.** This word is used re the body (Matt. 6:23; Luke 11:34, 36). ¶

DARNEL (*zizanion*) **Poisonous plant causing intoxication; it resembles wheat and grows in a similar fashion; also transl.: tares, weeds.** In a parable, the tares are the sons of the evil one (Matt. 13:25–27, 29, 30, 36, 38, 40). ¶

DAVID (*Dauid*: beloved, in Heb.) **King in the O.T. from whom Jesus Christ, the Messiah, is descended.** He is a type of the Lord as the rejected king and then as conqueror. He is mentioned in the genealogy of Jesus Christ (Matt. 1:1; Luke 3:31). He was a man after the heart of God (Acts 13:22). Jesus is the root and the offspring of David (Rev. 22:16). Other refs.: Matt. 1:6, 17; Mark 2:25; 10:47, 48; 11:10; Luke 1:27, 32, 69; John 7:42; Acts 1:16; Rom. 1:3; 4:6; 11:9; 2 Tim. 2:8; Heb. 4:7; Rev. 3:7; 5:5.

DAY OF THE LORD (day: *hēmera*; Lord: *Kurios*; from *kuros*: supremacy) **Future day of the Lord's dominion on earth.** The day of the Lord will come as a thief in the night (1 Thes. 5:2; 2 Thes. 2:2; 2 Pet. 3:10, 12). There are other expr. equivalent to the day of the Lord (Acts 2:20): the day of Christ (Phil. 1:10; 2:16), the day of Jesus Christ (Phil. 1:6), the day of the Lord Jesus (1 Cor. 5:5;

2 Cor. 1:14), the day of the Lord Jesus Christ (1 Cor. 1:8), the days of the Son of Man (Luke 17:22, 26), the day of God the Almighty (Rev. 16:14), the day (2 Pet. 1:19).

DAYSPRING FROM ON HIGH (dayspring: *anatolē*; from *anatellō*: to rise; high: *hupsos*) **Full light (rising sun) coming to enlighten a world of darkness.** This is a figure of speech related to Zacharias prophecy of the coming of the Lord Jesus to earth (Luke 1:78).

DEACON → SERVANT

DEATH (*thanatos*; from *thnēskō*: to die) **Death is the separation of the soul and spirit of a human being from the physical body.** At the coming of Jesus, light sprang up for those who sat in the shadow of death (Matt. 4:16; Luke 1:79). The word designates the spiritual state of man at birth, as separated from God (John 5:24; Rom. 5:12; see Eph. 2:1) and far from God (see Luke 15:24). Christians are identified with Christ in His death. It is compared to sleep (see 1 Cor. 15:6, 17, 18; 1 Thes. 4:13, 15). The second death is mentioned in Rev. 2:11; 20:6, 14; 21:8. This last enemy will be destroyed (1 Cor. 15:26).

DECAPOLIS (*Dekapolis*: ten cities) **Roman region composed of a group of ten cities east of Samaria and southeast of Galilee.** Great crowds from Decapolis followed Jesus (Matt. 4:25). A demoniac healed by Jesus proclaimed there all that Jesus had done for him (Mark 5:20). Jesus also healed a deaf man in that region (Mark 7:31). ¶

DEDICATION → FEAST OF DEDICATION

DEMAS (*Dēmas*; from Demeter, agrarian divinity) **Fellow worker of Paul.** He sent greetings to Philemon (Phm. 24) and the church at Colossae (Col. 4:14). He later forsook Paul (2 Tim. 4:10). ¶

DEMETRIUS (*Dēmētrios*; from Demeter, agrarian divinity) **a. Ephesian who made silver shrines of the goddess Diana.** He stirred up other artisans against Paul (Acts 19:24, 38). **b. Believing man of the N.T.** This man had a good report of all and of the truth itself (3 John 12). ¶

DEMON 1. (*daimonion*; from *daimōn*: demon, evil supernatural spirit) **For the pagans, they are inferior divinities, demigods; according to the word of God, they are fallen angels who have followed Satan in his fall; also transl.: devil.** Demons remain under the authority of Satan, awaiting the day when they will be thrown into the everlasting fire (see Matt. 25:41). They are deceiving spirits inciting men to do evil (1 Tim. 4:1). They were cast out by Jesus (Matt. 9:33; 17:18; Mark 1:34, 39; 7:26, 29, 30; 16:9; Luke 9:42; 11:14; 13:32), the twelve disciples (Mark 6:13; Luke 10:17) with the authority of the Lord (Matt. 10:8; Mark 3:15; Luke 9:1). Jesus was accused of casting out demons by their ruler (Matt. 9:34; 12:24, 27, 28; Mark 3:22; Luke 4:33, 35; 8:2; 11:15, 18–20) and of having a demon (John 7:20; 8:48, 49, 52; 10:20, 21). Demons believe that there is one God, and they tremble (Jas. 2:19). **2.** (*daimōn*) **See defin. above.** Demons were beseeching Jesus to send them away into the herd of swine (Matt. 8:31; Mark 5:12 in some mss.). They will incite the kings of the world to make war against Christ (Rev. 16:14). **3.** (to be possessed by a demon: *daimonizomai*; from *daimōn*: demon) **To be (a person) under the influence of a demon, which can lead that person astray mentally and physically; also transl.: demoniac.** This verb is used re the words of Jesus (John 10:21), the daughter of a woman of Canaan (Matt. 15:22), people brought to the Lord (Matt. 4:24; 8:16; Mark 1:32; Luke 8:36), and people healed by Jesus (Matt. 8:28, 33; 9:32; 12:22; Mark 5:15, 16, 18). ¶

DEMONIC (*daimoniōdēs*; from *daimonion*: demon, evil supernatural spirit) **Which relates to demons, which proceeds from them.** The wisdom of bitter emulation and strife in the hearts is demonic (Jas. 3:15; see v. 14). ¶

DENARIUS (*dēnarion*) **Roman coin which was equivalent in value to the Greek drachma; a denarius (plur.: denarii) prob. represented the pay for a day's work of a laborer; also transl.: penny (plur.: pence), coin, silver coin.** This coin was used as tax money (Matt. 22:19; Mark 12:15; Luke 20:24). The Samaritan gave two denarii to the innkeeper (Luke 10:35). It will be used to pay for wheat and barley (Rev. 6:6).

DERBE 1. (*Derbē*) **City of Asia Minor in the plain of Lycaonia.** Paul and Barnabas preached the gospel there (Acts 14:6, 20). Paul returned there (Acts 16:1). ¶ **2.** (of Derbe: *Derbaios*) **Native of Derbe.** Timothy was of Derbe (Acts 20:4; see 16:1). ¶

DESOLATION (*erēmōsis*; from *erēmoō*: to desolate, which is from *erēmos*: desert, wilderness) **Devastation, destruction.** The abomination of desolation will stand in the holy place (Matt. 24:15; Mark 13:14). When Jerusalem is surrounded by armies, then its desolation is near (Luke 21:20). ¶

DESTRUCTION 1. (*apōleia*; from *apollumi*: to destroy completely, which is from *apo*: intens., and *ollumi*: to destroy) **Loss, perdition, ruin.** Destruction is the opposite of eternal life (Matt. 7:13; Phil. 1:28; 3:19). There are vessels of wrath fitted for destruction (Rom. 9:22). Heresies will bring swift destruction on false prophets (2 Pet. 2:1, 3). This word is used re ungodly men (2 Pet. 3:7), some people twisting the Scriptures (2 Pet. 3:16). It is used in the expr. "the one doomed to destruction" (John 17:12; 2 Thes. 2:3). Desiring to be rich can lead to destruction (1 Tim. 6:9). Other refs.: Heb. 10:39; 2 Pet. 2:2 in some mss.; Rev. 17:8, 11. **2.** (*kathairesis*; from *kata*: down, and *haireō*: to take) **Action of casting down, of demolishing.** The weapons of the Christian are mighty for the destruction of strongholds (2 Cor. 10:4). Paul's authority was not for destruction (2 Cor. 10:8; 13:10). ¶ **3.** (*olethros*; from *ollumi*: to destroy) **Ruin, suppression, wiping out.** This word is used re the flesh (1 Cor. 5:5), men saying “Peace and safety” (1 Thes. 5:3), and those who do not obey the gospel (2 Thes. 1:9). Other ref.: 1 Tim. 6:9 (ruin). ¶ **4.** (*suntrimma*; from *sun*: intens., and *tribō*: to break) **Crushing, ruin.** Destruction and misery are in the ways of evil men (Rom. 3:16). ¶

DEVIL (*diabolos*; from *diaballō*: to accuse) **One of the names characterizing Satan; the word means an “accuser,” and more specifically a “slanderer”.** The devil is the great enemy of God and of man. He tempted Jesus at the beginning of His public ministry (Matt. 4:1, 5, 8, 11; Luke 4:2, 3, 5, 6, 13). He sows the tares (Matt. 13:39); he removes the word of God from the hearts (Luke 8:12). The eternal fire was prepared for him and his angels (Matt. 25:41). Jews were of their father, the devil (John 8:44). He put into the heart of Judas to betray Jesus (John 13:2). He was defeated by Jesus at the cross (Heb. 2:14). He is the adversary of the Christian (1 Pet. 5:8); he is the serpent of old, also called Satan (Rev. 12:9), who oppresses men (Acts 10:38). Pride is his sin (1 Tim. 3:6, 7; see Ezek. 28:1–19). Christians must stand against his artifices (Eph. 6:11), resist him (Jas. 4:7), not give place to him (Eph. 4:27). He will have great rage (Rev. 12:12). He will be bound for a thousand years (Rev. 20:2). He will go out to deceive the nations, but he will be cast into the lake of fire (Rev. 20:10). The word is also used concerning Judas who betrayed Jesus (John 6:70). Other refs.: Acts 13:10; 1 Tim. 3:11; 2 Tim. 2:26; 3:3; Titus 2:3; 1 John 3:8, 10; Jude 9; Rev. 2:10. ¶

DIANA (*Artemis*) **Goddess of hunting and fertility, mother goddess of Asia Minor, among the Romans; Artemis is her Greek name.** She was the goddess of the Ephesians (Acts 19:28, 34, 35). Her temple was one of the seven wonders of the time (Acts 19:27); miniature copies of it were made (v. 24). ¶

DIDYMUS (*Didumos*: twin) **Surname of Thomas; also transl.: the Twin.** He was one of the twelve apostles (John 11:16; 20:24; 21:2). ¶

DINNER (*ariston*) **Meal usually taken earlier in the day, but not necessarily.** Jesus told the one who had invited Him whom to invite when making a dinner (Luke 14:12). Jesus had not first washed before a dinner (Luke 11:38). A king prepared a dinner for the wedding of his son (Matt. 22:4). Other ref.: Luke 14:15 in some mss. ¶

DIONYSIUS (*Dionusios*; from Dionysius, Greek god of wine) **Member of the Areopagus, tribunal court of Athens.** He believed the preaching of Paul and joined him (Acts 17:34). ¶

DIOSCURI → TWIN BROTHERS

DIOTREPHES (*Diotrephēs*: nourished by Zeus) **Member of a gathering of Christians.** He loved to have the first place in the church (3 John 9). ¶

DISCIPLE 1. (*mathētēs*; from *manthanō*: to learn, to understand) **One who follows a teacher, learns his teachings, and puts them into practice.** The disciple is not above his teacher (Matt. 10:24). This word is used re John the Baptist (Matt. 9:14; John 1:35), the Pharisees (Matt. 22:16), the apostles of the Lord (Matt. 10:1–4; Luke 6:13–16). A disciple is an individual who receives by faith the teachings of Jesus and of the apostles, and puts them into practice (e.g., Acts 1:15). The word appears more than 250 times in the four Gospels and in the Acts. **2.** (*mathētria*; fem. of *mathētēs* above) **A woman who follows the teachings of a teacher and puts them into practice.** Dorcas (or: Tabitha) was a disciple (Acts 9:36). ¶ **3.** (to become a disciple, to be a disciple, to make a disciple, to be discipled, to win disciples, to instruct, to teach: *mathēteuō*; from *mathētēs*: disciple) **To become a disciple or to make someone else a disciple.** This word is used re a scribe (Matt. 13:52), Joseph of Arimathea (Matt. 27:57), Jesus' disciples (Matt. 28:19). Paul and Barnabas made many disciples (Acts 14:21). ¶

DIVINATION → PYTHON

DIVORCE (noun) (*apostasion*; from *aphistēmi*: to set aside, to separate) **Official dissolution of marriage.** Divorcing had been allowed by Moses (Matt. 5:31; 19:7; Mark 10:4; but see Matt. 19:6). ¶

DIVORCE (verb) **1.** (*apoluō*; from *apo*: from, away from, and *luō*: to let go) **To send one's spouse away, breaking off the marriage.** Joseph had decided to divorce Mary secretly (Matt. 1:19). Divorce was not acknowledged by Jesus except for cause of adultery (Matt. 5:31, 32; 19:3, 7–9; Mark 10:2, 4, 11, 12; Luke 16:18). **2.** (*aphiēmi*; from *apo*: from, and *hiēmi*: to send) **See previous defin.** See 1 Cor. 7:11–13.

DOG 1. (*kuōn*) **Unclean and despised animal in Israel.** See Deut. 23:18; 1 Sam. 17:43. This word is used with its usual meaning (Luke 16:21; 2 Pet. 2:22). It also designates people who cannot appreciate what is holy in the eyes of God (Matt. 7:6), are unclean morally (Phil. 3:2), and will be found as such in the judgment day (Rev. 22:15). ¶ **2.** (dog, little dog: *kunarion*; dimin. of *kuōn*: dog; lit.: little dog) **See defin. above.** It was a deprecatory term used by the Jews to designate the Gentiles. Jesus used it to show the grace of God toward Gentiles (Matt. 15:26, 27; Mark 7:27, 28). ¶

DONKEY 1. (*onos*) **Domesticated beast of burden.** Its owner takes care of it even on the Sabbath day (Luke 13:15; 14:5 in some mss.). Jesus entered Jerusalem on one that He had sent for (Matt. 21:2, 5, 7; John 12:15). ¶ **2.** (young donkey: *onarion*; dimin. of *onos*: donkey) **See defin. above.** Jesus sat upon one (John 12:14). ¶ **3.** (of a donkey: *onikos*; from *onos*: donkey) **Which pertains to a donkey.** Refs.: Matt. 18:6; Mark 9:42; Luke 17:2. ¶ **4.** (*hupozugion*; from *hupo*: under, and *zugos*: yoke; lit.: animal under the yoke) **Animal used to carry burdens.** This word is used re the king of the daughter of Zion (Matt. 21:5). A donkey reprimanded Balaam (2 Pet. 2:16). ¶

DOOR (*thura*) **That which permits entering in and going out; also transl.: doorway, entrance, gate.** A door designates Jesus Christ by whom one enters to obtain salvation (John 10:9). This word is used re a person's heart (Rev. 3:20), the door of faith opened to the nations (Acts 14:27). A great door was opened to Paul to preach the gospel (1 Cor. 16:9; 2 Cor. 2:12; Col. 4:3). God is the Judge standing before the door (Jas. 5:9). The door was shut in the parable of the ten virgins (Matt. 25:10).

DOORKEEPER (*thurōros*; from *thura*: door, and *ouros*: keeper) **Person, responsible for keeping watch at a door and permitting people to enter.** A doorkeeper was commanded to keep watch (Mark 13:34). The doorkeeper opens the door to the Shepherd (John 10:3). John spoke to the doorkeeper of the palace of the high priest (John 18:16, 17). ¶

DORCAS (*Dorkas*: gazelle; the word is associated with *derkomai*: to see clearly) **Christian woman of the city of Joppa.** She was a disciple full of good works and charitable deeds (Acts 9:36, 39). She died, but Peter prayed for her, and she returned to life (see Acts 9:40). Her name was Tabitha in Hebrew and Dorcas in Greek. ¶

DOVE (*peristera*) **Pigeon; this bird symbolizes purity, simplicity, and peace.** The disciples were to be guileless as doves (Matt. 10:16). The Spirit of God descended as a dove on Jesus (Matt. 3:16; Mark 1:10; Luke 3:22; John 1:32). Doves were sold in the temple to be offered in sacrifice (Matt. 21:12; Mark 11:15; Luke 2:24; John 2:14, 16). ¶

DRAGON (*drakōn*; from a form of *derkomai*: to see clearly) **Monstrous animal in mythology; very big serpent.** Satan is represented as a great red dragon in Revelation, having seven heads and ten horns (12:3). The dragon stands before the woman (Israel) to devour her child (Christ) (v. 4). Michael and his angels will fight against the dragon; he, with his angels, will be cast to the earth (12:7,

9). He will persecute Israel (12:13, 16, 17). He will give his power, his throne, and great authority to the first beast (13:2). People will worship him (13:4). The other beast will speak like him (13:11). Unclean spirits will come out of his mouth (16:13). He will be bound for a thousand years (20:2) and cast into the lake of fire (see v. 10). ¶

DRUSILLA (*Drousilla*) **Jewish woman.** She was the wife of the governor Felix (Acts 24:24). She died with her son during the eruption of Mount Vesuvius in A.D. 79. Other ref.: Acts 24:27 in some mss. ¶

E

EAGLE (*aetos*) **Large, strong bird of prey with sharp vision.** The eagle symbolizes the rapidity of God's judgment on corrupted humanity (Matt. 24:28; Luke 17:37; Rev. 4:7; 8:13). Other ref.: Rev. 12:14. ¶

EARNEST (noun) (*arrabōn*; from a similar Heb. word: security pledge) **What is given or done as an assurance of something to come.** The Holy Spirit is the earnest of the Christians' heavenly inheritance (2 Cor. 1:22; 5:5; Eph. 1:14). In modern Greek, *arrabōna* means an engagement ring. ¶

EGYPT (*Aiguptos*) **Country of North Africa, located southwest of Israel.** Jews from Egypt were present in Jerusalem at Pentecost (Acts 2:10). The Israelites sojourn in Egypt at the time of Joseph (Acts 7:9, 10–12, 15; 13:17) and their exodus from there was under the leadership of Moses (Acts 7:17, 18, 34, 36, 39, 40; Heb. 3:16; 8:9; 11:26, 27; Jude 5). Joseph and Mary with their child Jesus were obliged to flee there (Matt. 2:13–15, 19). It is the spiritual name of Jerusalem (Rev. 11:8). ¶

EGYPTIAN (*Aiguptios*) **Inhabitant of Egypt, a country of North Africa.** This name is used re Moses (Acts 7:22, 24, 28), the drowning in the Red Sea (Heb. 11:29). Paul was mistaken for one (Acts 21:38). ¶

ELAMITE (*Elamitēs*) **Inhabitant of Elam in Asia, a country north of the Persian Gulf; its capital was Susa.** They heard the gospel preached in their own language at Pentecost (Acts 2:9). ¶

ELDER 1. (*presbuteros*; from *presbus*: old man, ambassador; elder woman: *presbutera*) **a. Older person in general.** The elder son was in the field when the prodigal son came back (Luke 15:25). Elders are not to be rebuked sharply (1 Tim. 5:1, 2). Other ref.: Acts 2:17. **b. A representative of the people.** There were elders among the Jews (e.g., Matt. 21:23; Acts 4:8). Some elders were members of the council in Jerusalem. Other refs.: Matt. 16:21; Mark 7:3; Luke 7:3; John 8:9; Acts 4:5, 23. **c. Much respected ancestor among the Israelites.** Jesus' disciples transgressed their tradition (Matt. 15:2). They obtained a good testimony (Heb. 11:2). **d. Christian with spiritual maturity and experience that qualify him to oversee and respond to the spiritual needs of other Christians in a local church.** Elders were established by the apostles or their delegates (Titus 1:5). They are responsible to feed the flock of God (1 Pet. 5:1); younger people must submit to them (v. 5). Other refs.: Acts 11:30; 1 Tim. 5:17, 19; Titus 1:5; Jas. 5:14. **e. Priestly company of redeemed people glorified in heaven and characterized by spiritual wisdom and intelligence.** We read about these elders in the Book of Revelation (Rev. 4:4, 10; 5:5; 11:16; 14:3; 19:4). ¶ **2.** (council of elders: *presbuterion*; from *presbuteros*: elder) **Assembly of elders.** There were assemblies of elders among the Jews (Luke 22:66; Acts 22:5). Other ref.: 1 Tim. 4:14. **3.** (elder with: *sumpresbuteros*; from *sun*: together, and *presbuteros*: elder) **See d. in 1. above.** Peter was an elder himself (1 Pet. 5:1). ¶

ELEAZAR (*Eleazar*: God has helped, in Heb.) **Man of the O.T.** Eleazar is mentioned in the genealogy of Jesus Christ (Matt. 1:15). ¶

ELECTION (*eklogē*; from *ek*: from, and *legō*: to choose) **Free and sovereign choice of God; also transl.: choice.** This word is used re Paul (Acts 9:15), Jacob (Rom. 9:11), a remnant among the Jews (Rom. 11:5), Israel (Rom. 11:7, 28), the Thessalonians (1 Thes. 1:4), Christians (2 Pet. 1:10). ¶

ELI 1. (*Ēli*: my God, in Heb.) **Personal form of the name of God; also written: *Eloi*.** At the cross, Jesus cried "*Eli, Eli, lama sabachthani?* That is to say: My God, My God, why have You forsaken Me?" (Matt. 27:46). ¶ **2.** (*Hēli*: height, in Heb.) **Father of Joseph, himself the foster father of Jesus; also transl.: Heli.** Eli is mentioned in the genealogy of Jesus (Luke 3:23). ¶

ELIAKIM (*Eliakim*: God-appointed, in Heb.) **Name of two men in the O.T.** They are mentioned in the genealogy of Jesus Christ (Matt. 1:13; Luke 3:30). ¶

ELIEZER (*Eliezer*: God of help, in Heb.) **Man of the O.T.** He is mentioned in the genealogy of Jesus (Luke 3:29). ¶

ELIJAH (*Ēlias*: my God is Jehovah, in Heb.) **Prophet in Israel.** He is mentioned in connection with John the Baptist (Matt. 11:14; Luke 1:17; John 1:21, 25) and the Lord Jesus (Matt. 16:14; Mark 6:15; 8:28; Luke 9:8, 19). He had the same passions as we have; God answered his prayer (James 5:17). He was sent to a widow in a foreign land (Luke 4:25, 26). He thought he was the only one faithful to the Lord (Rom. 11:2). He appeared with Moses at the transfiguration of the Lord (Matt. 17:3, 4, 10–12; Mark 9:4, 5, 11–13; Luke 9:30, 33). Other refs.: Matt. 27:47, 49; Mark 15:35, 36; Luke 9:54. ¶

ELISHA (*Elisaios*: my God is deliverance, in Heb.) **Prophet in Israel.** He is mentioned in relation to Naaman, a leper who was cleansed (Luke 4:27). ¶

ELIUD (*Elioud*: God of majesty, in Heb.) **Man of the O.T.** He is mentioned in the genealogy of Jesus Christ (Matt. 1:14, 15). ¶

ELIZABETH (*Elisabet*: God of the oath, in Heb.) **Wife of the priest Zacharias and mother of John the Baptist.** She was from the daughters of Aaron (Luke 1:5). She conceived a son in her old age (Luke 1:7, 13, 24, 25, 36, 57). She was filled with the Holy Spirit and recognized Mary as the mother of the Lord (Luke 1:40, 41). ¶

ELMADAM (*Elmadam*; also spelled: *Elmōdam*) **Man of the O.T.** He is mentioned in the genealogy of Jesus (Luke 3:28). ¶

ELYMAS (*Elumas*: wise man) **Another name of the sorcerer Bar-Jesus.** He tried to turn away Sergius Paulus from the faith (Acts 13:8). ¶

EMERALD 1. (*smaragdos*) **Bright-green transparent precious stone.** One of the foundations of the wall of the heavenly Jerusalem is adorned with emerald (Rev. 21:19). ¶ **2.** (of emerald: *smaragdinos*) **See above.** The rainbow around the throne was like the appearance of an emerald (Rev. 4:3). ¶

EMMAUS (*Emmaous*: warm spring, in Heb.) **Village located about 7 miles (11 kilometers) northwest of Jerusalem.** Jesus conversed with two disciples from Emmaus (Luke 24:13). ¶

EMMOR → HAMOR

ENOCH (*Henōch*: initiated, instructed, in Heb.) **Faithful man of the O.T.** He is mentioned in the genealogy of Jesus (Luke 3:37). He had the testimony of having pleased God, who took him up so that he should not see death (Heb. 11:5). He prophesied about the wicked (Jude 14). ¶

ENOS → ENOSH

ENOSH (*Enōs*: man, in Heb.) **Man of the O.T.** He is mentioned in the genealogy of Jesus (Luke 3:38). He was the grandson of Adam (see Gen. 4:26). ¶

EPAENETUS (*Epainetos*: praise) **Believing man of the church of Rome.** He was the firstfruits of Asia for Christ (Rom. 16:5). ¶

EPAPHRAS (*Epaphras*; from Epaphroditus: devoted to Aphrodite) **Fellow servant of the apostle Paul.** He was a faithful servant of Christ for the Colossians (Col. 1:7), combating for them in prayer (4:12). He was a fellow prisoner of Paul (Phm. 23). ¶

EPAPHRODITUS (*Epaphroditos*: devoted to Aphrodite) **Fellow worker and fellow soldier of Paul.** He had been sent to bring a gift to Paul (Phil. 4:18). He was sent to the Philippians (Phil. 2:25). ¶

EPHESIAN (*Ephesios*) **Inhabitant of the city of Ephesus, capital of the Roman province of Asia.** They were devoted to the worship of Diana (Acts 19:28, 34, 35). Trophimus was an Ephesian (Acts 21:29). ¶

EPHESUS (*Ephesos*) **City of Lydia on the west coast of Asia Minor.** Paul reasoned with the Jews in the synagogue of Ephesus (Acts 18:19, 21). Apollos came there (Acts 18:24). Paul taught there for at least three years (Acts 19:1, 17, 26); he gave his recommendations to its elders (Acts 20:16, 17). He mentions his visits to Ephesus to the Corinthians (1 Cor. 15:32; 16:8). He addressed a letter to the church of Ephesus (Eph. 1:1). Timothy had remained there (1 Tim. 1:3); Paul sent Tychicus there (2 Tim. 4:12). Onesiphorus had rendered much service at Ephesus (2 Tim. 1:18). It is one of the seven churches to which a letter is addressed (Rev. 1:11; 2:1). ¶

EPHPHATHA (*ephphatha*) **Aram. term meaning "Be opened".** Jesus used this word when healing a deaf person (Mark 7:34). ¶

EPHRAIM (*Ephraim*: double fruitfulness, in Heb.) **City located approx. 15 miles (25 kilometers) from Jerusalem, near the desert.** Jesus stayed there (John 11:54). ¶

EPICUREAN (*Epikoureios*) **Epicureans were philosophers seeking happiness in pleasure and avoidance of sufferings; for them, the soul died with the body and there was no future retribution.** Epicurean and stoic philosophers attacked Paul verbally in Athens (Acts 17:18). ¶

EPILEPTIC (to be epileptic: *selēniazomai*; from *selēnē*: moon; lit.: to be affected by the moon) **Someone afflicted by periodical seizures; prob. a**

person suffering from epilepsy which was believed to be influenced by the moon. Jesus healed epileptic persons (Matt. 4:24; 17:15). ❡

EPISTLE (*epistolē*; from *epi*: to, and *stellō*: to send) It is the name given to the 21 books of the N.T. which are letters to local churches or to individuals.

EPISTLE OF COMMENDATION (letter: *epistolē*; of commendation: *sustatikos*; from *sunistaō*: to approve, to recommend) **Letter facilitating the favorable introduction of a Christian to other Christians.** It facilitated the reception of a Christian, including assistance in practical matters and participation in the Lord's Supper, at another local church (see Rom. 16:1, 2 where Phoebe is commended). Other ref.: 2 Cor. 3:1. ❡

ER (*Ēr*: watchful, in Heb.) **Man of the O.T.** He is mentioned in the genealogy of Jesus (Luke 3:28). ❡

ERASTUS (*Erastos*: beloved) **a. Treasurer of the city of Corinth.** He sent his greetings to the Christians at Rome (Rom. 16:23). **b. The same as the preceding or another Christian brother.** He ministered to Paul, who sent him to Macedonia (Acts 19:22). Later, he remained at Corinth (2 Tim. 4:20). ❡

ESAIAS → ISAIAH

ESAU (*Ēsau*: hairy, in Heb.) **Son of Isaac and Rebecca, and twin brother of Jacob.** He sold his birthright (Heb. 12:16). Isaac blessed him (Heb. 11:20). God hated Esau (Rom. 9:13), most likely because of his contempt for the divine promises of blessing made to his fathers. ❡

ESLI → HESLI

ESROM → HEZRON

ETERNAL 1. (*aidios*; from *aei*: always) **a. Without beginning or end, self-existent.** The eternal power and divinity of God are apprehended by the mind through the things that are made (Rom. 1:20). **b. Perpetual, without end, everlasting.** The angels who did not keep their original state (see Gen. 6) are being kept in eternal chains (Jude 6). ¶ **2.** (*aiōnios*; from *aiōn*: age, duration) **Without end, outside of time; also transl.: everlasting.** This word is used re the ages (Rom. 16:25), the nature of God Himself (Rom. 16:26; 1 Tim. 6:16; Heb. 9:14; 1 Pet. 5:10), salvation (Heb. 5:9), redemption (Heb. 9:12), glory (2 Cor. 4:17; 2 Tim. 2:10), things (2 Cor. 4:18), inheritance (Heb. 9:15), encouragement (2 Thes. 2:16), grace given (2 Tim. 1:9), dwellings (Luke 16:9), the kingdom of the Lord (2 Pet. 1:11), the future body of glory of Christian (2 Cor. 5:1), the eternal fire (Matt. 18:8; 25:41), condemnation (Mark 3:29; Heb. 6:2), punishment and destruction (Matt. 25:46; 2 Thes. 1:9), fire (Jude 7), the gospel (Rev. 14:6). Other refs.: Titus 1:2; Heb. 13:20; Phm. 15. **3** See **LIFE ETERNAL**.

ETERNAL LIFE → LIFE ETERNAL

ETHIOPIAN (*Aithiops*: burned by the sun) **Inhabitant of Ethiopia, a country of eastern Africa.** An Ethiopian of the royal court was converted through the preaching of Philip (Acts 8:27) and was baptized by him (see Acts 8:26–40). ¶

ETHNARCH → GOVERNOR

EUBULUS (*Euboulos*: well-intentioned, prudent) **Christian man of Rome.** He sends his greetings to Timothy (2 Tim. 4:21). ¶

EUNICE (*Eunikē*: happily victorious; from *eu*: good, and *nikos*: victory) **Mother of Timothy.** She was a believing Jewish woman who had married a Greek man (see Acts 16:1). The sincere faith in her son Timothy had first dwelt in her (2 Tim. 1:5). ¶

EUNUCH (eunuch: *eunouchos*; to make eunuch: *eunouchizō*; from *eunē*: bed, and *echō*: to keep; lit.: keeper of the bed) **Man who cannot have a normal sexual life or procreate because of a forced or voluntary castration or birth defect; to become such.** There are those who were born as such, those who were made eunuchs by men, and those who have made themselves eunuchs (figur. speaking) for the kingdom of heaven (Matt. 19:12). Philip preached Jesus to a eunuch from Ethiopia (Acts 8:27, 34, 36, 38, 39). ¶

EUODIA (*Euodia*: pleasant journey or fragrant; from *eu*: good, and *odos*: journey) **Christian woman of Philippi.** Paul urged Euodia and Syntyche to have the same mind in the Lord (Phil. 4:2). ¶

EUODIAS → EUODIA

EUPHRATES (*Euphratēs*: the abounding) **River in western Asia, approx. 1,740 miles (2,800 kilometers) in length, located east of Israel; Babylon was built near the Euphrates River; it flows into the Persian Gulf.** Four angels bound there will be released; they will kill the third part of men (Rev. 9:14). Other ref.: Rev. 16:12. ¶

EURAQUILO → EUROCLYDON

EUROCLYDON (*Eurokludōn*; from *euros*: east wind, and *kludōn*: wave) **Very violent wind blowing from the east or from the northeast.** This wind endangered the ship on which Paul was traveling to Italy (Acts 27:14). ¶

EUTYCHUS (*Eutuchos*: fortunate; from *eu*: good, and *tuchē*: fortune) **Young man of Troas.** He fell from the third floor and was taken up dead (Acts 20:9), but he came back to life (see vv. 10, 12). ¶

EVANGELIST (*euangelistēs*; from *eu*: well, and *angellō*: to bring a message; lit.: one who announces good news) **This spiritual gift is for the preaching of**

the gospel concerning Jesus Christ, the Son of God. It is given by the Lord (Eph. 4:11) for the edifying of the body of Christ (see v. 12). Philip is the only one to be called an evangelist (Acts 21:8). Timothy was to do the work of an evangelist (2 Tim. 4:5). ¶

EVE (*Eua*: life, in Heb.) **Name of the first woman.** God created Eve from Adam (see Gen. 2:22); she was the mother of all living (3:20). God formed her after Adam (1 Tim. 2:13). She was deceived by the craftiness of the serpent (2 Cor. 11:3). ¶

EXPOSITION OF THE LOAVES (exposition: *prothesis*; from *pro*: before, and *tithēmi*: to place; loaf: *artos*) **There were twelve loaves of bread in the holy place of the tabernacle, which were arranged in two rows on the table of showbread.** The showbread was in the Holy Place of the tabernacle (Heb. 9:2). David ate the showbread reserved for the priests under the law (Matt. 12:4; Mark 2:26; Luke 6:4; see 1 Sam. 21:6).

EYE SALVE (*kollourion*; from *kolla*: glue) **Medicinal ointment applied to the eye for healing, collyrium.** The angel of the church of Laodicea was to buy eye salve from the Lord (Rev. 3:18). ¶

EZECHIAS → HEZEKIAH

F

FABLE (*muthos*; close to *mutheō*: to say, to tell) **Invented story, imaginary event; also transl.: myth.** Fables seem to have been common among the Jews; Paul exhorts not to be attached to them (1 Tim. 1:4; Titus 1:14). They should be rejected (1 Tim. 4:7). There are those who will turn aside to fables (2 Tim. 4:4). The coming of the Lord was not made known by imagined fables (2 Pet. 1:16). ¶

FAIR HAVENS (*Kaloi Limenes*; from *kalos*: beautiful, good, and *limēn*: port) **Seaport of southern Crete, near the city of Lasea.** Paul's ship came there (Acts 27:8). ¶

FAITH 1. (*pistis*; from *peithō*: to convince, to believe) **Trust, confidence; Heb. 11:1 says that faith is the assurance of things hoped for and the conviction of things not seen.** Faith comes by hearing and hearing by the word of God (Rom. 10:17). It is a gift of God (Eph. 2:8). Faith is presented in various aspects: **a.** the means by which one acquires salvation (e.g., Rom. 10:17; Eph. 2:8); **b.** the inner energy of the Christian fed by the word of God and directed by the Holy Spirit (e.g., 1 Tim. 4:12); **c.** the whole range of Christian truths and divine blessings received by faith (e.g., Eph. 4:5); **d.** a particular gift of grace of use in the church (e.g., 1 Cor. 12:9). **2.** (of little faith: *oligopistos*; from *oligos*: little, and *pistis*: conviction, faith) **Not believing or trusting very much.** The disciples were people of little faith (Matt. 6:30; 8:26; 16:8; Luke 12:28), Peter in particular (Matt. 14:31). ¶

FAITHFUL (*pistos*; from *peithō*: to believe, to have confidence) **a. Which is reliable, sure; trustworthy.** Paul uses the expr. "this is a faithful saying" (1 Tim. 1:15; 3:1; 4:9; 2 Tim. 2:11; Titus 3:8). The words spoken to John were faithful and true (Rev. 21:5; 22:6). **b. Worthy of confidence, person worthy of confidence; one who believes.** The term designates those who have faith (e.g., Col. 1:7). It is used re a servant (Matt. 24:45; 25:21, 23), a manager (Luke 12:42), men who will be able to teach others (2 Tim. 2:2), the circumcision (Acts 10:45), being in Christ Jesus (Eph. 1:1), those with the Lamb (Rev. 17:14). It is used often in 1 Tim. (4:3, 10, 12; 5:16; 6:2). It characterizes God (e.g., 1 Cor. 1:9) and Jesus (e.g., Heb. 3:2).

FAITHFULLY (*piston*; from *peithō*: to believe, to have confidence) **With faith, inspiring confidence.** Gaius was acting faithfully in what he did toward the brothers (3 John 5).

FAITHFULNESS 1. (*pistis*; from *peithō*: to believe, to have confidence; lit.: faith, firm conviction) **Loyalty, trustworthiness; also transl.: faith, fidelity.** Faithfulness is one of the more important matters of the law (Matt. 23:23). The faithfulness of God remains (Rom. 3:3). It is part of the fruit of the Spirit (Gal. 5:22). Servants are to show faithfulness (Titus 2:10). **2.** See **FAITH**.

FAITHLESS 1. (*asunthetos*; from *a*: neg., and *suntithēmi*: to concur) **Oath breaker, disloyal.** Some men are faithless (Rom. 1:31). ¶ **2.** (to be faithless: *apisteō*; from *a*: neg., and *pistos*: believing, faithful) **To disbelieve, to be unfaithful.** If Christians are faithless, Jesus Christ remains faithful (2 Tim. 2:13).

FAST (noun), **FASTING** (noun), **FAST** (verb) (fast, fasting: *nēsteia*; to fast: *nēsteuō*; from *nē*: neg. particle, and *esthiō*: to eat) **Voluntary deprivation of food; to voluntarily deprive oneself of food.** The Lord fasted at the beginning of His ministry (Matt. 4:2). He gave instructions on how to conduct oneself when fasting (Matt. 6:16, 17, 18). The disciples of John fasted often, but not those of Jesus (Matt. 9:14, 15; Mark 2:18, 19, 20; Luke 5:33–35). A Pharisee fasted twice a week (Luke 18:12). Fasting is associated with prayer (Matt. 17:21; Mark 9:29; Luke 2:37; Acts 10:30; 13:2, 3; 14:23). Paul fasted (2 Cor. 6:5; 11:27). Other refs.: Acts 27:9; 1 Cor. 7:5 in some mss. ¶

FATHOM (*orguia*; from *oregō*: to stretch) **Measure of length or depth of about six feet (1.8 meters).** Ref.: Acts 27:28. ¶

FEAR (*phobos*; from *phebomai*: to fear, to be afraid) **Feeling of trouble and worry in the soul caused by danger, evil, pain; also transl.: awe, respect, reverence.** The guards at the tomb of Jesus trembled for fear (Matt. 28:4). This word is also used re the Gerasenes (Luke 8:37), the disciples (Matt. 14:26), shepherds (Mark 4:41; Luke 2:9), those who will be ready to die (Luke 21:26).

FEAST 1. (*dochē*; from *dechomai*: to receive) **Banquet, reception.** Levi gave a great feast (Luke 5:29). The poor, the crippled, the lame, the blind should be invited to a feast (Luke 14:13). ¶ **2.** (*heortē*) **Celebration, commemoration; also transl.: festival.** This word designates the Israelite celebrations: the Passover (Matt. 26:5; 27:15; Mark 14:2; 15:6; Luke 2:41, 42; 23:17; John 2:23; 6:4; 13:1, 29), the Feast of Unleavened Bread (Luke 22:1), the Feast of Tabernacles (John 7:2), and the Feast of the Dedication (John 10:22). Other refs.: John 4:45; 5:1; 7:8, 10, 11, 14, 37; 11:56; 12:12, 20; Acts 18:21; Col. 2:16. ¶ **3.** to celebrate the feast: *heortazō*; from *heortē*: feast) **To keep a feast or a festival, a special occasion by a ceremony.** Christians are to celebrate the feast of unleavened bread with sincerity and truth (1 Cor. 5:8), in separation of evil (see v. 7). ¶ **4.** (governor of the feast, master of the feast: *architriklinos*; from *archi*: denoting rank or degree, and *triklinos*: room with three couches) **Person responsible for arranging the table and couches, guiding guests, organizing the meal as well as tasting food and wine at a feast.** Water that had been transformed into wine was brought to the master of the feast (John 2:8, 9). ¶

FEAST OF DEDICATION (*enkainia*; from *en*: in, and *kainos*: new) **Jewish feast lasting eight days and celebrated in the middle of the month of December.** This feast was celebrated in Jerusalem (John 10:22). It perpetuated the memory of the dedication of the temple purified and rebuilt after its profanation by Antiochus Epiphanes. It was instituted by Judas Maccabeus in 164 B.C. Jews today still celebrate the rededication of the temple during the Festival of Lights (Hanukkah). ¶

FELIX (*Phēlix*: happy, in Lat.) **Governor of Judea.** Paul was brought to him (Acts 23:24, 26; 24:3, 22, 24, 25). He left Paul prisoner to gain the favor of the Jews (Acts 24:27; 25:14). ¶

FELLOW PRISONER (*sunaichmalōtos*; from *sun*: together, and *aichmalōtos*: captive) **One who is held captive together with another**. Andronicus and Junias were fellow prisoners of Paul (Rom. 16:7), as were also Aristarchus (Col. 4:10) and Epaphras (Phm. 23). ¶

FELLOW REBEL (*sustasiastēs*; from *sun*: together, and *stasis*: insurrection, revolt) **Accomplice with others during an insurrection, a rebellion.** Barabbas was bound with his fellow rebels (Mark 15:7). ¶

FELLOW SERVANT (*sundoulos*; from *sun*: together, and *doulos*: slave, servant) **a. Collaborator, associate in the work of the Lord.** Paul uses this term re Epaphras (Col. 1:7) and Tychicus (4:7). **b. Slave with someone else.** This term is used re men (Matt. 18:28, 29, 31, 33; 24:49; Rev. 6:11) and angels (Rev. 19:10; 22:9). ¶

FELLOW SLAVE → FELLOW SERVANT

FELLOW SOLDIER (*sustratiōtēs*; from *sun*: together with, and *stratiōtēs*: soldier) **Collaborator in the service for Christ.** Epaphroditus was a fellow soldier with Paul (Phil. 2:25), as was also Archippus (Phm. 2). ¶

FELLOW TRAVELER (*sunekdēmos*; from *sun*: together, and *ekdēmos*: traveler) **Person who journeys with another one.** Paul uses this term re Gaius and Aristarchus (Acts 19:29), a brother preaching the gospel (2 Cor. 8:19). ¶

FELLOW WORKER (*sunergos*; from *sun*: together, and *ergon*: work) **One who exercises an activity with someone else to achieve something, collaborator, companion.** This word is used re Paul and others (2 Cor. 1:24), Prisca and Aquila (Rom. 16:3), Urbanus (Rom. 16:9), Timothy (Rom. 16:21; 1 Thes. 3:2), Titus (2 Cor. 8:23), Epaphroditus (Phil. 2:25), Clement and others (Phil. 4:3), Aristarchus, Mark and Jesus called Justus (Col. 4:11), as well as Philemon, Demas, and Luke (Phm. 1, 24), those who have gone forth for the name of Jesus (3 John 8). Other ref. (laborer together): 1 Cor. 3:9. ¶

FELLOWSHIP 1. (*koinōnia*; from *koinōneō*: to share) **Common interest and portion, association; also transl.: communion.** This word is used re the apostles (Acts 2:42), the blood and the body of Christ (1 Cor. 10:16), darkness (2 Cor. 6:14), the gospel (Phil. 1:5), the Father and the Son (1 Cor. 1:9; 1 John 1:3, 6), the Holy Spirit (2 Cor. 13:14; Phil. 2:1), Christians (1 John 1:7). **2.** (to have fellowship with: *sunkoinōneō*; from *sun*: together, and *koinōneō*: to share) **To have something in common with, to associate with.** Christians should not have fellowship with the unfruitful works of darkness (Eph. 5:11). **3.** (to give the right hand of fellowship; right: *dexios*; to give: *didōmi*; fellowship: *koinōnia*; from *koinōnos*: common) **To give the hand (lit.: the right) as a token of support, communion; the right hand is a sign of a loyal engagement.** James, Cephas, and John gave the right hand of fellowship to Paul and Barnabas in their service for the Lord (Gal. 2:9).

FESTUS (*Phēstos*: festive) **Procurator of Judea.** He succeeded Felix (Acts 24:27). Paul defended himself before him (see Acts 25 and 26). Other refs.: Acts 25:1, 4, 9, 12–14, 22–24; 26:24, 25, 32. ¶

FIG 1. (*sukon*) **Edible fruit of the fig tree; the fleshy receptacle has seeds on the inside.** Figs are not gathered from thistles (Matt. 7:16) or thornbushes (Luke 6:44). Jesus found no figs on a fig tree (Mark 11:13). Figs are not produced by a grapevine (Jas. 3:12). ¶ **2.** (unseasonable fig: *olunthos*) **Fig that is not ripe.** Ref.: Rev. 6:13. ¶

FIG TREE (*sukē*; from *sukon*: fig) **Fruit tree which is the most common in Israel and which can live up to 200 years.** The fig tree produces its leaves at the end of spring (Matt. 24:32; Mark 13:28; Luke 21:29). Its flowers are invisible to the human eye, but one can obtain several harvests of figs each year. The Lord's curse upon a fig tree which bore no fruit, only leaves (Matt. 21:19a, b, 20, 21; Mark 11:13, 20, 21), is an illustration of Israel which bore no fruit for God. Jesus had seen Nathanael under the fig tree (John 1:48, 50). Other refs.: Luke 13:6, 7; Jas. 3:12; Rev. 6:13. ¶

FIGURE 1. (*antitupon*; from *anti*: in place of, instead of, and *tupos*: type) **That which is foreshadowed, represented by a type.** Baptism is the figure of Noah's ark going through the water (1 Pet. 3:21). Other ref. (copy): Heb. 9:24. ¶ **2.** (*parabolē*; from *para*: along, near, and *ballō*: to throw) **Symbolic narrative or comparison of everyday life to illustrate more clearly a moral or spiritual lesson.** The tabernacle is a figure for the present time (Heb. 9:9). Abraham received Isaac in a figure as risen from among the dead (Heb. 11:19).

FINE LINEN (fine linen: *bussos*; from a Heb. verb: to be white; with or in fine linen: *bussinos*) **Fabric made from high quality linen.** The following are clothed in fine linen: a rich man (Luke 16:19), the Lamb's bride (Rev. 19:8), Babylon (Rev. 18:12, 16), and the armies that follow the Lord (Rev. 19:14). ¶

FIRSTBORN (*prōtotokos*; from *protos*: first, and *tiktō*: to give birth) **First in order of birth; preeminent; also transl.: firstbegotten.** This word is used re

Jesus Christ (Matt. 1:25; Luke 2:7), the Israelites (Heb. 11:28), the preeminence of the Lord Jesus (Heb. 1:6) over creation (Col. 1:15), as the Creator (see v. 16), among many brothers (Rom. 8:29), in resurrection (Col. 1:18; Rev. 1:5). The church is called the church of the firstborn (Heb. 12:23). ¶

FIRSTFRUITS (*aparchē*; from *apo*: from, and *archē*: beginning) **First ripe fruits of the harvest; also transl.: first convert.** This was the occasion of a feast instituted by the Lord (see Lev. 23:9–14). Believers, who have the firstfruits of the Spirit, groan inwardly as they wait eagerly for adoption as sons (Rom. 8:23). This word is used re the first Christians (Rom. 16:5; 1 Cor. 16:15), Jesus Christ raised from among the dead (1 Cor. 15:20, 23), the 144,000 (Rev. 14:4), Israel (Rom. 11:16), Christians (Jas. 1:18). Other ref.: 2 Thes. 2:13 in some mss. ¶

FLAX (*linon*) **Fiber of a plant from which linen is obtained; lamp wicks made from braided flax.** The Lord will not quench smoking flax (Matt. 12:20; see Is. 42:3). Other refs.: Mark 1:18 in some mss.; Rev. 15:6. ¶

FLESH 1. (*sarx*) **In the N.T., this word has different meanings: a. the substance of the body, whether of animals or men** (1 Cor. 15:39); **b. the human body** (2 Cor. 10:3; Gal. 2:20; Phil. 1:22); **c. the human nature, which includes the spirit, the soul, and the body** (Matt. 24:22; John 1:13; Rom. 3:20); **d. the holy humanity of the Lord Jesus, which includes His spirit, His soul, and His body** (John 1:14; 1 Tim. 3:16; 1 John 4:2, 3; 2 John 7); in Heb. 5:7, the expr. "the days of his flesh" refers to the life of the Lord spent on the earth in contrast to His present life in resurrection; **e. the complete person** (2 Cor. 7:5; Jas. 5:3); **f. the weakest element of the human nature** (Matt. 26:41; Rom. 6:19; 8:3); **g. the non-regenerated state of men** (Rom. 7:5; 8:8, 9); **h. the seat of sin in the inward man** (2 Pet. 2:18; 1 John 2:16); **i. the inferior and temporal element in the Christian** (Gal. 3:3; 6:8) **and in the ordinances of the flesh** (Heb. 9:10); **j. the human person with its natural abilities** (1 Cor. 1:26; 2 Cor. 10:2, 3); **k. circumstances** (1 Cor. 7:28); concerning what is external to

Christians (2 Cor. 7:1; Eph. 6:5; Heb. 9:13); **l. what is external and visible in contrast with the spirit, which is internal and true** (John 6:63); **m. natural relationships** (1 Cor. 10:18; Gal. 4:23) **or marital ones** (Matt. 19:5, 6; Mark 10:8; 1 Cor. 6:16; Eph. 5:31). (After Walter Biggar Scott.) **2.** (*kreas*) **Meat.** It is right not to eat flesh, whereby one's brother is scandalized (Rom. 14:21). Paul would never again eat flesh if it made his brother stumble (1 Cor. 8:13). ¶

FLOOD 1. (*kataklusmos*; from *katakluzō*: to overflow) **Overflowing of water, which becomes a cataclysm.** The flood happened during the days of Noah. We read that "all the fountains of the great deep were broken up, and the windows of heaven were opened" (Gen. 7:11), to such an extent that "the high hills under the whole heaven were covered" (v. 19). The flood was a judgment of God upon the world of the ungodly (2 Pet. 2:5). Only Noah, the righteous, and his household were saved (Matt. 24:38, 39; Luke 17:27; see also 1 Pet. 3:20). ¶ **2.** (*plēmmura*; *pimplēmi* means to fill) **Rise in the water level, overflow of a river.** In a parable, when a flood came, the stream beat with violence against the house (Luke 6:48). ¶

FORNICATION → SEXUAL IMMORALITY

FORTRESS 1. (*parembolē*; from *para*: beside, and *emballō*: to interpose) **Lit.: soldier's quarters, barracks; hence, fortified castle, stronghold.** Paul was brought into a fortress (Acts 21:34, 37; 22:24; 23:10, 16, 32). **2.** (*ochurōma*; from *ochuroō*: to fortify) **Fortified place, stronghold.** Reasonings against the knowledge of God are compared to fortresses; but the Christian, by spiritual weapons, can destroy such fortresses (2 Cor. 10:4). ¶

FORTUNATUS (*Phortounatos*: happy, fortunate, in Lat.) **Christian man of Corinth.** His coming had gladdened Paul (1 Cor. 16:17; see v. 18). ¶

FORUM OF APPIUS → MARKET OF APPIUS

FOX (*alōpēx*) **Carnivorous mammal of the same family as the dog, which customarily makes a den for itself.** Foxes have a dwelling place, but Jesus did not (Matt. 8:20; Luke 9:58). Herod Antipas was like one (Luke 13:32). ¶

FRANKINCENSE (*libanos*; from a Heb. word: white) **White and fragrant gum obtained by making an incision in a certain tree.** Frankincense was presented to Jesus (Matt. 2:11). Babylon will no longer buy frankincense (Rev. 18:13). ¶

FREE (adj.) **1.** (*eleutheros*) **Liberated, not bound by an obligation; unconstrained, independent.** This word is used re the Jews (John 8:33), the Son (John 8:36), custom or tribute (Matt. 17:26). Paul often uses this word in his letters (Rom. 6:20; 7:3; 1 Cor. 7:21, 22, 39; 9:1, 19; 12:13; Gal. 3:28; 4:26, 31; Eph. 6:8; Col. 3:11); see also 1 Pet. 2:16, Rev. 13:16; 19:18. The word is transl. "free woman" (*eleuthera*) in Gal. 4:22, 23, 30, and "free man" (*eleutheros*) in Rev. 6:15. ¶ **2.** (to set free, to make free, to free: *eleutheroō*; from *eleutheros*: free) **To liberate, to deliver from slavery or bondage.** The truth and the Son of God set free (John 8:32, 36). The Christian is set free from sin (Rom. 6:18, 22) by the law of the Spirit of life (Rom. 8:2). The creation will be set free from the bondage of corruption (Rom. 8:21. Christians are to stand fast in the liberty by which Christ has set them free (Gal. 5:1). ¶

FREEDMAN 1. (*apeleutheros*; from *apo*: from, and *eleutheros*: free) **Man released from slavery or bondage.** The servant called in the Lord is the Lord's freedman (1 Cor. 7:22). ¶ **2.** (*Libertinos*: person who has been liberated) **Person made prisoner and freed later; also transl.: Libertine.** Some men from the Synagogue of the Freedmen argued with Stephen (Acts 6:9). ¶

FRINGE (*kraspedon*; from *kras*: head, summit, and *pedon*: ground, earth) **Strip of cloth used to border a garment; also transl.: border, edge, hem,**

tassel. This word is used re the Pharisees' garments (Matt. 23:5). Other refs.: Matt. 9:20; 14:36; Mark 6:56; Luke 8:44. ¶

FROG (*batrachos*) **Amphibian known for its croaking; symbol of impurity due to the fact it lives nears swamps and in the mud.** The unclean spirits coming out of the mouths of the dragon, the beast, and the false prophet are like frogs (Rev. 16:13). ¶

G

GABBATHA (*Gabbatha*: elevated place, in Aram.) **Place where there was a tribunal, and judgments were delivered.** Pilate sat there, presenting and delivering Jesus over to the Jews (John 19:13). ¶

GABRIEL (*Gabriēl*: hero of God, in Heb.) **Angel of God.** He was sent to Zechariah, announcing the birth of his son, John, the Messiah's forerunner (Luke 1:19), and to Mary, announcing the conception of Jesus, God's Son (v. 26; see v. 31). ¶

GAD (*Gad*: good fortune, in Heb.; see Gen. 30:11, 12) **A son of Jacob and the tribe descending from him.** Twelve thousand out of Gad will be sealed (Rev. 7:5). ¶

GADARENE → See **GERASENE**

GAIUS (*Gaios*) **a. Macedonian Christian man.** He was a traveling companion of Paul (Acts 19:29). **b. Christian man of Derbe.** He accompanied Paul to Asia (Acts 20:4). **c. Christian man of Corinth.** He was Paul's host (Rom. 16:23). Paul baptized him (1 Cor. 1:14). **d. Christian man dear to John.** Ref.: 3 John 1. ¶

GALATIA 1. (*Galatia*) **Central province of Asia Minor.** Churches had been established there (1 Cor. 16:1; Gal. 1:2). Crescens departed there (2 Tim. 4:10); other mss.: *Gallia* (Gaul in Western Europe). Other ref.: 1 Pet. 1:1. ¶ **2.** (of Galatia: *Galatikos*) **Which concerns the province of Galatia in Asia Minor;**

also transl.: Galatian. Paul traversed this region (Acts 16:6); he later strengthened disciples there (18:23). ¶

GALATIAN (*Galatēs*) **Inhabitant of Galatia, a province of central Asia Minor.** They foolishly abandoned the gospel of grace and returned to works (Gal. 3:1). ¶

GALILEAN (*Galilaios*) **Inhabitant of Galilee, most northern province of Israel.** Jesus was a Galilean (Matt. 26:69; Mark 14:70: see v. 71; Luke 22:59: see v. 60); as such, He was sent to Herod (Luke 23:6; see v. 7). Galileans received Jesus (John 4:45). They witnessed His ascension (Acts 1:11) and spoke in other tongues at Pentecost (2:7). Other refs.: Luke 13:1, 2. ¶

GALILEE (*Galilaia*: circle, circuit) **Most northern province of Israel.** Jesus spent His childhood in Nazareth of Galilee (Matt. 2:22) and the greater part of His ministry in that province (4:23). It is called "Galilee of the nations" (Matt. 4:15). Later, there were churches in Galilee (Acts 9:31), where the good news had begun to be announced (10:37).

GALL (*cholē*; comp. *chloē*: green, *cheō*: to pour) **Bile of animals or birds; this liquid is secreted by the liver to facilitate absorption and digestion.** Gall was mingled with wine and offered to Jesus to drink before His crucifixion (Matt. 27:34). Simon the magician was in the gall of bitterness (Acts 8:23). ¶

GALLIO (*Galliōn*) **Proconsul (i.e., governor or military commander) of Achaia.** Paul was brought before his tribunal (Acts 18:12, 14); Sosthenes was beaten in front of him (v. 17). ¶

GAMALIEL (*Gamaliēl*: reward of God, in Heb.) **Pharisee, doctor of the law and a man held in honor by all the Jewish people.** He advised in the Sanhedrin to let the apostles alone (Acts 5:34; see v. 39). Paul was instructed at his feet (Acts 22:3). ¶

GAZA (*Gaza*: strong, in Heb.) **City near the Mediterranean Sea and southwest of Jerusalem.** Philip met an Ethiopian on the road from Jerusalem to Gaza (Acts 8:26). ¶

GEHENNA → HELL

GENERATION (*genea*; from *ginomai*: to become) **a. Descendants of a man, counted by lifespan.** There are 14 generations from Abraham to David; 14 from David to the captivity in Babylon; 14 from the captivity in Babylon to the Christ (Matt. 1:17). **b. Group of people living during a given length of time: 30 to 35 years on the average.** See e.g., Acts 14:16; 15:21. Generations may be marked by moral characteristics: wicked (Matt. 12:45; Luke 11:29), unbelieving and perverted (Matt. 17:17; Mark 9:19; Luke 9:41), wicked and adulterous (Matt. 12:39; 16:4), adulterous and sinful (Mark 8:38), perverse (Acts 2:40), crooked and perverted (Phil. 2:15).

GENNESARET (*Gennēsaret*) **Very fertile plain near the Sea of Galilee (or Lake of Gennesaret).** Jesus healed many sick people (Matt. 14:34; Mark 6:53) and taught crowds (Luke 5:1; see vv. 2, 3) in Gennesaret. ¶

GENTILE, GENTILES → GREEK, NATION

GERASENE (*Gerasēnos*) **Inhabitant of a region east of Lake Tiberias; also written: Gadarene, Gergesene.** Jesus was met in their region by two demon-possessed men (Matt. 8:28), of whom one is mentioned by Mark and Luke (Mark 5:1; see vv. 1–13; Luke 8:26; see vv. 26–33). People of the surrounding area, terrified after Jesus commanded the unclean spirit to depart, begged Him to leave (Luke 8:37). ¶

GERGESENE → GERASENE

GETHSEMANE (*Gethsēmani*: oil press, in Aram.; also spelled: *Gethsēmanē*) **Garden located near Jerusalem, at the foot of the Mount of Olives.** Jesus prayed in Gethsemane before His betrayal (Matt. 26:36; Mark 14:32). ¶

GIDEON (*Gedeōn*: a hewer, in Heb.) **Judge of Israel.** He delivered and judged Israel (see Judg. 6–8); he is mentioned among O.T. people of faith (Heb. 11:32). ¶

GIFT 1. (*doma*; from *didōmi*: to give) **Good thing offered voluntarily and freely.** Christ has given gifts to men (Eph. 4:8). Paul was not seeking a gift from the Philippians (Phil. 4:17). **2.** (*dōrea*; from *didōmi*: to give) **Free present from God; also transl.: free gift.** This word is used re God (John 4:10), the Holy Spirit (Acts 2:38; 8:20; 10:45; 11:17), Jesus Christ (Rom. 5:15), righteousness (v. 17), God's grace (Eph. 3:7), God's unspeakable gift (2 Cor. 9:15), the measure of the gift of Christ (Eph. 4:7), and the heavenly gift (Heb. 6:4). ¶ **3.** (*dōrēma*; from *dōreō*: to make a gift) **Thing given, present, offering.** Every good gift (*dosis*) and every perfect gift (*dōrēma*) comes down from the Father of lights (Jas. 1:17). In Rom. 5:16, the gift (*dōrēma*) is through Jesus Christ. ¶ **4.** (*dōron*; from *didōmi*: to give) **Present, sacrifice; also transl.: offering.** A gift was offered to Jesus by wise men (Matt. 2:11), presented at the altar (5:23, 24), ordained by Moses (8:4), hypocritically said to be given to God (15:5; Mark 7:11), cast into the treasury by the rich (Luke 21:1) out of their wealth (v. 4). The gift of God is salvation by grace, through faith (Eph. 2:8). **5.** (generous gift: *eulogia*; from *eulogeō*: to bless, to praise, which is from *eu*: well, and *logos*: word) **Blessing; monetary gift.** The Corinthians had prepared a gift (2 Cor. 9:5). **6.** (*merismos*; from *merizō*: to divide into parts, which is from *meris*: part) **What is being shared, distributed; the act of sharing.** Salvation has been confirmed by the gifts of the Holy Spirit (Heb. 2:4). **7.** (*charis*; from *chairō*: to rejoice; lit.: grace) **Generous present.** A gift was to be sent by the Corinthians to Jerusalem (1 Cor. 16:3). **8.** (gift, free gift, spiritual gift: *charisma*; from *charizomai*: to freely give, which is from *charis*: gift, grace, which is from *chairō*: to rejoice) **Free present from God; spiritual capacity.** This word is used re spiritual instruction (Rom. 1:11), salvation of repenting sinners (5:15, 16; 6:23), God's calling of Israel (11:29), self-control (1 Cor. 7:7), answer to prayer (2 Cor. 1:11). There are different gifts for building the church (Rom. 12:6, 1 Cor. 1:7; 12:4, 9, 28, 30, 31). Timothy was not to neglect the gift that was in him (1 Tim. 4:14), he was to rekindle that gift (2 Tim. 1:6), and he was to use it to minister to fellow Christians (1 Pet. 4:10). **¶ 9.** (spiritual gift: *pneumatikos*; from *pneuma*: spirit) Paul wrote concerning spiritual gifts (1 Cor. 12:1).

GOD (*Theos*) **The supreme, eternal Being.** God is known by His works in His eternal power and divinity (Rom. 1:19, 20). He is the Lord God, the Almighty (Rev. 4:8). He is God in three Persons: Father, Son, and Holy Spirit. He is revealed in the Lord Jesus Christ, God manifested in flesh (John 1:13, 14; 1 Tim. 3:16). God is light (1 John 1:5) and love (4:8, 16), revealed to Christians as Father (John 20:17). His principal characteristics and attributes are holiness (Luke 1:49), incorruptibility (Rom. 1:23), wisdom (11:33–36), patience (15:5), faithfulness (1 Cor. 1:9), eternal being (1 Tim. 1:17), invisibility (v. 17; 6:16), immortality (6:16), righteousness (2 Tim. 4:8), omniscience (Heb. 4:13), omnipresence (Jer. 23:23, 24; Heb. 13:5), immutability (Jas. 1:17), grace and mercy (2 John 1:3), omnipotence (Rev. 19:6), and sovereignty (6:15). (After Walter Biggar Scott.)

GOD (other god) **1.** (*daimonion*; dimin. of *daimōn*: demon) **Pagan divinity.** Philosophers said that Paul was proclaiming foreign gods to Athenians (Acts 17:18). See **DEMON**. **2.** (*theos*) **Superior spiritual being or its representation.** The Israelites desired to have false gods (Acts 7:40), a certain Remphan among others (v. 43). Paul and Barnabas were mistaken for god(s) (Acts 14:11; 28:6). Paul saw an altar to the unknown God in Athens (Acts 17:23). Satan is the god of this age (2 Cor. 4:4). Other refs.: John 10:34, 35; Acts 12:22; 19:26; 1 Cor. 8:5; Gal. 4:8; Phil. 3:19.

GODHEAD 1. (*theiotēs*; from *Theos*: God) **Term that characterizes the nature of God and His infinite power.** The eternal power and Godhead of God are understood through what has been made (Rom. 1:20). ¶ **2.** (*theotēs*; from *Theos*: God) **God, in all the plenitude of His being, without restriction.** All the fullness of the Godhead dwells in Christ bodily (Col. 2:9). ¶

GODLINESS 1. (*eusebeia*; from *eusebēs*: devout, godly, which is from *eu*: well, and *sebomai*: to experience a sense of religious fear, to adore) **Living relationship of the Christian with God characterized by fear, respect, and confidence.** The godliness of Peter was not the means of curing a lame man (Acts 3:12). A quiet life is characterized by it (1 Tim. 2:2). Its mystery is related to the person of Christ (1 Tim. 3:16). Timothy was to exercise himself unto godliness (1 Tim. 4:7); it is profitable for everything (v. 8). The teaching of Jesus Christ is according to it (1 Tim. 6:3), as is the knowledge of the truth (Titus 1:1). It is esteemed a source of gain by corrupt men (1 Tim. 6:5); but, for believers, it is a great gain (v. 6) and is to be pursued (v. 11). It is to characterize Christian conduct (2 Pet. 1:3, 6, 7; 3:11), in contrast to a mere form of it (2 Tim. 3:5). ¶ **2.** (*theosebeia*; from *theosebēs*: God-fearing, devout, which is from *Theos*: God, and *sebomai*: see **1.**) **Fear of God, piety, reverence toward God.** Good works are proper for women who profess godliness (1 Tim. 2:10). ¶

GODLY (*eusebōs*; from *eusebēs*: devout, godly, which is from *eu*: well, and *sebomai*: to venerate, to adore) **With reverence toward God, piously.** All who desire to live godly in Christ will be persecuted (2 Tim. 3:12). Christians are called to live godly (Titus 2:12). ¶

GOG (*Gōg*; from Gog, the chief prince of Meshech and Tubal in Ezek. 38:2; 39:1) **Gog and Magog are the symbolical names of nations that are enemies of God.** They will be gathered by Satan for the great battle at the end of the millennium (Rev. 20:8); the fire of God will come down from heaven and devour them (see v. 9). ¶

GOLD 1. (*chrusos*) **Precious metal of a brilliant yellow color, very ductile and malleable; in virtue of its brilliance and costliness, it symbolizes divine righteousness.** The wise men gave the child Jesus gold (Matt. 2:11). The disciples were not to acquire any for the way (10:9). Some swore by the gold of the temple (Matt. 23:16, 17). The Divine Nature is not like gold (Acts 17:29). Gold is eclipsed by good works (1 Tim. 2:9, 10). The gold and silver of the rich were eaten away (Jas. 5:3). The great prostitute Babylon will be adorned with gold (Rev. 17:4; 18:16); she will not buy merchandise of gold anymore (18:12). Other refs.: 1 Cor. 3:12; Rev. 9:7. ¶ **2.** (*chrusion*; dimin. of **1.**) **Object or money made of gold.** Peter had no gold (Acts 3:6); he coveted none (20:33). The ark of the covenant was covered with gold (Heb. 9:4). The word is also used re faith (1 Pet. 1:7), redemption by Christ's blood (v. 18), the adornment of a quiet spirit (3:3). The heavenly Jerusalem and its street are pure gold (Rev. 21:18, 21). Other ref.: Rev. 3:18. ¶

GOLGOTHA (*Golgotha*: skull, in Aram.) **Place of the crucifixion of Jesus.** See **SKULL**.

GOMORRAH (*Gomorra*: submersion, in Heb.) **City of the plain of the Jordan which was destroyed at the same time as Sodom; its inhabitants were destroyed because their sin was grievous.** See Gen. 18:20, 21; 19:24, 25. It was judged and condemned as an example (Matt. 10:15; Mark 6:11; Rom. 9:29; 2 Pet. 2:6; Jude 7). ¶

GOSPEL 1. (*euangelion*; from *euangelos*: who brings a good news, which is from *eu*: well, and *angelos*: who brings news, messenger) **Good news, good message; also transl.: glad tidings. a. The Gospel of God's grace** (Acts 20:24) calls for faith in the person and work of Jesus Christ (see 1 Cor. 15:1–4). It brings salvation (Eph. 1:13) and peace (6:15) to sinners. **b. The Gospel of the kingdom** was preached by Jesus (Matt. 4:23; 9:35; Mark 1:14) and will be preached preceding His return to reign (Matt. 24:14; Mark 13:10; 16:15). **c. The everlasting Gospel** (Rev. 14:6) proclaims the Creator God (see v. 7).

d. Other uses of the word Gospel: of Jesus Christ, the Son of God (Mark 1:1), of God (Rom. 1:1), of His (God's) Son (v. 9), of Paul (2:16), of Christ (15:19), of the glory of Christ (2 Cor. 4:4), to the uncircumcised (committed to Paul), to the circumcised (committed to Peter) (Gal. 2:7), of our Lord Jesus Christ (2 Thes. 1:8), of the glory of the blessed God (1 Tim. 1:11). **2. Name later given to each of the four accounts of the life of Jesus Christ narrated in the N.T.** Each gospel presents a particular aspect of Christ's person: Matthew, the King of Israel; Mark, the humble and perfect Servant; Luke, the Son of Man; John, the Son of God.

GOVERNING (from *huperechō*: to surpass, which is from *huper*: over, above, and *echō*: to have) **Which is above.** Governing authorities are established by God (Rom. 13:1).

GOVERNOR 1. (*ethnarchēs*; from *ethnos*: people, nation, and *archō*: to begin, to reign, which is from *archē*: beginning, domination; lit.: ethnarch) **Ruler of people, chief.** There was a governor in Damascus (2 Cor. 11:32). ¶ **2.** (*hēgemōn*; from *hēgeomai*: to lead, to administer) **He to whom one has entrusted an administration.** This word is used in a general sense (Matt. 2:6; 10:18; Mark 13:9; Luke 20:20; 21:12; 1 Pet. 2:14). Particularly, there were Roman procurators exercising civil and military authority: Pontius Pilate (Matt. 27:2, 11, 14, 15, 21, 23, 27; 28:14), Felix (Acts 23:24, 26, 33; 24:1, 10), and Porcius Festus (Acts 26:30). ¶ **3.** (to be the governor: *hēgemoneuō*; from *hēgemōn*: governor, ruler) **To guide, to direct; also transl.: to govern, to have the government.** Cyrenius was governor of Syria (Luke 2:2); Pontius Pilate, of Judea (Luke 3:1; *epitropeuō* in some mss.: to be the administrator). ¶ **4.** (to govern: *hēgeomai*; from *agō*: to lead) **To rule, to administer.** Pharaoh established Joseph over Egypt and all his household (Acts 7:10, lit.: governing).

GRACE 1. (*charis*; from *chairō*: to rejoice; the word *chara* (joy) is also derived from *chairō*) **Unmerited favor which God, in His love, extends to the sinner who repents.** Grace is an unmerited favor granted without expectation of return; it is the free expression of God's loving kindness to men, motivated only by His bounty and benevolence. Its direct antithesis is *erga*, works (Eph. 2:8, 9). Grace forgives the repentant sinner, producing joy and thankfulness. Grace introduces a new creation (2 Cor. 5:17). (After S. Zodhiates). It brings salvation to the sinner (Eph. 2:5, 8; Titus 2:11), justifying this individual (Rom. 3:24; Titus 3:7). It accompanies Christians on earth (1 Cor. 15:10; 2 Cor. 12:9). Grace and truth came (sing. in Greek) by Jesus Christ (John 1:17). A gift of grace (1 Pet. 4:10) is for God's service. "Grace be with you" is a frequent closing salutation in N.T. epistles (Col. 4:18; Heb. 13:25; et al.). **2.** (*euprepeia*; from *euprepēs*: beautiful, decent, which is from *eu*: well, and *prepō*: to be suitable) **Beauty, noble appearance.** The grace of the flower has perished (Jas. 1:11). ¶

GRAIN OF MUSTARD (*kokkos sinapeōs*; *kokkos*; *sinapi*) **Kernel of seed of a plant, black or white mustard, which abounds in Israel; its size is approx. three millimeters (0.1 inch), which makes it the smallest grain of seed among those that were sown in N.T. times.** The resulting plant can grow to over ten feet (three meters) and attract birds. It illustrates the rapid development of the kingdom of the heavens (Matt. 13:31; Mark 4:31; Luke 13:19). It is used in a simile of faith (Matt. 17:20; Luke 17:6).

GRAIN OF WHEAT (*kokkos tou sitou*; *sitos*) **Cereal originating from the Middle East; wheat is used for making bread.** Man sows a bare grain of wheat (1 Cor. 15:37), but God gives it a body (see v. 38). It falls into the ground, dies, and bears much fruit: it is an image of Jesus (John 12:24). It is used in a simile for Satan sifting believers (Luke 22:31).

GRANDCHILD (*ekgonos*; from *ekginomai*: to be born of, which is from *ek*: out, and *ginomai*: to become) **Child of one's son or daughter; also transl.: descendant, nephew.** They must repay their family elders (1 Tim. 5:4). ¶

GREAT TRIBULATION (*thlipsis megalē*; tribulation: *thlipsis*; from *thlibō*: to afflict; great: *megas*) **Great distress, severe trouble.** This future great tribulation will be unequalled (Matt. 24:21: great tribulation; Mark 13:19: tribulation). It will come on Jezebel and her paramours (Rev. 2:22). An innumerable crowd will come out of it (Rev. 7:14).

GREAT WHITE THRONE (throne: *thronos*; from *thraō*: to sit; great: *megas*; white: *leukos*) **Seat of judgment, set up immediately after the millennium.** Earth and heaven fled away from Him sitting on it (Rev. 20:11); those dead in sins will be judged there (see v. 12) according to their works.

GREECE (*Hellas*) **Region of Southern Europe; see ACHAIA.** Paul sojourned there three months (Acts 20:2; see v. 3). ¶

GREEK 1. (*Hellēn*) **Person inhabiting Greece (*Hellas*) or of the Greek race.** Certain Greeks wanted to see Jesus (John 12:20; see v. 21). The Lord Jesus was announced to them (Acts 11:20 in some mss.), as was also the gospel (Rom. 1:14, 16; 1 Cor. 1:22, 24). Many Greeks believed (Acts 14:1; 17:4, 12); Paul reasoned with them (Acts 18:4); they heard the Lord's word (19:10, 17; 20:21). God does not show partiality to Jews or to Greeks (Rom. 2:9, 10) for both are under sin (3:9), but God is rich to all who call on Him, Jew or Greek (10:12). Greeks sought wisdom (1 Cor. 1:22). Christian liberty was not to be a stumbling block for them (1 Cor. 10:32); Jew and Greek are baptized into one body: God's church (1 Cor. 12:13; Gal. 3:28; Col. 3:11). Other refs.: Mark 7:26. John 7:35; Acts 16:1, 3; 21:28, Gal. 2:3. ¶ **2.** (*Hellēnikos*; from *Hellas*: Greece) **Which pertains to Greece; Greek language.** The inscription above Jesus on the cross was in Greek, Latin, and Hebrew letters (Luke 23:38). The name of the angel of the abyss is Apollyon in Greek (Rev. 9:11). ¶ **3.** (*Hellēnisti*; from *Hellas*: Greece) **Greek language.** The title above Jesus on the cross was in Greek and other languages (John 19:20). Paul knew Greek (Acts 21:37). ¶

H

HADES (*hadēs*; from *a*: neg., and *eidon*: conjugated form of "to see") **Invisible place where the souls of men go after death; KJV translates: hell, but see the meaning of that word.** Capernaum will be brought down to Hades (Matt. 11:23; Luke 10:15). Its gates shall not prevail against the church (Matt. 16:18). A rich man was in torment there (Luke 16:23). As David prophesied (Acts 2:27), Christ was not left in Hades (v. 31). The Son of Man has the keys of Hades (Rev. 1:18); Hades accompanies Death (6:8; 20:13) and will be cast into the lake of fire (20:14). Other ref.: 1 Cor. 15:55 (in some mss.). ¶

HAGAR (*Hagar*) **Egyptian bondservant, handmaid of Sarah, by whom Abraham begat Ishmael; also spelled: Agar.** She illustrates the bondage of the law (Gal. 4:24, 25). ¶

HARRAN (*Charran*: parched, in Heb.) **City of Mesopotamia located northeast of Canaan; also transl.: Charran.** Abraham lived there during his journey from Mesopotamia to Canaan (Acts 7:2, 4). ¶

HARVEST (*therismos*; from *therizō*: to reap, which is from *theros*: hot season, summer) **The season for gathering in crops.** Lit., it is the time or act of reaping (Mark 4:29; John 4:35). Spiritually, it is the time when souls are gathered in by the gospel (Matt. 9:37, 38; Luke 10:2) and the time of judgment at the end of the age (Matt. 13:30, 39; Rev. 14:15). ¶

HEALING 1. (*therapeia*; from *therapeuō*: to serve, to heal) **Curing, restoring of health.** Jesus healed people who had need of healing (Luke 9:11). The leaves of the tree of life will be for the healing of the nations (Rev. 22:2). Other refs.: Matt. 24:45; Luke 12:42. ¶ **2.** (*iama*; from *iaomai*: to heal) **Result or means of curing.** Physical healing was a "sign gift" in the early church (1 Cor. 12:9, 28, 30). ¶ **3.** (*iasis*; from *iaomai*: to heal) **Process or act of restoring to health.** Healing was performed on a lame man (Acts 4:22). Early Christians asked the Lord to stretch out His hand to heal (Acts 4:30; lit.: for healing). Other ref.: Luke 13:32. ¶

HEAVEN 1. (*ouranos*) **a. Atmosphere above the earth, firmament; also transl.: air, sky.** Refs.: Matt. 6:26; 16:3. **b. Interstellar space of the creation.** Ref.: Acts 4:24. The new heavens (2 Pet. 3:13) will replace the present heavens (v. 10). **c. Abode of God and the angels.** Refs.: Matt. 5:16; 21:25; 24:36; John 3:13, 31. The Lord Himself will descend from thence (1 Thes. 4:16). **d. Abode of Christians.** The Christian's habitation is from heaven (2 Cor. 5:2). **e. Term designating the divine origin of something.** This word is used re the kingdom (Matt. 19:14), John's baptism (Matt. 21:25; Luke 20:4, 5), a gift (John 3:27). **2.** (from heaven: *ouranothen*; from *ouranos*: heaven, and suffix *then*: from a place) Refs.: Acts 14:17; 26:13. ¶ **3.** (midst of heaven: *mesouranēma*; from *mesos*: midst, and *ouranos*: heaven) **Mid-sky; also transl.: midair, midheaven.** Refs.: Rev. 8:13; 14:6; 19:17. ¶

HEAVENLY 1. (*ouranios*; from *ouranos*: heaven) **Which relates to heaven, celestial.** This word is used re God the Father (Matt. 5:48; 6:14, 26, 32; 15:13), the host of angels praising God (Luke 2:13), and Paul's vision (Acts 26:19). ¶ **2.** (*epouranios*; from *epi*: upon, in, and *ouranos*: heaven) **Who, which is in heaven.** This word is used re God the Father (Matt. 18:35), things known by Jesus (John 3:12), bodies (1 Cor. 15:40), the Lord Jesus and Christians (1 Cor. 15:48, 49), places (Eph. 1:3, 20; 2:6, 3:10; 6:12; lit.: the heavenlies), knees of such beings (Phil. 2:10), a kingdom (2 Tim. 4:18), a calling (Heb. 3:1), a gift (6:4), things (8:5; 9:23), a country (11:16), and the heavenly Jerusalem (12:22). ¶

HEBER (*Eber*: beyond, in Heb.) **Hebrew patriarch.** He is mentioned in Jesus' genealogy (Luke 3:35). ¶

HEBREW 1. (*Hebraios*: from Eber; see Gen. 10:21) **The Hebrews are the ancestors of the Israelites who came from the east bank of the Euphrates River; the Jews called themselves by this name because they spoke Hebrew, or rather Aramaic, a related language.** The Hellenists murmured against the Hebrews (Acts 6:1). Paul was a Hebrew (2 Cor. 11:22; Phil. 3:5). ¶ **2.** (*Hebraikos*) **Hebraic.** The letters written above Jesus on the cross were in Hebrew, Greek, and Latin (Luke 23:38). ¶ **3.** (*Hebrais*) **Term describing the language of the Hebrews.** Paul spoke in Hebrew to people of Jerusalem (Acts 21:40; 22:2). The Lord spoke to Saul in Hebrew on the road to Damascus (Acts 26:14). ¶ **4.** (in Hebrew: *Hebraisti*) **In the Hebraic language.** This word is used re a pool (John 5:2: Bethesda) a stone pavement (19:13: Gabbatha), the place of a skull (19:17: Golgotha), a teacher (20:16: Rabboni in some mss.), the angel of the abyss (Rev. 9. 11: Abaddon), a gathering place of armies (16:16: Armageddon). The inscription above Jesus on the cross was written in Hebrew, Greek, and Latin (John 19:20). ¶

HELI → ELI

HELL 1. (*geenna*; from the Heb.: valley of Hinnom) **This term represents the lake of fire, the place of eternal torment.** The unbeliever's body and soul suffer eternal destruction in hell (Matt. 5:29, 30; 10:28). God has power to cast into it (Luke 12:5). Jesus speaks of: "judgment of hell" (Matt. 23:33), "hell of fire", "hell, the fire unquenchable" (Matt. 5:22; 18:9; Mark 9:43, 45, 47). The tongue is set on fire by hell (Jas. 3:6). Other ref.: Matt. 23:15. ¶ **2.** (to cast to hell, to cast down to hell: *tartaroō*; from *tartaros*: the Tartar; lit.: to precipitate into the Tartarus, or bottom of gloom) **In Greek mythology, Tartarus was a part of Hades where evil persons were kept and tormented.** God has cast angels who sinned down to hell (2 Pet. 2:4). ¶ **3** See **HADES**.

HELLENISTIC JEW (*Hellēnistēs*; from *Hellas*: Greece) **Israelite who spoke the Greek language and adopted Greek customs; also transl.: Hellenist.** They murmured against Hebrews (Acts 6:1); Saul disputed against them (9:29). Other ref.: Acts 11:20 in some mss. ¶

HELP 1. (*antilēmpsis*; from *antilambanō*: to come to the rescue, which is from *anti*: against, and *lambanō*: to take; lit.: laying hold; also spelled: *antilēpsis*) **Aid, assistance to anyone.** Help is a service of aiding other Christians in their needs (1 Cor. 12:28). ¶ **2.** (*boētheia*; from *boētheō*: to help, which is from *boē*: cry, and *theō*: to run) **Aid, assistance in response to the cry of a person in distress.** We can receive seasonable help at the throne of grace (Heb. 4:16). Other ref.: Acts 27:17. ¶ **3.** (*epikouria*; from *epikouros*: one who helps, especially during war) **Assistance provided by an ally, succor.** Paul had obtained help from God (Acts 26:22). ¶ **4.** (*epichorēgia*; from *epichorēgeō*: to supply, which is from *epi*: moreover, and *chorēgeō*: to provide) **Aid, assistance.** Help was given by the Spirit of Jesus Christ (Phil. 1:19). Other ref.: Eph. 4:16. ¶

HERESY → SECT

HERMAS (*Hermas*; perhaps from Hermes, a Greek god) **Christian man of Rome.** Paul sent him greetings (Rom. 16:14). ¶

HERMES (*Hermēs*; name of a Greek god) **Messenger and interpreter of the messages of the gods in Greek mythology (known as Mercurius among the Romans, or Mercury in Engl.); also, a Christian man.** People of Lystra called Paul, the lead speaker: "Hermes" (Acts 14:12). Paul sends greetings to Hermes, a believer (Rom. 16:14). ¶

HERMOGENES (*Hermogenēs*: born of Hermes, a Greek god) **Christian man of Asia.** He turned away from Paul (2 Tim. 1:15). ¶

HEROD (*Hērōdēs*) **a. Herod the Great, king of Judea.** Jesus was born during his reign (Matt. 2:1; Luke 1:5). He sent soldiers to kill all male infants in Bethlehem (Matt. 2:3, 7, 12, 13, 15, 16, 19, 22). **b. Herod Antipas, son of Herod the Great; tetrarch of Galilee.** He had John the Baptist beheaded (Matt. 14:1, 3, 6; Mark 6:14, 16, 18, 20–22; Luke 3:1, 19; 9:7, 9) and wanted to kill Jesus (Luke 13:31). Pilate sent Jesus to him. This Herod hoped to see Jesus perform some sign, questioned Him, mocked Him, and sent Him back to Pilate (Luke 23:7, 8, 11, 12, 15). He was gathered with others against Jesus (Acts 4:27). Johanna, wife of his steward, followed Jesus (Luke 8:3). Manaen, a believer, was brought up with him (Acts 13:1). **c. Herod Agrippa I, grandson of Herod the Great, nephew of Herod Antipas.** King of Judea (Acts 12:1), he laid hands on certain Christians; he imprisoned Peter, who was delivered out of his hand by the Lord (vv. 6, 11, 19, 21); Paul was kept under guard in his courtroom (23:35). **d. Herod Agrippa II, son of Herod Antipas.** Ref.: Acts 25:13. ¶

HERODIANS (*Hērōdianoi*) **Sectarian followers of King Herod.** They attempted to lead the people into the practices and leisure entertainment of the people of the nations; refs.: Matt. 22:16; Mark 3:6; 12:13. ¶

HERODIAS (*Hērōdias*) **Wife of Philip, the brother of Herod Antipas.** Herod married her while her husband lived, for which John the Baptist reproved him (Matt. 14:3 (see v. 4); Mark 6:17 (v. 22 in some mss.); Luke 3:19). She resented John and wanted to have him killed (Mark 6:19). Her daughter danced, pleasing Herod (Matt. 14:6; Mark 6:22). ¶

HERODION (*Hērōdiōn*) **Christian man of Rome.** Paul sent greetings to him, his relative (Rom. 16:11). ¶

HESLI (*Hesli*: reserved by Jehovah, in Heb.; also spelled and transl.: Esli) **Man of the O.T.** He is mentioned in the genealogy of Jesus (Luke 3:25). ¶

HEZEKIAH (*Ezekias*: strength from Jehovah, in Heb.) **King of Judah; also transl.: Ezechias.** He is mentioned in the genealogy of Jesus (Matt. 1:9, 10). ¶

HEZRON (*Hesrōm*: walled in, in Heb.) **Man of the O.T.; also transl.: Esrom.** He is mentioned in the genealogy of Jesus (Matt. 1:3; Luke 3:33). ¶

HIERAPOLIS (*Hierapolis*: holy city; from *hieros*: holy, sacred, and *polis*: city) **City near Colossae and Laodicea in Asia Minor.** Epaphras was deeply concerned for believers there (Col. 4:13). ¶

HIGH PRIEST (*archiereus*; from *archē*: denoting dignity, rank, and *hiereus*: priest) **Chief priest who was to exercise the priesthood until his death (see Num. 35:25).** He alone might enter the Most Holy Place once a year with blood (Heb. 9:7, 25; 13:11; see Lev. 16). The N.T. refers to the high priest (e.g., Matt. 26:3; Acts 4:6; Heb. 9:11). The word is used concerning Christ who is the High Priest in heaven (Heb. 2:17) after the order of Melchizedek (see Heb. 5:6; 7:3, 23, 24; 10:21). He sustains Christians (Heb. 7:26). He presents them and their offerings to God, sanctifying them (see Heb. 13:15). He intercedes for them (see Rom. 8:34).

HOLINESS 1. (*hagiasmos*; from *hagiazō*: to sanctify, which is from *hagios*: holy, which is from *hagos*: religious respect, reverence toward God) **Sanctification, moral purity.** Holiness is associated with righteousness (Rom. 6:19) and fruit (v. 22). Christ Jesus is made holiness to Christians (1 Cor. 1:30). This word is used re the sanctification of Christians in chaste living (1 Thes. 4:3, 4), Christians being called to holiness by God (v. 7) and being chosen for salvation through sanctification by the Spirit (2 Thes. 2:13; 1 Pet. 1:2), Christians continuing in holiness (1 Tim. 2:15) and pursuing holiness (Heb. 12:14). ¶ **2.** (*hagiotēs*; from *hagios*: holy) **Separation from evil according to the character and the nature of God.** Christians are disciplined that they may share in the holiness of God

(Heb. 12:10). ¶ **3.** (*hagiōsunē*; from *hagios*: holy) **Setting apart, separation in moral purity.** The Holy Spirit is called the Spirit of holiness (Rom. 1:4). The hearts of believers should be established in holiness (1 Thes. 3:13). They should perfect it in the fear of God (2 Cor. 7:1). ¶ **4.** (*hosiotēs*; from *hosios*: holy, sacred) **Godliness, obedience to God.** Israel served God in holiness (Luke 1:75). The new man is created in holiness (Eph. 4:24). ¶

HOLY 1. (*hagios*; from *hagos*: religious respect, reverence toward God; same root as *hagnos*: pure) **Quality of one who or of that which is consecrated to God, set apart for Him; holiness is also an attribute of God Himself who is separate from evil; other transl.: sacred.** This word is used re God the Father (John 17:11), Jesus the Servant of God (Acts 4:27), God (1 Pet. 1:15, 16; Rev. 4:8; 6:10), God's name (Luke 1:49), His temple (1 Cor. 3:17; Eph. 2:21), His law (Rom. 7:12), His commandment (Rom. 7:12; 2 Pet. 2:21), His covenant (Luke 1:72), His calling (2 Tim. 1:9), John the Baptist (Mark 6:20), angels who have not sinned (Mark 8:38; Luke 9:26; Acts 10:22; Rev. 14:10), prophets (Luke 1:70; Acts 3:21; 2 Pet. 3:2), apostles (Eph. 3:5), men of God (2 Pet. 1:21), Christians (Eph. 1:4; Col. 1:22; 3:12; 1 Thes. 5:27; Heb. 3:1; 1 Pet. 1:15, 16; Rev. 20:6), children of a believer who is married to an unbeliever (1 Cor. 7:14), a kiss (Rom. 16:16; 1 Cor. 16:20; 2 Cor. 13:12; 1 Thes. 5:26), bodies as a living sacrifice (Rom. 12:1), priesthood (1 Pet. 2:5), nation (v. 9), the church as Christ's bride (Eph. 5:27), Israel (Rom. 11:16), the first sanctuary of the tabernacle called Holy (Heb. 9:2) and the second called Holy of Holies (v. 3), the city of the new Jerusalem (Rev. 11:2; 21:2, 10; 22:19: *hagion*), myriads coming with the Lord (Jude 14), the ground (Acts 7:33), Scriptures (Rom. 1:2), the unmarried woman, in body and spirit (1 Cor. 7:34), lives (2 Pet. 3:11), faith (Jude 20), every male opening the womb (Luke 2:23). **2.** (that which is holy, what is holy, what is sacred: *hagion*; neuter of *hagios*) **The sacred.** It was not to be given to dogs (unappreciative people) (Matt. 7:6). **3.** (*hieros*) **Sacred.** The O.T. writings are called the Holy Scriptures (2 Tim. 3:15). Other ref.: 1 Cor. 9:13. ¶ **4.** (*hosios*) **Godly, righteous.** Men should lift holy hands in prayer

(1 Tim. 2:8). The Son of God, as high priest, is holy (Heb. 7:26). The Lord God only is holy (Rev. 15:4; 16:5). Other ref.: Acts 13:34.

HOLY SPIRIT (*Hagion Pneuma*; holy: *agios*; from *hagos*: religious respect, reverence toward God; spirit: *pneuma*; from *pneō*: to breath) **Third person of the Trinity.** The Holy Spirit is named with the Father and the Son in Matt. 28:19. He was sent by God the Father and by the Lord Jesus (John 14:26; 15:26). His personality and divine authority are evidenced in many passages. Ananias lied to Him (Acts 5:3). He forbade Paul and Timothy to preach in Asia and did not permit them to go into Bithynia (16:6, 7). Saints are built together to be a habitation of God by the Spirit (Eph. 2:22; 1 Cor. 3:16). He gives life to the saved (John 6:63) and seals them (Eph. 1:13). He dwells in them and baptizes them into one body in Christ (1 Cor. 12:13). He is their Comforter (*paraklētos*) or Advocate on the earth (John 14:16, 26). He did not come to earth as a Person before Christ's ascension (see John 16:7). His presence on earth after the Lord's crucifixion brings demonstration to the world of sin, righteousness, and judgment (see John 16:8–11). (After Walter Biggar Scott.)

HOPE 1. (*elpis*; comp. *elpō*: to give hope, to believe) **Contrary to human hope which includes uncertainty, the Christian hope has been described as a happy and confident expectation.** This word is used re what is invisible and future (Rom. 8:24; see v. 25), God for the Christians (Acts 24:15; 1 Pet. 1:21), God being the God of hope (Rom. 15:13), Jesus Christ who is the Christian's hope (Col. 1:27; 1 Tim. 1:1; 1 John 3:3), Israel (Acts 23:6; 26:6, 7; 28:20), Abraham (Rom. 4:18). Before their conversion, Christians had no hope (Eph. 2:12); unbelievers have no hope (1 Thes. 4:13). Christians now have the hope of glory (Rom. 5:2; 2 Cor. 3:12), of righteousness (Gal. 5:5), of the calling of God (Eph. 1:18; 4:4), of the gospel (Col. 1:23), of salvation (1 Thes. 5:8), and of eternal life (Titus 1:2; 3:7). Our hope is good (2 Thes. 2:16) and living (1 Pet. 1:3). The blessed hope (Titus 2:13) is the coming of the Lord for His saints (see 1 Thes. 4:15–18). **2.** (to have hope: *elpizō*; from *elpis*: hope, trust) **To**

have confidence, to trust. We have hope in Christ in this life and afterwards (1 Cor. 15:19).

HORN (*keras*; akin to *kara*: head) **Bony projection on the head of an animal, or object with the same shape; symbol of strength, power.** The horn represents the power of deliverance wrought by God (Luke 1:69), the great strength of the Lamb (Rev. 5:6), the dragon (Rev. 12:3), and the two beasts (Rev. 13:1, 11; 17:3, 7, 12, 16). The golden altar had four horns (Rev. 9:13). ¶

HOSANNA (*Hōsanna*) **Hebrew term composed of two words meaning: "Save, we pray!" (see Ps. 118:25); it became an expr. of praise, a wish for prosperity.** Jesus, entering Jerusalem, was greeted with this cry (Matt. 21:9, 15; Mark 11:9, 10; John 12:13). ¶

HOSEA (*Hōsēe*: liberator, in Heb.) **Prophet of the O.T.** His prophecy was applied by Paul (Rom. 9:25). ¶

HOUR (*hōra*; *hora*, in Lat.) **Unit of measurement of time corresponding to one twelfth of the day or night.** Hours are counted in the familiar Roman manner in John's Gospel; they are counted in the Jewish manner in the others (Matthew, Mark, Luke), i.e., the day beginning at six o'clock in the morning; e.g., the ninth hour corresponds to three o'clock in the afternoon. Jesus was crucified at the third hour (Mark 15:25). Pilate presented Jesus to the Jews as king about the sixth hour (John 19:14). There was darkness over the whole land from the sixth hour until the ninth hour while He was on the cross (Matt. 27:45; Mark 15:33; Luke 23:44). At the ninth hour, Jesus cried out: "My God, My God, why have You forsaken Me?" (Matt. 27:46; Mark 15:34).

HOUSEHOLD 1. (*therapeia*; from *therapeuō*: to serve, to heal, which is from *therapōn*: servant) **Group of servants working in a house.** A master's household was ruled by a faithful steward (Luke 12:42); some mss.: Matt. 24:45. Other refs.: Luke 9:11; Rev. 22:2. ¶ **2.** (one of the household: *oikiakos*; from *oikia*: house, dwelling, which is from *oikos*: house) **Those who belong to the house.** Refs.: Matt. 10:25, 36. ¶ **3.** (of the household: *oikeios*; from *oikos*: house) **Who belongs to a family.** Scripture refers to the household of faith (Gal. 6:10), of God (Eph. 2:19), and of a Christian (1 Tim. 5:8). ¶ **4.** (*oiketeia*; from *oiketēs*: domestic servant) **Group of servants working in a house.** A master's household was ruled by a faithful servant (Matt. 24:45). ¶ **5.** (with all the household: *panoikei*; from *pas*: all, and *oikos*: house) **With all the members of the family.** The jailer rejoiced, believing in God with all his household on hearing the preaching of Paul (Acts 16:34). ¶

HUSK (*keration*; dimin. of *keras*: horn; lit.: little horn) **Horn-shaped seed pod from the carob tree.** The prodigal son longed to eat this food eaten by the pigs (Luke 15:16). ¶

HYMENAEUS (*Humenaios*; from *Humēn*, the god of marriage) **Man of the N.T.** Paul delivered him to Satan to be taught not to blaspheme (1 Tim. 1:20). He strayed from the truth (2 Tim. 2:17; see v. 18). ¶

HYSSOP (*hussōpos*) **Small aromatic plant.** A sponge filled with vinegar was put on hyssop and presented to Jesus (John 19:29). It was used to sprinkle the blood of sacrifices (Heb. 9:19). ¶

I

ICONIUM (*Ikonion*: like an image) **Major city of Lycaonia in Asia Minor.** A great number of Jews and Greeks believed the gospel preached there by Paul and Barnabas. Persecution obliged the two apostles to leave, pursued to Lystra by Jews of Iconium who stoned Paul and dragged him out of the city. But Paul rose up and returned to Iconium to strengthen the disciples (Acts 13:51; 14:1, 19, 21; 2 Tim. 3:11). Timothy had a good testimony of the brothers of Iconium (Acts 16:2). ¶

IDOL 1. (*eidōlon*; from *eidos*: appearance, what one sees) **Material representation of a false god for the purpose of religious worship; the false god itself.** Sacrifices were offered to idols (Acts 7:41; 1 Cor. 8:4, 7; 10:19). Gentile Christians were cautioned to abstain from things polluted by idols (Acts 15:20). The Jew in Rom. 2:22 abhors idols. Before conversion, the Corinthians were led away to mute idols (1 Cor. 12:2). There is no agreement between God's temple and idols (2 Cor. 6:16). The Thessalonians had turned to God from idols (1 Thes. 1:9). Men will not repent of worshiping idols (Rev. 9:20). The injunction to keep oneself from idols (i.e., anything that would displace worship due to God) still applies to Christians today (1 John 5:21). ¶ **2.** (idol's temple: *eidōleion*; from *eidōlon*: see **1.**) **Place of pagan religious worship.** Eating in an idol's temple can wound the conscience of a weak brother (1 Cor. 8:10). ¶ **3.** (thing sacrificed to the idol, thing offered to idols: *eidōlothuton*; from *eidōlon*: see **1.**, and *thuō*: to sacrifice) **Remains of victims sacrificed to idols (i.e., false gods).** Paul speaks of things sacrificed to idols (1 Cor. 8:1, 4, 7, 10). Balaam and Jezebel would induce the Lord's people to eat things sacrificed to idols (Rev. 2:14; 2:20). Other refs.: Acts 15:29; 21:25; 1 Cor. 10:19, 28 in some mss. ¶ **4.** (full of idols: *kateidōlos*; from *kata*: intens., and *eidōlon*: see **1.**) **Filled with idols (i.e., false gods), given up to idolatry.** Athens was full of idols (Acts 17:16). ¶

IDOLATER (*eidōlolatrēs*; from *eidōlon*: idol, and *latris*: worshiper, servant) **One who worships idols (i.e., false gods).** A Christian cannot always avoid associating with this world's idolaters (1 Cor. 5:10) but is not to associate with anyone called brother who is an idolater (v. 11). Idolaters will not inherit the kingdom of God (1 Cor. 6:9; Eph. 5:5). The Christian must not be an idolater (1 Cor. 10:7). The part of idolaters will be in the lake of fire (Rev. 21:8); they will be outside the heavenly Jerusalem (22:15). ¶

IDOLATRY (*eidōlolatreia*; from *eidōlon*: idol, and *latreia*: divine service, which is from *latreuō*: to worship) **Religious worship of idols.** God's word condemns idolatry (Gal. 5:20; Col. 3:5; 1 Pet. 4:3). The Christian is to flee idolatry (1 Cor. 10:14). ¶

IDUMEA (*Idoumaia*: belonging to Edom, in Heb.) **Region occupied by the descendants of Edom (or Esau, the twin brother of Jacob), located southwest of the Dead Sea.** People from there followed Jesus (Mark 3:8). ¶

ILLYRICUM (*Illurikon*) **Region located northeast of the Adriatic Sea.** Paul fully preached the gospel of Christ as far as Illyricum (Rom. 15:19). ¶

IMMORTALITY (*athanasia*; from *a*: neg., and *thanatos*: death) **Quality of that which cannot die.** The Christian's mortal body will put on immortality (1 Cor. 15:53, 54). Immortality characterizes God's nature (1 Tim. 6:16). ¶

INCORRUPTIBILITY 1. (*aphtharsia*; from *a*: neg., and *phtartos*: corruptible) **a. Purity, sincerity.** Scripture speaks of all who love the Lord in incorruptibility (Eph. 6:24) and of incorruptibility in teaching (Titus 2:7). **b. Quality of**

that which cannot be corrupted, i.e., decomposed; also transl.: immortality, imperishable, incorruption. Some people by perseverance in good works seek for incorruptibility (Rom. 2:7). At the resurrection, the bodies of believers in the Lord who have died will be resurrected in incorruptibility (1 Cor. 15:42, 50, 53, 54). Jesus Christ has brought incorruptibility to light (2 Tim. 1:10). ¶ **2.** (*adiaphthoria*; from *a*: neg., and *diaphtheirō*: to corrupt) **Purity, sincerity.** Ref.: Titus 2:7 in certain mss.; see **1.** ¶

INSTRUCTION (*didaskalia*; from *didaskō*: to teach, which is from *daō*: to teach, to learn) **Teaching, learning.** Things (of the O.T.) were written before for our instruction (Rom. 15:4).

ISAAC (*Isaak*: one who laughs, in Heb.) **Patriarch of the O.T.** He was Abraham's son and the father of Jacob (Matt. 1:2) and Esau (see Gen. 25:25, 26). Christians, like Isaac, are children of promise (Gal. 4:28). Isaac is mentioned among O.T. people of faith (Heb. 11:9, 17, 18, 20). Tested by God, Abraham offered up his son Isaac on the altar (James 2:21; Heb. 11:17).

ISAIAH (*Ēsaias*: Jehovah's salvation, in Heb.) **Prophet of the O.T.; also transl.: Esaias.** John the Baptist quotes the prophet Isaiah (Matt. 3:3; John 1:23), as does also Jesus (Matt. 13:14; 15:7; Mark 7:6) and Paul (Rom. 9:27, 29; 10:16, 20; 15:12). Philip heard an Ethiopian court official reading the prophet Isaiah (Acts 8:28, 30).

ISRAEL (*Israēl*: wrestler, or prince of God, in Heb.) **Name of the earthly people of God, descended from Jacob, who himself received this name after having struggled with God (see Gen. 32:28); the people of Israel are formed of twelve tribes, essentially corresponding to the twelve sons of Jacob.** Jesus was acclaimed king of Israel (John 1:49; 12:13). He commanded His disciples to go to the lost sheep of the house of Israel (Matt. 10:6), to whom He Himself had been sent (Matt. 15:24; Acts 13:23). During the period of grace, Israel is partially hardened to the gospel, but later all true Israel shall be saved (Rom. 11:25, 26).

ISRAELITE (*Israēlitēs*: from Israel, in Heb.) **Descendant of Israel, i.e., of Jacob, grandson of Abraham (see Gen. 32:28).** Christ comes from this people who had received various favors and promises from God (Rom. 9:4; see v. 5). Jesus calls Nathanael a true Israelite (John 1:47). The expr. "men of Israel" is used as an appellation in the Acts by Peter (2:22; 3:12), Gamaliel (5:35), Paul (13:16), and the Jews from Asia (21:28). Paul was an Israelite (Rom. 11:1; 2 Cor. 11:22). ¶

ISSACHAR (*Isachar*: he will bring a reward, in Heb.; see Gen. 30:18) **Son of Jacob and one of the 12 tribes descended from him.** Ref.: Rev. 7:7. ¶

ITALIAN (*Italikos*: which belongs to Italy) **Name of a cohort; also transl.: Italic.** Cornelius was a centurion of a cohort called Italian (Acts 10:1). ¶

ITALIC → ITALIAN

ITALY (*Italia*) **Country of Europe whose capital is Rome.** Aquila and Priscilla came from Italy to Athens (Acts 18:2). Paul was brought to Italy as a prisoner (Acts 27:1, 6). The author of the epistle to the Hebrews sends greetings from those of Italy (Heb. 13:24). ¶

ITURAEA (*Itouraia*; prob.: encircled) **Province northeast of Galilee.** Philip was its tetrarch (Luke 3:1). ¶

J

JACINTH 1. (*huakinthos*) **Precious stone whose color resembles the hyacinth flower.** The eleventh foundation of the heavenly Jerusalem's wall was adorned with jacinth (Rev. 21:20). ¶ **2.** (of jacinth: *huakinthinos*) **Which resembles the precious stone; see 1.** The breastplates in Rev. 9:17 are of jacinth, i.e., they look like this stone. ¶

JACOB (*Iakōb*: supplanter, in Heb.) **a. Son of Isaac.** He is mentioned in the genealogy of Jesus Christ (Matt. 1:2; Luke 3:34). Following a famine, his sons went down to Egypt to buy wheat; later his son Joseph sent for him (Acts 7:12, 14, 15). Dying, Jacob worshiped, leaning on the top of his staff (Heb. 11:21). **b. Another man of the O.T.** This Jacob is mentioned in the genealogy of Jesus Christ and is the father of Joseph, Mary's husband (Matt. 1:15, 16). ¶

JAILER (*desmophulax*; from *desmos*: bond, and *phulax*: guardian) **Prison keeper, person responsible for a jail; also spelled: jailor.** The Philippian jailer guarding Paul and Silas feared the prisoners had fled. Converted and baptized, he brought news of release to Paul (Acts 16:23, 27, 36). ¶

JAILOR → JAILER

JAIRUS (*Iairos*: whom Jehovah enlightens) **Chief of a synagogue.** He came to Jesus (Mark 5:22; Luke 8:41), and Jesus resurrected his daughter (see Mark 5:41, 42; Luke 8:54, 55). ¶

JAMBRES (*Iambrēs*) **Egyptian magician.** Jannes and Jambres opposed Moses, imitating the miracles that he performed before Pharaoh (2 Tim. 3:8; see Ex. 7:11, 22; 8:7, 18). ¶

JAMES (*Iakōbos*; Greek name of Jacob) **a. Father of Judas.** This James is the father of Judas (Luke 6:16; Acts 1:13), not Judas Iscariot (see John 14:22), but Judas otherwise known as the Thaddaeus of Matt. 10:3; Mark 3:18. **b. James the brother of John and one of the twelve apostles (Matt. 10:2; Mark 3:17; Luke 6:14; Acts 1:13).** James and John, Zebedee's sons, were repairing nets when Jesus called them to follow Him (Matt. 4:21, 22; Mark 1:19, 20; Luke 5:10). James was with Jesus when He was transfigured (Matt. 17:1; Mark 9:2; Luke 9:28) and at Gethsemane (Mark 14:33). James and John asked to sit one at the Lord's right hand and the other at His left hand in glory (Mark 10:35, 41). King Herod had James killed with the sword (Acts 12:2). Other refs.: Mark 1:29; 5:37; 13:3; Luke 8:51; 9:54. **c. Son of Alphaeus.** This James was also one of the twelve apostles (Matt. 10:3; Mark 3:18; Luke 6:15; Acts 1:13). He is called James the Less, i.e., the smaller (Matt. 27:56; Mark 15:40; 16:1; Luke 24:10). **d. James the Lord's brother.** This James is mentioned in Matt. 13:55; Mark 6:3. He gave Paul and Barnabas the right hand of fellowship to preach to the nations (Gal. 2:9). The Epistle of James was most likely written by this brother of the Lord (Jas. 1:1).

JANNA → JANNAI

JANNAI (*Ianna*: whom Jehovah bestows) **Man of the O.T.; also spelled: Janna.** He is mentioned in the genealogy of Jesus (Luke 3:24). ¶

JANNES (*Iannēs*) **Egyptian magician.** See **JAMBRES**.

JARED (*Iared*: descent, in Heb.) **Man of the O.T., father of Enoch; see Gen. 5:18.** He is mentioned in the genealogy of Jesus (Luke 3:37). ¶

JASON (*Iasōn*: who heals) **a. Christian man of Thessalonica.** He received Paul and Silas. Jews attacked his house and dragged him before city rulers; these rulers made Jason and others give money as security and then released them (Acts 17:5–7, 9). **b. Relative of the apostle Paul.** In Paul's letter, Jason greets the Christians of Rome (Rom. 16:21). ¶

JASPER (*iaspis*) **Precious stone colored by spots or bands.** The appearance of the One on the throne (Rev. 4:3) and the shining of the heavenly Jerusalem are likened to jasper stone (Rev. 21:11). The wall of the heavenly Jerusalem is built of jasper (Rev. 21:18); this wall's first foundation is adorned with jasper (21:19). ¶

JECHONIAH, JECHONIAS → JECONIAH

JECONIAH (*Iechonias*: Jehovah will establish, in Heb.) **Name of a King of Judah (Jehoiachin or Coniah; see 2 Kgs. 24:8; Jer. 22:24–30).** He is mentioned in the genealogy of Jesus Christ (Matt. 1:11, 12). ¶

JEHOSHAPHAT (*Iōsaphat*: Jehovah is judge, in Heb.) **King of Judah; also transl.: Josaphat.** He is mentioned in the genealogy of Jesus Christ (Matt. 1:8). ¶

JEPHTHAH (*Iephthae*: he delivered, in Heb.) **Judge of Israel.** His brothers drove illegitimate Jephthah from his father's house; he delivered Israel (see Judg. 11:1 to 12:7). He was distinguished by faith (Heb. 11:32). ¶

JEREMIAH (*Ieremias*: appointed of Jehovah, in Heb.) **Prophet of the O.T.** Some said that Jesus was Jeremiah (Matt. 16:14). Matthew's Gospel reports two prophecies of Jeremiah which were fulfilled in the Lord's time: the massacre of the little children at Herod's order (2:17) and the price of the betrayal by Judas (27:9). ¶

JERICHO (*Ierichō*: fragrance, in Heb.) **Major city of Israel, located approx. 17 miles (27 kilometers) northeast of Jerusalem and 787 feet (2410 meters) below the level of the Mediterranean Sea.** It was the first city taken by the Israelites during the conquest of Canaan; its walls fell after the Israelites had encircled them for seven days (Heb. 11:30). Jesus healed two blind men as He exited Jericho (Matt. 20:29), including Bartimaeus (Mark 10:46; Luke 18:35). In the parable of the "Good Samaritan," a man went down to Jericho (Luke 10:30). Passing through Jericho, Jesus met Zaccheus (Luke 19:1). ¶

JERUSALEM 1. (*Hierosoluma, Ierousalēm*: habitation of peace, in Heb.) **Capital of Israel, located in Judea at 2,460–2,620 feet (750–800 meters) above sea level.** Jesus went there several times. He reproached Jerusalem, the city that kills the prophets and stones those sent to her (Matt. 23:37; Luke 13:34). Jesus was crucified there. **2.** (people of Jerusalem: *Hierosolumitēs*; from *Hierosoluma*: see **1.**) **Inhabitant of this city.** Refs.: Mark 1:5; John 7:25. ¶

JESSE (*Iessai*: strong, in Heb.) **Man of the O.T.; see 1 Sam. 17:17.** He is David's father (Acts 13:22) and mentioned in the genealogy of Jesus Christ (Matt. 1:5, 6; Luke 3:32). Jesus arose from Jesse's root (Rom. 15:12). ¶

JESTING (*eutrapelia*; from *eu*: easily, and *trepō*: to turn) **Coarse pleasantry; remarks intended to make people laugh, but of a light and even vulgar character; also transl.: coarse jesting, coarse joking, crude joking.** Jesting is not to be named among Christians (Eph. 5:4). ¶

JESUS (*Iēsous*: Jehovah saves, in Heb.) **a. Name of the Son of God manifested in flesh.** Jesus is the personal name of the Lord as man (Matt. 1:21). Conceived by the Holy Spirit (Matt. 1:20), He was born of the virgin Mary (v. 20). The child Jesus grew and became strong, being full of wisdom, and the grace of God was upon Him (Luke 2:40). As a twelve-year-old occupied in His Father's business, his parents found Him in the temple listening and asking questions in the midst of doctors, who were astonished at His intelligence and answers (Luke 2:41–49). Growing up in Nazareth, He was subject to His parents. He advanced in wisdom and in stature, and in favor with God and man (Luke 2:52). At about thirty years of age, He came to John the Baptist to be baptized by him; there, the Holy Spirit descended on Him, and the Father declared that He was His beloved Son in whom He had found His pleasure (Matt. 3:13–17). He was then tempted by the devil and overcame him by God's word (Matt. 4:1–11; Luke 4:1–13). After being presented as the Lamb of God who takes away the sin of the world (John 1:29), Jesus began His public ministry. He preached the gospel of the kingdom, healed the sick, cast out demons, and raised the dead. He fulfilled O.T. prophecies predicting what the Messiah would do. Jesus was also on earth for the purpose of saving souls; to all those who received Him, He gave to them the right to be children of God (John 1:12). He revealed God to them as Father and gave them eternal life. Christ was the second Man, the last Adam, the Head of a new race. Those who are sanctified in Him are delivered from sin and their former condition in Adam; they are justified and given a new position in Christ. By the baptism of the Holy Spirit at Pentecost, they have become one body, united to the Lord in glory: He is the Head of the church. Leaders in Israel rejected the Lord Jesus: "His own did not receive Him" (John 1:11). But some believers were gathered around Him; He chose among them twelve apostles. After a ministry of about three and a half years, the time came for Jesus to offer Himself as a sacrifice for sin, according to the counsel of God. In Gethsemane, He was filled with dread at the prospect of bearing sin. He asked His Father: "My Father, if it is possible, let this cup pass from me"; but that was not possible, and He bowed before His Father's will. He was arrested and crucified; His blood was shed, and by His blood redemption was accomplished. On the third day, He rose from among the dead; He breathed into the apostles the Holy Spirit as the power of life (John 20:19–23). Having appeared on several occasions to many witnesses, He ascended to heaven. The Scriptures clearly demonstrate by direct affirmations and by the works of the Lord Jesus that He was at the same time God and man;

He indeed accomplished what no mere man could do, e.g., read the thoughts of men, forgive sins, raise the dead by His own power, and raise Himself from among the dead (John 10:18). The Lord Jesus is truly God and man. This mystery surrounding His person is beyond human comprehension. No one knows the Son except the Father; no one knows the Father except the Son, and he to whom the Son may be pleased to reveal Him (Matt. 11:27; Luke 10:22). This is not to be a stumbling block, but calls forth reverence, praise, and adoration. (After Walter Biggar Scott.) **b. Disciple at Rome, also called Justus.** Paul commends Jesus called Justus, who was a consolation to Paul (Col. 4:11); this Jesus greets the Colossians (see v. 10). **c. Name or surname of Barabbas in some mss.** Refs.: Matt. 27:16, 17.

JEW 1. (*Ioudaios*: man of Judea) **At the beginning, member of the tribe of Judah; later, person of this race.** The name "Jew" (or: Judean) was first used after the division of Israel into two kingdoms of ten tribes and two tribes (see 2 Kgs. 16:6). It is thought to be derived from "Judah," the kingdom formed of the tribes of Judah and of Benjamin. Those returned from the captivity belonged to these two tribes. After the captivity, the descendants of the twelve tribes were called Jews; the Lord is called "King of the Jews" (Matt. 27:37). Salvation is of the Jews (John 4:22). In John's Gospel, the "Jews" designate the inhabitants of Judea, in contrast with people from elsewhere, gathered for the feast. The expr. "those who say they are Jews" is used regarding religious groups claiming to represent Judaism or Christianity and seeking to give a Judaic form to Christianity; they are under the influence of Satan ("the synagogue of Satan") and oppose the faithful represented by two churches: Smyrna and Philadelphia (Rev. 2:9; 3:9). (After Walter Biggar Scott.) **2.** (like the Jews: *Ioudaikōs*) **According to the customs of the Jewish people.** Peter lived like the Gentiles and not like the Jews (Gal. 2:14). ¶ **3.** See **JUDAISM** and **JUDAIZE**.

JEWISH (*Ioudaikos*; from *Iouda*: Judah) **Pertaining to Judaism.** Christians should beware of heeding Jewish myths (Titus 1:14). ¶

JEZEBEL (*Iezabel*: chaste, in Heb.) **Daughter of a king of the Sidonians and wife of Ahab (see 1 Kgs. 16:29–31).** This wicked queen exterminated the Lord's prophets (see 1 Kgs. 18:4) and had Naboth murdered so Ahab might usurp his vineyard (see 1 Kgs. 21). In Rev. 2:20, Jezebel incites Christians to commit sexual immorality and to eat things sacrificed to idols. She symbolizes those in Christendom who join idolatrous practices to true Christianity. ¶

JOANAN (*Iōannas*; also spelled: *Iōanan*) **Man of the O.T.; also transl.: Joanna, Joannas, Joannes.** He is mentioned in the genealogy of Jesus (Luke 3:27). ¶

JOANNA (*Iōanna*) **Wife of Chuza, Herod's steward.** She ministered to Jesus (Luke 8:3). With other women, she announced the Lord's resurrection to the apostles (Luke 24:10). ¶

JOATHAM → JOTHAM

JOB (*Iōb*: persecuted, poorly treated, in Heb.) **Patriarch of the O.T. which contains a book bearing his name.** He suffered affliction with patience; the Lord was full of compassion and tender mercy toward him (James 5:11). ¶

JOEL (*Iōēl*: Jehovah is God, in Heb.) **Prophet of the O.T., which contains a book bearing his name.** Fulfilling his prophecy, at Pentecost the Holy Spirit descended from heaven and disciples prophesied (Acts 2:16; see 17–21). ¶

JOHN (*Iōannēs*: Jehovah has been gracious, in Heb.) **a. John the Baptist or John the Baptizer, cousin of Jesus.** John's father, Zacharias, and mother, Elizabeth, were righteous before God (see Luke 1:5, 6); they were very old when John was born (see v. 7). John was sent from God to bear witness of Christ (John 1:6; see v. 7). He preached repentance and the coming of the kingdom of the heavens; he baptized with water for repentance. Jesus came to be baptized by John: although righteous and having nothing to confess, He associated Himself with the repentant remnant of Israel (Matt. 3:13; see v. 15). After a short ministry, John was beheaded in prison by Herod's order (Matt. 14:10). Although John the Baptist performed no miracle (John 10:41), Jesus says there is no greater prophet than he (Luke 7:28). **b. Son of Zebedee, brother of James and disciple of the Lord.** The apostle John describes himself as the disciple whom Jesus loved (John 13:23; 19:26; 20:2; 21:7, 20). Jesus surnamed John and his brother James "Boanerges," i.e., "Sons of Thunder" (see Mark 3:17), perhaps because of their impetuous character (Matt. 20:20–24; Mark 10:35–41; see Luke 9:49, 54). On the cross, Jesus entrusted His mother to John (see John 19:25–27). The Gospel of John presents the Lord Jesus as the Son of God. John wrote three epistles bearing his name and, when in exile on the island Patmos, he wrote the book of Revelation (Rev. 1:1, 4, 9; 22:8). Other refs.: Mark 9:38; Luke 9:49; 22:8; Acts 3:1, 4, 11; 4:13, 19; 8:14; Gal. 2:9. **c. John, called Mark.** See **MARK**. **d. Important Jewish man, of the high priestly family.** Peter and John, and others appeared before him (Acts 4:6). **e. Father of Peter.** Refs.: John 1:42; 21:15–17 in some mss.; see **JONAH**. ¶

JONAH (*Iōnas*: dove, in Heb.) **a. Prophet of the O.T., which contains a book bearing his name; also transl.: Jonas.** As he was a sign, being three days and three nights in the belly of the great fish, so Jesus would remain in death for three days (Matt. 12:39–41; 16:4; Luke 11:29, 30, 32). **b. Father of Simon Peter; also transl.: Jona, Jonas.** Refs.: John 1:42; 21:15–17; other mss.: John. ¶

JONAM (*Iōnam*: Jehovah is gracious, in Heb.) **Man of the O.T.; also spelled: Jonan.** He is mentioned in the genealogy of Jesus (Luke 3:30). ¶

JONAN → JONAM

JONAS → JONAH

JOPPA (*Ioppē*: beauty, in Heb.) **Seaport city of Israel facing the Mediterranean Sea, located northwest of Jerusalem; its present name is Jaffa.** Dorcas, a disciple, was resurrected by Peter there (Acts 9:36, 38, 42). In Joppa, Peter had a vision preparing him to go to Cornelius, a Gentile (Acts 9:43; 10:5, 8, 23, 32; 11:5, 13). ¶

JORAM (*Iōram*: Jehovah is exalted, in Heb.) **Name of a king of Judah, son of Jehoshaphat (see 2 Kgs. 8:16, 17).** He is mentioned in the genealogy of Jesus Christ (Matt. 1:8). ¶

JORDAN (*Iordanēs*: the descender, in Heb.) **River which the Israelites crossed when they entered the promised land (see Josh. 3); it is the main river of Israel.** John baptized in the Jordan; he baptized Jesus there (Matt. 3:5, 6, 13; Mark 1:5, 9; Luke 3:3; 4:1; John 1:28). Several times we find the expr. "across the Jordan," "beyond the Jordan" (or similar expr.) (Matt. 4:15, 25; 19:1; Mark 3:8; 10:1; John 1:28; 3:26; 10:40). ¶

JOREIM (*Iōreim*; also spelled and transl.: Jorim) **Man of the O.T.** He is mentioned in the genealogy of Jesus (Luke 3:29). ¶

JORIM → JOREIM

JOSAPHAT → JEHOSHAPHAT

JOSEPH (*Iōsēph*: He will add, in Heb.; see Gen. 30:24) **a. Son of Jacob and name of one of the twelve tribes descended from him.** He received from Jacob a plot near Sychar (John 4:5). Full of envy against him, Joseph's brothers sold him for twenty pieces of silver, and he was led away to Egypt. In that land, he prospered, for God was with him; he saved his family from famine (Acts 7:9, 13, 14, 18). Dying, Jacob blessed Joseph's sons (Heb. 11:21); before dying, Joseph spoke of the Israelites' exodus and gave orders to carry away his bones (v. 22). In Canaan, Joseph's descendants became two tribes, Ephraim and Manasseh (see Josh. 14:4). Twelve thousand out of the tribe of Joseph will be sealed (Rev. 7:8). **b. Husband of Mary, the mother of Jesus.** This Joseph is mentioned in the genealogy of Jesus Christ (Matt. 1:16; Luke 1:27). An angel appeared to him and told him not to fear to take Mary as his wife, for the child she was expecting had been conceived by the Holy Spirit (Matt. 1:18–20, 24; see v. 25; Luke 2:33 and, in some mss., v. 43). Joseph went to Bethlehem with Mary, who was pregnant, on the occasion of a census (Luke 2:4). Shepherds found Mary and Joseph, and the baby lying in a manger (Luke 2:16). An angel appeared to him to tell him to flee to Egypt, for Herod was going to seek the little child to kill him (Matt. 2:13). An angel appeared to him so that he would return to Israel after Herod's death (Matt. 2:19; see v. 20); he lived in Nazareth (see 2:19–23). People regarded Jesus as the son of Joseph (Luke 3:23; 4:22; John 1:45; 6:42). **c. Man of the N.T. originally from Arimathea.** Joseph of Arimathea, a rich man, was a disciple of Jesus (Matt. 27:57), an honorable counsellor, waiting for the kingdom of God, a good and righteous man (Mark 15:43; Luke 23:50). He asked for Jesus' body, wrapped it in clean linen cloth, and put it in his new tomb (Matt. 27:57, 59; Mark 15:45, 46). This Joseph and Nicodemus wrapped Jesus' body in linen with aromatic spices, with a mixture of myrrh and aloes weighing about 100 pounds (45 kilograms) (John 19:38; see 38–42). **d. Name of three men of the O.T.** Their names are mentioned in the genealogy of Jesus (Luke 3:24, 26 (other mss.: *Iōsēch*), 30). **e. Christian man at the beginning of Acts.** Joseph was a disciple called Barsabbas and surnamed Justus (Acts 1:23), proposed to replace Judas; but the lot fell on Matthias (see v. 26). **f. Levite from Cyprus, surnamed Barnabas.** Ref.: Acts 4:36; see BARNABAS. **g.** Other refs.: Matt. 13:55; 27:56; see **JOSES.** ¶

JOSES (*Iōsēs*: adding, in Heb.) **a. One of the brothers of the Lord; also transl.: Joseph.** Refs.: Matt. 13:55; Mark 6:3. **b. Another name of Jude, son of Mary and brother of James; also transl.: Joseph.** Refs.: Matt. 27:56; Mark 15:40, 47. **c. Another name of Joseph, surnamed Barnabas.** See **BARNABAS.**

JOSHUA 1. (*Iēsous*: Jehovah saves, in Heb.; same spelling in Greek of the name of Jesus) **Leader of Israel who succeeded Moses.** He brought the Israelites into Canaan, the promised land (Acts 7:45). Joshua did not bring this people into rest (Heb. 4:8); there remains a rest to come for God's people (v. 9). **2.** (*Iōsē*: adding, in Heb.) **Man of the O.T.; also transl.: Jose, Joses.** Joshua is mentioned in the genealogy of Jesus (Luke 3:29). ¶

JOSIAH (*Iōsias*: Jehovah heals, in Heb.) **King of Judah (see 2 Kgs. 22:1).** He is mentioned in the genealogy of Jesus Christ (Matt. 1:10, 11). ¶

JOSIAS → JOSIAH

JOTHAM (*Iōatham*: Jehovah is perfect, in Heb.) **Name of a king of Judah (Jotham, son of Uzziah, or Azariah: 2 Kgs. 15:32, 33); also transl.: Joatham.** He is mentioned in the genealogy of Jesus Christ (Matt. 1:9a, b). ¶

JUDAISM (*Ioudaismos*; from *Iouda*: Judah) **Religious system based on the law of Moses, to which the Jews had added traditional practices.** Paul speaks of his behavior in Judaism before his conversion and of his progress in Judaism (Gal. 1:13, 14). ¶

JUDAIZE (*ioudaizō*; from *Ioudaios*: Jewish) **To impose Jewish customs and ways; also transl.: to live like Jews, to follow Jewish customs.** Paul reproved Peter who compelled the nations to Judaize (Gal. 2:14). ¶

JUDAS (*Ioudas*: form of Judah, in Heb.) **a. One of the brothers of Jesus.** He is mentioned in Matt. 13:55; Mark 6:3. **b. The brother of James and prob. the same as Lebbaeus surnamed Thaddaeus (Matt. 10:3; Mark 3:18).** This Judas was one of the twelve apostles (Luke 6:16; John 14:22; Acts 1:13) and author of the book bearing his name (Jude 1). **c. Disciple of Jesus.** Judas Iscariot was one of Jesus' twelve disciples (Matt. 26:14, 47; Mark 14:10, 43; Luke 22:47; John 12:4) and had the money bag (John 13:29), but he was a thief (see

John 12:6). The devil put it into his heart to betray Jesus (John 13:2) and Satan entered into him (Luke 22:3). He then betrayed Jesus (Matt. 10:4; 26:25; Mark 3:19; Luke 6:16; 22:48; John 6:71; 13:26; 18:2, 3, 5; Acts 1:16) for thirty pieces of silver (see Matt. 26:15). Filled with remorse, Judas brought back the thirty pieces of silver, confessing he had sinned by betraying innocent blood, went away, and hanged himself (Matt. 27:3–5). Matthias replaced Judas as an apostle (Acts 1:25; see v. 26). **d. Believing man of Jerusalem.** Refs.: Acts 15:22, 27, 32; see **BARSABBAS**. **e. Inhabitant of Damascus.** Saul of Tarsus stayed with this Judas (Acts 9:11). **f. Man of Galilee.** Judas of Galilee led many people after him in a revolt (Acts 5:37). ¶

JUDE → JUDAS b.

JUDEA (*Ioudaia*) **Region of southern Israel, west of the Dead Sea and the Jordan River; Judea corresponds to the territory assigned to the tribe of Judah.** Bethlehem (Matt. 2:1) and Jerusalem (3:5) are in Judea. Large crowds from Judea followed Jesus (Matt. 4:25; Mark 3:7). There were several churches in Judea (Acts 9:31; 10:37; Gal. 1:22; 1 Thes. 2:14). Paul solicited prayer that he might be delivered from unbelievers in Judea (Rom. 15:31).

JUDGMENT SEAT 1. (*bēma*; from *bainō*: to go; lit.: step) **Place where justice is dispensed, tribunal; also transl.: court, judge's seat.** Scripture speaks of Pilate's judgment seat (Matt. 27:19; John 19:13), that of Galio (Acts 18:12, 16, 17), and that of Festus (25:6, 10, 17). All men will stand before the judgment seat of God (of Christ, in some mss.) (Rom. 14:10); Christians will not be judged, because Jesus Christ has suffered God's judgment in their place at the cross. Nevertheless, the works of Christians will be judged when manifested before Christ's judgment seat. Believers will be rewarded for faithfulness, but they will suffer loss regarding anything not done for the Lord and His glory (2 Cor. 5:10; see 1 Cor. 3:15). **2.** (*kritērion*; from *kritēs*: he who decides, judge, which is from *krinō*: to judge) **See defin. in 1.; also transl.: court, law court, tribunal.** Saints will judge the world and should be competent to constitute the smallest law courts (1 Cor. 6:2). The rich drag the oppressed before judgment seats (Jas. 2:6).

JULIA (*Ioulia*; fem. of Julius) **Christian woman of Rome.** Paul sends greetings to her (Rom. 16:15). Other ref.: Rom. 16:7 in some mss. rather than Junia (or Junias, a masc. name). ¶

JULIUS (*Ioulios*) **Centurion of the cohort of Augustus.** Paul and other prisoners were delivered to him (Acts 27:1); he treated Paul with consideration (v. 3). ¶

JUNIAS (*Iounias*) **Christian man of Rome; also transl.: Junia, a fem. name.** He was Paul's kinsman and former fellow prisoner (Rom. 16:7); some mss. have Julia, a fem. name, rather than Junias. ¶

JUPITER → ZEUS

JUSTICE (person) (*Dikē*: Justice) **Personification of divine justice among the Greeks; also transl.: vengeance, Nemesis, the goddess Justice.** A viper seizing Paul's hand, natives of Malta believed he was a murderer whom Justice would not allow to live (Acts 28:4).

JUSTIFICATION 1. (*dikaiōma*; from *dikaioō*: to justify, which is from *dikaios*: just, righteous, which is from *dikē*: justice) **Result of being justified, acquittal.** The free gift of God's grace was in justification (Rom. 5:16). **2.** (*dikaiōsis*; from *dikaioō*: see **1. Acquittal of an individual from all charges that could weigh on him.** He is then considered as being without fault. In His death, Jesus Christ accomplished all that was necessary for our justification (Rom. 5:18). Jesus was raised for the justification of believers (Rom. 4:25). ¶ **3.** See **JUSTIFY**.

JUSTIFY (*dikaioō*; from *dikaios*: just, righteous, which is from *dikē*: justice) **To render just, righteous by acquitting an individual from all charges that**

could weigh on him or her; also transl.: to free, to consider righteous, to declare righteous, to practice righteousness, to vindicate. Before God, man is justified freely by His grace (Rom. 3:24), by faith without works of law (v. 28); it is God who justifies (Rom. 3:30; 4:5; 8:30, 33; Gal. 3:8). Fulfilling the law of Moses or works of the law cannot justify a man before God (Acts 13:39; Rom. 2:13; 3:20; 4:2; Gal. 2:16; 3:11; 5:4). The man who has died is justified from sin (Rom. 6:7) by God's grace, by faith in Jesus Christ (Acts 13:39; Rom. 3:24, 26, 28; 5:1, 9; 1 Cor. 6:11; Gal. 2:16, 17; 3:24; Titus 3:7). Abraham (James 2:21, 24) and Rahab (v. 25) were justified by their works which proved their faith (see v. 18).

JUSTUS (*Ioustos*: just) **a. Surname of Joseph, called Barsabbas.** Joseph, surnamed Justus, was proposed to replace Judas (Acts 1:23). **b. Man who served God and whose house was next to the synagogue.** Paul lodged at his home (Acts 18:7); other mss.: Titius Justus. **c. Surname of a man called Jesus.** Ref.: Col. 4:11. ¶

K

KIDRON (*Kedrōn*: dark, confused, in Heb.) **Ravine where a brook flowed east of Jerusalem, separating the city from the Mount of Olives.** On the night He was betrayed, Jesus went beyond this brook into a garden (John 18:1). ¶

KINGDOM OF GOD (kingdom: *basileia*; from *basileus*: king; God: *Theos*) **Sphere in which God reigns and exercises His authority (moral authority currently).** The expr. "kingdom of God" occurs frequently in the N.T., particularly in the Gospel of Luke and in the Acts (approx. forty times). To enter the kingdom of God, one must be born anew, born of water and of the Spirit (John 3:3, 5); see **BORN AGAIN (BE).** The kingdom of God is righteousness, peace, and joy in the Holy Spirit (Rom. 14:17). Jesus preached the kingdom of God (e.g., Mark 1:14) as did His disciples (Luke 9:2). Other servants will preach this gospel before the reign of Christ is established (see Matt. 24:14). The kingdom of God was in the midst of men when Jesus Christ (the king) was on earth (Luke 17:21). Presently Jesus is represented as a nobleman who has gone to a far country to receive for Himself a kingdom and return (see Luke 19:12). During the age of the new covenant, the kingdom of God also morally bears the character of the kingdom of heaven.

KINGDOM OF HEAVEN (kingdom: *basileia*; from *basileus*: king; heaven: *ouranos*) **The kingdom of heaven (lit.: of the heavens) emphasizes the present session of the king, the Lord Jesus, in heaven.** Matthew alone uses the expr. "kingdom of heaven" in his Gospel to designate the kingdom of God. The ten parables of the kingdom of heaven (see Matt. 13:24–50; 18:23–35;

20:1–16; 22:1–14; 25:1–13) illustrate the fact that there are presently in this kingdom those who serve the king who is in heaven, and there are those who deny Him by their conduct. At the coming of Jesus, the kingdom of heaven had drawn near (Matt. 3:2; 4:17; 10:7). Jesus gives the characteristics of those who will and of those who will not enter the kingdom of heaven (Matt. 5:3, 10, 19, 20; 7:21; 8:11; 11:11; 18:1, 3, 4; 19:12, 14, 23). He says that the violent seize on the kingdom of heaven (Matt. 11:12), for John the Baptist had preached repentance necessary for entering it. Scribes and Pharisees shut up the kingdom of heaven against men (Matt. 23:13). To Jesus' disciples, it was given to know the mysteries of the kingdom of heaven (Matt. 13:11).

KIS → KISH

KISH (*Kis*: bow, in Heb.) **Man of the O.T.; also transl.: Cis, Kis.** He was the father of King Saul (Acts 13:21). ¶

KORAH (*Kore*; from *korah*: bald, in Heb.) **Man of the tribe of Levi.** Jude 11 speaks of his rebellion: he incited the Israelites to revolt against Moses' authority (see Num. 16:1–19). ¶

L

LAKE (*limnē*; comp. *limēn*: harbor) **a. An expanse of water surrounded by land.** Jesus stood by the lake of Gennesaret (Luke 5:1) and saw two boats by the lake (v. 2). With His disciples, He set out to the other side of the lake (Luke 8:22); a squall came down on the lake (v. 23). A herd of swine rushed into the lake and drowned (Luke 8:33). **b. The lake of fire is a place of eternal suffering and damnation reserved for unbelievers as well as fallen angels.** The beast and the false prophet (Rev. 19:20), the devil (20:10), death and Hades (20:14), and anyone not found written in the book of life (20.15) will all be cast into the lake of fire. The lake burns with fire and brimstone: the second death (Rev. 21:8). ❡

LAMA (*lama*) **Heb. word meaning "Why?".** Refs.: Matt. 27:46; Mark 15:34; see **SABACHTHANI.** ❡

LAMECH (*Lamech*: strong, in Heb.) **Father of Noah (see Gen. 5:28, 29).** He is mentioned in Jesus' genealogy (Luke 3:36). ❡

LAODICEA (*Laodikeia*; from *laos*: people, and *dikē*: justice) **City in western Asia Minor, in Phrygia.** Paul mentions Christians there (Col. 2:1; 4:13), greets brothers there (4:15), and encourages the Colossians to read the letter sent to them (4:16). The church of Laodicea, marked by a lukewarm condition, is the last of seven churches to which a letter is addressed (Rev. 1:11; 3:14). ❡

LAODICEAN (*Laodikeus*; from *laos*: people, and *dikē*: justice) **Inhabitant of Laodicea, in Asia Minor, near Colossae and Hierapolis.** Paul asked the Colossians and Laodiceans to read the respective letters from each other (Col. 4:16). Other ref.: Rev. 3:14 in some mss. ¶

LASEA (*Lasaia*) **City in southern Crete near Fair Havens.** Paul's ship approached this city (Acts 27:8). ¶

LAW (*nomos*; from *nemō*: to distribute) **Rules that allow, restrict, or prohibit individual and institutional behavior.** The term describes a law in general (Rom. 4:15; 5:13). Most frequently, it describes the divine law given through Moses (Matt. 5:17, 18; 7:12; 23:23; Luke 2:22; John 7:51; 8:5). Sometimes it means the books of Moses or the Pentateuch containing the law (Luke 24:44; 1 Cor. 14:21). The gospel method of justification is called the "law of faith," the opposite of the "law of works" (Rom. 3:27). The "law of the Spirit of life" is the opposite of the law of sin and death (Rom. 8:2). In James we find the "royal law" (2:8). The "perfect law of liberty" (Jas. 1:25; 2:12) frees Christians from ceremonial observances and from the slavery of sin; it is contrasted to the Mosaic law which made nothing perfect (Heb. 7:19; 10:1).

LAWLESS (noun) (*anomos*; from *a*: neg., and *nomos*: law) **Which does not observe any moral rule; without faith or law.** The Lord was counted among the lawless (Mark 15:28; Luke 22:37). In 2 Thes. 2:8, the lawless one refers to the antichrist. The law is for the lawless (1 Tim. 1:9).

LAWLESS MAN (*athesmos*; from *a*: neg., and *thesmos*: law, ordinance) **Without restriction, disobedient to rules; also transl.: godless, unprincipled man, wicked.** Lot was distressed with the filthy conduct of lawless men in Sodom and Gomorrah (2 Pet. 2:7). Peter spoke of the error of lawless men (2 Pet. 3:17). ¶

LAWLESSNESS (*anomia*; from *a*: neg., and *nomos*: law) **Conduct without law, unrestrained, characterized by wickedness.** The man of lawlessness will be revealed before the return of the Lord to reign on the earth (2 Thes. 2:3). Other ref.: 2 Thes. 2:7.

LAYING ON OF HANDS (laying on: *epithesis*; to lay on, to lay upon: *epitithēmi*; from *epi*: upon, and *tithēmi*: to put; hand: *cheir*) **a. Practice consisting of laying hands on the sick and the infirm to heal them, invoking upon them the power of God.** Jesus laid on hands (Mark 5:23; 6:5; 7:32; 8:25; Luke 4:40). He speaks of others laying hands on the sick (Mark 16:18). In a vision, Ananias laid his hands on Saul (Acts 9:12); after Ananias laid hands on him, Saul again saw (v. 17). Paul laid hands on Publius' father and healed him (Acts 28:8). **b. Practice for publicly recognizing Christians having received a gift of grace for a service.** The expr. is used of seven men chosen to serve tables (Acts 6:6), Barnabas and Saul (13:3), Timothy (1 Tim. 4:14; 2 Tim. 1:6) and those on whom he was to lay hands (1 Tim. 5:22). **c. Practice through which a person receives the Holy Spirit.** Christians of Samaria received the Holy Spirit thus (Acts 8:17); Simon offered money to receive this power (v. 19; see v. 18). When Paul laid hands on Christians of Ephesus, the Holy Spirit came on them (Acts 19:6). **d. Practice of O.T. times.** The Christian is to go on to perfection, not laying again a foundation of this practice (Heb. 6:2). **e. Practice of Jesus' times,** Jesus laid His hands on little children (Matt. 19:13, 15).

LAZARUS (*Lazaros*: God is my help, in Heb.) **a. Poor man in an account.** He was laid at a rich man's gate (Luke 16:20); after his death, he was comforted in Abraham's bosom (vv. 23–25). **b. Brother of Martha and Mary.** He was sick and died; Jesus resurrected him (John 11:1, 2, 5, 11, 14, 43). Afterwards, Lazarus sat at table with Jesus (John 12:1, 2). Chief priests wanted to kill him; on his account many Jews believed in Jesus (John 12:9, 10, 17). ¶

LEADER (one who rules over: *hēgoumenos*, from: *hēgeomai*: to rule) **One who guides, who commands.** In the church, "one who rules over" is an elder caring for brothers and sisters in the Lord by giving direction. Christians are to remember them (Heb. 13:7) and to obey them (v. 17). A special greeting is addressed to those who rule (Heb. 13. 24). This word is used re Christ who will shepherd Israel (Matt. 2:6, transl. "Ruler").

LEBBAEUS (*Lebbaios*) **One of the twelve apostles of Jesus; this name appears in some mss.** He was surnamed Thaddaeus and was the brother of James (Matt. 10:3). This is prob. Jude, author of the epistle of the same name (see Mark 3:18; Acts 1:13). ¶

LEGION (*legiōn*; from Lat.: *legio*) **a. The most important unit of the Roman army, consisting of 5,000 to 6,000 men and divided into 10 cohorts of 500 to 600 men each.** In Matt. 26:53, "twelve legions of angels" is synonymous with a significantly high number. **b. Evil spirits.** Because there were many demons in a possessed man, Legion was the name of those evil spirits (Mark 5:9, 15; Luke 8:30). ¶

LEPER (*lepros*; from *lepō*: to peel, or *lepos*: scale; lit.: scaly) **Person afflicted with leprosy; also transl.: man with leprosy, one with leprosy.** Jesus healed many lepers in Israel (Matt. 8:2; 11:5; Mark 1:40; Luke 7:22; 17:12). He sent out the twelve disciples to cleanse lepers (Matt. 10:8). He went to the house of Simon the leper (Matt. 26:6; Mark 14:3). There were many lepers in Israel in Elisha's time, but only Naaman the Syrian was cleansed (Luke 4:27). ¶

LEPROSY (*lepra*; from *lepis*: scale, which is from *lepō*: to peel) **Contagious and incurable illness.** Leprosy symbolizes sin especially since the leper gradually loses feeling in the afflicted members. Jesus healed various individuals of their leprosy (Matt. 8:3; Mark 1:42; Luke 5:12, 13). See **LEPER.** ¶

LETTER OF COMMENDATION (letter: *epistolē*; of commendation: *sustatikos*; from *sunistaō*: to approve, to recommend) **Letter introducing a Christian to other Christians.** It facilitated his or her reception, including assistance in practical matters and participation in the Lord's Supper, at another church (see Rom. 16:1, 2 where Phoebe is commended). Other ref.: 2 Cor. 3:1. ¶

LEVI (man of the N.T.) (*Leuis*: joining, in Heb.; see Gen. 29:34) **One of the twelve apostles of Jesus.** He was a tax collector (Mark 2:14; Luke 5:27). He is also called Matthew (Matt. 9:9; 10:3; Mark 3:18; Luke 6:15; Acts 1:13). He left everything to follow Jesus and made Him a great feast in his house (Luke 5:29). ¶

LEVI (men of the O.T.) (*Leui*: joining, in Heb.; see Gen. 29:34) **a. Son of Jacob and name of one of the twelve tribes descended from him.** A family of his sons received the service of the priesthood (Heb. 7:5, 9). Twelve thousand out of the tribe of Levi will be sealed (Rev. 7:7). **b. Name of two men of the O.T.** They are mentioned in Jesus' genealogy (Luke 3:24, 29).

LIBYA (*Libuē*) **Region of northeast Africa, bordering Egypt and near Cyrene.** Jews from there were in Jerusalem at Pentecost (Acts 2:10). ¶

LICTOR → OFFICER

LIFE (TO GIVE) (to come to life, to give life: *zōopoieō*; from *zōos*: alive, and *poieō*: to make) **To communicate life, especially eternal life, to vivify; also transl.: to make alive, to quicken.** The Father and the Son give life (John 5:21), as does the Holy Spirit (John 6:63; 2 Cor. 3:6; 1 Pet. 3:18; v. 19 in some mss.). God gives life to the dead (Rom. 4:17). This is also attributed to God by His Spirit (Rom. 8:11). The principle of giving life is the following: that which is sown must die before being given life (1 Cor. 15:36). The last Adam, Jesus Christ, is a life-giving spirit (1 Cor. 15:45); He will give life to the mortal bodies of Christians, whether living or fallen asleep, at His coming. The law cannot give life (Gal. 3:21). God preserves in life all things (1 Tim. 6:13).

LIFE ETERNAL (life: *zōē*; from *zaō*: to live; eternal: *aiōnios*; from *aiōn*: age) **Life eternal is communicated at new birth. It is new life, divine life transmitted by God.** God communicates life eternal to whoever believes in the Son of God (John 3:15, 16, 36; 6:40, 47, 54; 1 Tim. 1:16; 1 John 1:2). Jesus gives life eternal (John 10:28; 17:2). He who hears the word of the Lord and believes Him who sent Him has life eternal (John 5:24). God has given eternal life to the Christian, and this life is in His Son (1 John 5:11); Jesus Christ is the true God and eternal life (v. 20); the Christian already possesses eternal life while here on earth and enjoys it presently (v. 13). Perfect and definitive enjoyment of blessings related to this life is yet future (Matt. 19:29; Rom. 2:7; 6:22; Gal. 6:8; 1 Tim. 6:12).

LILY (*krinon*) **Prob. anemones which cover the hills of Israel at the end of winter; these flowers may be purple, blue, or pink in color.** Jesus said to consider the lilies of the field as a lesson in God's care (Matt. 6:28; Luke 12:27). ¶

LINEN, LINEN CLOTH 1. (*linon*; *linum*, in Lat.) **Plant (flax) from which fabric is made for clothing.** A linen garment may represent the holiness and moral purity of the person wearing it. In Rev. 15:6, seven angels are clothed in pure bright linen. Other ref.: Matt. 12:20. ¶ **2.** (*othonion*; dimin. of *othonē*: linen, sheet) **Linen bandage used to wrap a body; also transl. (plur.): linen clothes, linen wrappings, strips of linen.** Jesus' body was bound in linen (John 19:40). Peter saw these linen cloths lying by themselves (Luke 24:12; John 20:6), as did John (John 20:5). The handkerchief that had been upon His head was not lying with the linen cloths (John 20:7). ¶ **3.** (*sindōn*) **a. Clothing made of linen.** A youth who followed Jesus to Gethsemane was covered with a linen cloth, which he left behind when he fled his pursuers (Mark 14:51, 52). **b. Piece of linen used for wrapping the dead; also transl.: fine linen.** Joseph wrapped Jesus' body in a clean linen cloth (Matt. 27:59; Mark 15:46; Luke 23:53). ¶

LINUS (*Linos*; perhaps from *linon*: flax, linen) **Christian man of Rome.** Paul sends the greetings of Linus to Timothy (2 Tim. 4:21). ¶

LITTLE FAITH (OF) (*oligopistos*; from *oligos*: little, and *pistis*: conviction, faith) **Not believing or trusting very much.** The disciples were people of little faith (Matt. 6:30; 8:26; 16:8; Luke 12:28); also, Peter (Matt. 14:31). ¶

LOCUST (*akris*) **Type of insect (large grasshopper) invading Eastern countries and destroying vegetation; the Mosaic law permitted eating the locusts (Lev. 11:21, 22).** John the Baptist fed on locusts (Matt. 3:4; Mark 1:6). Locusts will receive power to injure those men who do not have the seal of God on their foreheads (Rev. 9:3); the locusts looked like horses prepared for battle (v. 7). The angel of the abyss is their king (see **ABADDON**). ¶

LOIS (*Lōis*) **Grandmother of Timothy.** The sincere faith in Timothy had first dwelt in his grandmother Lois (2 Tim. 1:5). ¶

LORD 1. *(Kurios, kurios*; from *kuros*: might, supremacy) **a. Title of God and of the Lord Jesus as those who have authority.** This title is used re God (e.g., Matt. 1:20, 22, 24; Rev. 21:22). Jesus uses "the Lord your God" when responding to Satan, (Matt. 4:7, 10). Jesus is Lord of all (Acts 10:36). Anticipating His return, Christians say: Come, Lord Jesus! (Rev. 22:20). **b. Person who has authority over another, master, sir.** The servant is not above his lord (Matt. 10:24; John 13:16); it is enough for the servant to be as his lord (Matt. 10:25). The term is used in parables (Matt. 18:25–27, 31, 32, 34; 21:30; 25:11; Luke 19:25). It designates Pilate (Matt. 27:63), Paul and Silas (Acts 16:30), Abraham (1 Pet. 3:6), and an elder (Rev. 7:14). The Lamb is Lord of lords (Rev. 17:14; 19:16). **c. Sovereign, emperor.** Festus referred to Augustus as his lord (Acts 25:26). **2.** (*Despotēs*) **Sovereign master, one possessing supreme authority.** The term is used in addressing God (Luke 2:29; Acts 4:24; Rev. 6:10). **3.** (Lord's: *kuriakos*; from *kurios*: see **1.**) **Which belongs particularly to the Lord.** This word is used only re the Lord's Supper (1 Cor. 11:20) and the Lord's day (Rev. 1:10). ¶ **4.** (lords: *megistanes*; plur. of *megistos*, superlative of *megas*) **People who are very important, e.g., politically.** Herod hosted his lords and others (Mark 6:21). Other refs.: Rev. 6:15; 18:23. ¶

LOT (*Lōt*: veil, in Heb.) **Nephew of Abraham.** God preserved him at the destruction of Sodom (Luke 17:28, 29). Lot's wife is to be remembered (Luke 17:32): she looked back and became a pillar of salt (see Gen. 19:26). God delivered righteous Lot, oppressed by the dissolute behavior of the wicked (2 Pet. 2:7). ¶

LOVE 1. (*agapē*; from *agapaō*: to love) **Deep feeling of affection, of attachment toward another person.** In the N.T., the term is used only concerning divine persons (e.g., John 15:9; Rom. 15:30; 1 John 2:15) and Christians (e.g., Phil. 1:9; 2 Thes. 1:3). Love has its source in God and is expressed only by God and by those who are born of God (e.g., John 15:13; 1 John 4:8, 16, 18). The word is sometimes transl. "charity" (e.g., 1 Thes. 3:6). **2.** (love of the brothers, brotherly love: *philadelphia*; from *philadelphos*: one who loves his brother, which is from *philos*: friend, and *adelphos*: brother) **Affection, friendship between the brothers and sisters in faith.** We must be kindly affectionate to one another with brotherly love (Rom. 12:10). Concerning brotherly love, the Thessalonians had no need that Paul should write to them (1 Thes. 4:9). Brotherly love must continue (Heb. 13:1). Peter speaks of unfeigned brotherly love (1 Pet. 1:22; 2 Pet. 1:7). ¶ **3.** (love, love toward man, love to man: *philanthrōpia*; from *philos*: friend, and *anthrōpos*: human being) **Benevolence toward, fondness for the human race.** The kindness and the love toward man of God the Savior appeared (Titus 3:4). Other ref.: Acts 28:2. ¶ **4.** (love of money: *philarguria*; from *philos*: friend, and *arguros*: money) **Avarice, inordinate greed for money.** The love of money is a root of every evil (1 Tim. 6:10). ¶

LUCIUS (*Loukios*; *lux*, in Lat.: light) **a. Christian man of Antioch.** Lucius of Cyrene was among the prophets and teachers in the church of Antioch (Acts 13:1). **b. Relative of Paul.** This Lucius sent his greetings to the Christians of Rome (Rom. 16:21). Perhaps the same as **a.** ¶

LUKE (*Loukas*; *lux*: light, in Lat.) **Author of the Gospel that bears his name.** He presents the Lord Jesus as the "Son of Man". He also wrote the Acts of the Apostles. Paul speaks of him as the beloved physician (Col. 4:14) and a fellow worker (Phm. 24). He was still with Paul when the latter wrote the second epistle to Timothy (2 Tim. 4:11). ¶

LYCAONIA (*Lukaonia*) **Region located in the center of Asia Minor.** Paul and Barnabas preached the gospel to the cities there (Acts 14:6). ¶

LYCIA (*Lukia*) **Province of Asia Minor.** On his way to Italy, Paul came to Myra in Lycia (Acts 27:5). ¶

LYDDA (*Ludda*; from Lod, in Heb.: a town situated near Joppa on the road to Jerusalem) **City of Judea northwest of Jerusalem.** Peter went down to the saints who lived there (Acts 9:32). There he healed Aeneas, a paralyzed man; the residents of Lydda and Sharon saw Aeneas and turned to the Lord (Acts 9:35). Lydda is near Joppa (Acts 9:38). ¶

LYDIA (*Ludia*; prob. "from Lydia," a coastal region of Asia Minor) **Christian woman of Thyatira in Lydia.** She was a seller of purple fabrics who served God; the Lord opened her heart to be attentive to the things Paul was saying (Acts 16:14). After she had been baptized, she urged Paul to come and stay at her house (see Acts 16:15). After Paul and Silas went out of the prison, they returned to her house (Acts 16:40). Lydia thus became the first Christian woman of Macedonia and of Europe. ¶

LYSANIAS (*Lusanias*: who drives away sorrow) **Tetrarch of the region of Abilene.** The word of God came to John the Baptist during his rule (Luke 3:1). ¶

LYSIAS (*Lusias*) **Chiliarch commanding the garrison of Jerusalem.** Claudius Lysias delivered Paul from hostile Jews and sent him to the governor Felix in Caesarea (Acts 23:26; 24:7, 22). ¶

LYSTRA (*Lustra*) **City of Lycaonia in Asia Minor, near Derbe)** Paul and Barnabas preached the gospel there (Acts 14:6) where Paul was deemed a god after he healed a man who had never walked (Acts 14:8; see v. 12). After he was stoned (see Acts 14:19), Paul returned to Lystra to strengthen the disciples (Acts 14:21). He revisited Derbe and Lystra, where he met Timothy (Acts 16:1, 2). At the end of his life, Paul spoke of persecutions he had endured at Lystra (2 Tim. 3:11). ❡

M

MAATH (*Maath*: small, in Heb.) **Man of the O.T.** He is mentioned in the genealogy of Jesus (Luke 3:26). ❡

MACEDONIA (*Makedonia*: extended land) **Region of northern Greece.** Having seen a vision (Acts 16:9, 10), Paul went there and preached the gospel, especially in the cities of Philippi (Acts 16:12) and Thessalonica (see 17:1–15). Later, he sent Timothy and Erastus there (Acts 19:21, 22) and returned himself on his third missionary journey (20:1, 3). Christians there sent a contribution to poor saints at Jerusalem (Rom. 15:26; 2 Cor. 8:1). The Philippians made a gift to supply Paul's need (2 Cor. 11:9; Phil. 4:15).

MACEDONIAN MAN (*Makedōn*: see **MACEDONIA**) **Inhabitant of Macedonia in northern Greece.** In a vision, a Macedonian man begged Paul to come to Macedonia (Acts 16:9; see v. 10). This word is used re Gaius and Aristarchus, traveling companions of Paul (Acts 19:29; 27:2). Paul boasted to the Macedonians of the Corinthians' zeal for service to the saints (2 Cor. 9:2, 4). ❡

MAGADAN (*Magadan*) **Locality situated west of the Sea of Galilee, perhaps incl. Magdala.** Jesus came there (Matt. 15:39) and reproached hypocritical Pharisees and Sadducees (see Matt. 16:3). See **MAGDALA.** ❡

MAGDALA 1. (*Magdala*: tower, in Heb.) **City situated on the western shore of the Sea of Galilee.** This name appears instead of "Magadan" (Matt. 15:39, in some mss.). ¶ **2.** (of Magdala: *Magdalēnē*: see **1.**) **Who lives at Magdala; also transl.: Magdalene.** This was the surname of a Mary in the gospels (Matt. 27:56, 61).

MAGDALENE → MAGDALA

MAGI → WISE MAN

MAGIC (*periergos*; from *peri*: around (intens.), and *ergō*: to work) **Marginal, strange activity, certainly linked to the occult; also transl.: curious arts, sorcery.** Magic was formerly practiced by many at Ephesus (Acts 19:19). Other ref.: 1 Tim. 5:13. ¶

MAGISTRATE 1. (*archē*) **Lit.: beginning; by metonymy: person in a position of authority, ruler.** Believers were interrogated before magistrates (Luke 12:11). **2.** (*archōn*; from *archō*: to rule, which is from *archē*: beginning) **Person in a position of authority; also transl.: authority, ruler.** This word is used re going to him with one's adversary (Luke 12:58). Paul and Silas were dragged before magistrates (Acts 16:19). They are not a terror to good works, but to evil (Rom. 13:3). **3.** (*stratēgos*; from *stratos*: army, and *agō*: to lead, to conduct) **Primary sense: military commander; also: principal magistrate of a Roman province.** Magistrates commanded officers (lictors) (Acts 16:35, 38) and dispensed justice at Rome or in her colonies (Acts 16:20, 22, 36).

MAGOG (*Magōg*) **Northern country whose people are descended from Japheth, one of the sons of Noah (see Gen. 10:2).** It will be gathered with Gog to war by Satan at the millennium's end (Rev. 20:8), only to be consumed by fire from heaven (see v. 9). ¶

MAHALALEEL (*Maleleēl*: praise of God, in Heb.) **Man of the O.T.** He is mentioned in the genealogy of Jesus (Luke 3:37; see Gen. 5:12, 15: Mahalalel). ¶

MALCHUS (*Malchos*: counsellor, in Aram.) **Servant of the high priest.** Peter struck him and cut off his right ear (John 18:10). Jesus healed him (see Luke 22:51). ¶

MALELEEL → MAHALALEEL

MALTA (*Melitē*) **Mediterranean island located south of Sicily; also transl.: Melita.** Paul was shipwrecked there and treated kindly by the inhabitants. He stayed there for three months (Acts 28:1; see also v. 11). ¶

MAMMON (*mamōnas*) **Aram. word; this term personifies material possessions or riches that enslave; also transl.: money, wealth.** Mammon cannot be served alongside God (Matt. 6:24; Luke 16:13). The word is used re unrighteousness (Luke 16:9), unrighteous (v. 11); it corresponds to the riches of this Christ-rejecting world. ¶

MANAEN (*Manaēn*: comforter, consoler, in Heb.) **Teacher in the church of Antioch.** He was brought up with Herod the tetrarch (Acts 13:1). ¶

MANASSEH (*Manassēs*: causing to forget, in Heb.) **a. Older son of Joseph and the tribe descended from him (see Gen. 41:50–52; 48:8–20).** Twelve thousand out of this tribe will be sealed (Rev. 7:6). **b. King of Judah.** This Manasseh is mentioned in the genealogy of Jesus (Matt. 1:10). He did evil in the Lord's eyes (see 2 Kgs. 21:2). ¶

MARANATHA (*marana tha*) **Aram. expr. meaning "the Lord comes".** This word is used at the end of Paul's letter to the Corinthians (1 Cor. 16:22). ¶

MARK (*Markos*; *Marcus*, in Lat.) **Surname of a Christian named John.** He was the son of a certain Mary (Acts 12:12). He was the nephew (or cousin) of Barnabas (Col. 4:10). He was Peter's son, in the spiritual sense no doubt (1 Pet. 5:13). Barnabas and Saul took him as their helper (Acts 12:25; see 13:5), but he abandoned them during their first journey (see 13:13). Later, Barnabas proposed to take him along again (15:37), but Paul refused (see v. 38), resulting in a rift; taking Mark with him, Barnabas sailed to Cyprus (v. 39). Yet later, Paul said Mark was useful to him for service (2 Tim. 4:11) and called him a fellow worker (Phm. 24). Mark authored the Gospel bearing his name; he presents the Lord Jesus as the perfect Servant.

MARKET OF APPIUS (*Appiou Phoron*) **A station 37 miles (60 kilometers) southeast of Rome.** Brothers from Rome came to meet Paul there (Acts 28:15). ¶

MARTHA (*Martha*: lady, lady of the household, in Aram.) **Sister of Lazarus and Mary of Bethany.** She received Jesus into her house; but was distracted with much serving (Luke 10:38, 40, 41). After witnessing the resurrection of Lazarus (John 11:1, 5, 19–21, 24, 30, 39; see vv. 42–44), she again served Jesus at supper (John 12:2). ¶

MARY (*Maria* or *Mariam*) **a. Mother of Jesus.** She conceived Jesus miraculously (Matt. 1:16, 18, 20), having found favor with God (Luke 1:30; see v. 31). She had four other sons and at least two daughters (Matt. 13:55; see also v. 56; Mark 6:3). On the cross, Jesus entrusted her to the disciple John (see John 19:26, 27). After the Lord's ascension, she persevered in prayer with others in the upper room (Acts 1:14). Other refs.: Matt. 2:11; Luke 1:27, 34, 38, 39, 41, 46, 56; 2:5, 16, 19, 34. **b. Mary Magdalene (Mary of Magdala).** Jesus cast seven demons out of her (Mark 16:9; Luke 8:2). She followed Jesus, ministering to Him (Matt. 27:56; see v. 55; Mark 15:40; see v. 41), stood by the cross, and saw where the Lord's body was laid (Matt. 27:61; Mark 15:47; John 19:25). An angel told her of His resurrection; Jesus appeared to her first; she carried news of His resurrection and pending ascension (Matt. 28:1; Mark 16:1; Luke 24:10; John 20:1, 11, 16, 18). **c. Mary of Bethany.** She sat at Jesus' feet, listening to His word (Luke 10:39, 42). A sister of Lazarus, she witnessed his resurrection by Jesus (John 11:1, 19, 20, 28, 31, 32, 45); she anointed Jesus with ointment and wiped His feet with her hair (11:2; 12:3). **d. Mary, the wife of Clopas.** She (*Maria* in Greek) is the sister of Mary (*Mariam*, in Greek), the mother of Jesus (John 19:25) and possibly the same person as Mary, the mother of James and Joseph (or Joses) (Matt. 27:56; Mark 15:40, 47; 16:1; Luke 24:10), and "the other Mary" (Matt. 27:61; 28:1). She was near the cross and the tomb; Jesus may have appeared to her also after His resurrection, since her husband's name may also be Cleopas (Luke 24:13–35). **e. Mary, mother of John surnamed Mark.** After his miraculous deliverance from prison, Peter went to her house where many were praying for him (Acts 12:12, see v. 5). **f. Christian woman of Rome.** Paul writes greetings to her (Rom. 16:6). ¶

MATHUSALA → METHUSELAH

MATTATHA (*Mattatha*: gift of Jehovah, in Heb.) **Man of the O.T.** He is mentioned in the genealogy of Jesus (Luke 3:31). ¶

MATTATHIAS (*Mattathias*: gift of Jehovah, in Heb.) **Name of two men of the O.T.** They are mentioned in the genealogy of Jesus (Luke 3:25, 26). ¶

MATTHAN (*Matthan*: gift, in Heb.) **Man of the O.T.** He is mentioned in the genealogy of Jesus (Matt. 1:15). ¶

MATTHAT (*Matthat*: gift of God, in Heb.) **Name of two men of the O.T.** They are mentioned in the genealogy of Jesus (Luke 3:24, 29). ¶

MATTHEW (*Matthaios*: gift of God, in Heb.) **One of the twelve apostles of Jesus.** See **LEVI** (man of the N.T.). His gospel presents the Lord Jesus as the King of Israel (Matt. 9:9).

MATTHIAS (*Matthias*: gift of Jehovah, in Heb.) **Disciple who replaced Judas Iscariot.** He was added to the eleven apostles (Acts 1:23, 26). ¶

MEASURE 1. (*batos*) **Bath, a liquid standard equaling 6 to 10 gallons (approx. 35 liters).** This word is used re oil (Luke 16:6). ¶ **2.** (*koros*) **Largest standard for dry things in Israel, of about 275 dry quarts (300 liters).** This word is used re wheat (Luke 16:7). ¶ **3.** (*metrētēs*; from *metreō*: to measure) **Standard of capacity for liquids of approx. 40 liters or 10 U.S. gallons.** Water pots had room for two or three measures (John 2:6). ¶ **4.** (*metron*) **Determination of the value of an object; portion.** With the measure a person uses, it will be measured back to him (Matt. 7:2; Mark 4:24; Luke 6:38). Scribes and Pharisees were completing the measure of their fathers (Matt. 23:32). God does not give the Spirit by measure (John 3:34). The word is used re faith that God has dealt to each one (Rom. 12:3), the sphere of ministry assigned by God (2 Cor. 10:13), the gift of Christ (Eph. 4:7), the stature of the fullness of Christ (v. 13), every part of the body of Christ, i.e.: the church (v. 16), man (Rev. 21:17). ¶ **5.** (*saton*; from the Heb. *seah*) **Standard of volume corresponding to between 8 to 11 liters.** This word is used re flour (Matt. 13:33; Luke 13:21). ¶ **6.** (excellent measures: *katorthōma*; from *katorthō*: to make straight) **Beneficial and valuable action; lit.: excellent attainments.** This word is used re the Jewish nation (Acts 24:2). ¶ **7.** (beyond measure, in surpassing measure: *huperbolē*; from *huperballō*: to throw beyond, which is from *huper*: beyond, and *ballō*: to throw) **Used as an adv., the Greek word has the meaning of "excessively".** Paul persecuted the church of God beyond measure (Gal. 1:13). **8.** (above measure, beyond measure: *huperperissōs*; from *huper*: above, and *perissōs*: abundantly) **Excessively, utterly.** People were astonished above measure by Jesus' healing power (Mark 7:37). ¶ **9.** (beyond, out of, without measure: *ametros*; from *a*: neg., and *metron*: see **4.**) **Beyond what is reasonable.** Paul would not boast out of measure (2 Cor. 10:13, 15). ¶

MEDE (*Mēdos*) **Inhabitant of Media, region situated south of the Caspian Sea and east of Israel.** They were present in Jerusalem at Pentecost (Acts 2:9). ¶

MEDIATOR (*mesitēs*; from *mesos*: middle, and *eimi*: to go) **Intermediary, conciliator.** Christ is mediator between God and men (1 Tim. 2:5). Moses was mediator between God and Israel (Gal. 3:19, 20; see Ex. 24:37). Jesus is mediator of the new and better covenant, founded on the glories of His Person and the perfection of His work (Heb. 8:6; 9:15; 12:24). ¶

MELCHI (*Melchi*: my king, in Heb.) **Name of two men of the O.T.** They are mentioned in the genealogy of Jesus (Luke 3:24, 28). ¶

MELCHIZEDEK (*Melchisedek*: king of righteousness, in Heb.) **King and priest of the O.T.** He blessed Abraham after Abraham's victory over kings (Heb. 7:1, 10; see Gen. 14:13–20). The Son of God is a priest forever according to the order of Melchizedek (Heb. 5:6, 10; 6:20; 7:11, 15, 17, 21; see Ps. 110:4). ¶

MELEA (*Meleas*) **Man of the O.T.; also transl.: Meleas.** He is mentioned in the genealogy of Jesus (Luke 3:31). ¶

MENNA (*Mainan*) **Man of the O.T.** He is mentioned in the genealogy of Jesus (Luke 3:31). ¶

MERCY 1. (*eleos*) **Compassion for the misery of others, forbearing disposition exercised toward others.** God is rich in mercy (Eph. 2:4); He saves according to His own mercy (Titus 3:5). Mary and Zacharias exalted the mercy of God (Luke 1:50, 54, 58, 72, 78). God expects man to exercise mercy (Matt. 9:13; 12:7; 23:23; Luke 10:37; Jas. 2:13). Christians look for the mercy of the Lord Jesus Christ unto eternal life (Jude 21). **2.** (to be object of, to enjoy, to find, to have, to obtain, to receive, to show mercy: *eleeō*; from *eleos*: see **1.**) **To show or be given compassion for the misery of others.** This verb is used re the merciful (Matt. 5:7), Jesus (Mark 5:19), God (Rom. 9:15, 16, 18), Gentile and Jewish believers (11:30, 31, 32), Paul (1 Tim. 1:13, 16). Showing mercy should be done with cheerfulness (Rom. 12:8). **3.** (*oiktirmos*; from *oikterō*: to have compassion, which is from *oiktos*: compassion, pity) **Compassion; attitude of**

one seeking to respond to the needs of others, to relieve their sufferings. God is the Father of mercies (2 Cor. 1:3). This word is used re God (Rom. 12:1), Christ (Phil. 2:1). The Christian is to put on tender mercies (Col. 3:12). One who despised Moses' law died without mercy (Heb. 10:28). ¶ **4.** (without mercy: *aneleos*; from *a*: neg., and *eleos*: see **1.**) **Without compassion or forbearance for the misery of others.** This verb is used re the judgment to one who has shown no mercy (Jas. 2:13). ¶

MERCY SEAT (*hilastērion*; from *hilaōs*: favorable, propitious) **a. Cover of the ark surmounted by cherubim.** The cherubim of glory overshadowed the mercy seat (Heb. 9:5; see Lev. 16). **b. He who is invested with propitiatory power.** God set forth Christ: the mercy seat to cover the believer's sins through faith in His blood (Rom. 3:25; see Ps. 32:1: the root of the equivalent Heb. word means "to cover"). ¶

MESSIAH (*Messias*: who is anointed, consecrated, in Heb.) **One of the titles of the Lord Jesus; see CHRIST.** Andrew told Peter, "We have found the Messiah!" (John 1:41); a Samaritan woman knew He was coming (4:25). ¶

METHUSELAH (*Mathousala*: man of the dart, in Heb.; see Gen. 5:25) **Man of the O.T.** He is mentioned in the genealogy of Jesus (Luke 3:37). He lived 969 years: the longest life recorded in the Bible (see Gen. 5:27). ¶

MICHAEL (*Michaēl*: who is like God?, in Heb.) **Archangel of God.** He disputed with the devil re Moses' body (Jude 9). With his angels he will fight Satan and his angels, who will be cast down to earth and will persecute Israel (Rev. 12:7; see vv. 8, 9, 13). He aids Israel in their battles (see Dan. 10:13, 21; 12:1). ¶

MILE (*milion*; *mille*, in Lat.: thousand, a measure of distance equivalent to 1,000 *passus* or paces) **Roman measure of distance of approx. 1,480 meters**

(1,600 yards). If one compels a disciple to go one mile, he is to go with him two (Matt. 5:41). ¶

MILETUS (*Milētos*) **City located in the southwest of Asia Minor, south of Ephesus.** Arriving there, Paul called the Ephesian elders to a meeting (Acts 20:15, 17). He left Trophimus sick there. (2 Tim. 4:20). ¶

MINA (*mna*) **Measure of weight and of money amounting to approx. 100 Greek drachmas or 100 Roman denarii; one mina weighed slightly less than 500 grams.** A nobleman gave one mina to each of his ten servants so that they might gain more by trading (Luke 19:13, 16, 18, 20, 24, 25). ¶

MIND (*nous*) **Understanding, as well as perception and judgment.** God gave over evil men to a reprobate mind (Rom. 1:28). The law of sin may war against the law of the mind (Rom. 7:23). One may serve the law of God with the mind (Rom. 7. 25). The mind of the Lord is unknowable to the natural man (Rom. 11:34; 1 Cor. 2:16). Believers are transformed by the renewing of their mind (Rom. 12:2); they are renewed in the spirit of their mind (Eph. 4:23). One is persuaded in one's own mind re matters of faith (Rom. 14:5). Christians are to be perfectly united in the same mind (1 Cor. 1:10); the spiritual man has the mind of Christ (2:16). Nations walk in the vanity of their mind (Eph. 4:17). Men are corrupted in mind (1 Tim. 6:5; 2 Tim. 3:8); their mind and conscience are defiled (Titus 1:15).

MINISTER 1. (*diakonos*) **Servant, deacon.** This word is used in the following contexts: ministers of the new covenant (2 Cor. 3:6), ministers of Satan (11:15), ministers of Christ (v. 23), and minister of sin (Gal. 2:17). **2.** (*leitourgos*; from *leitos*: of the people, and *ergon*: work) **He who exercises a public service; official administrator.** Rulers are God's ministers (Rom. 13:6); Paul was the minister of Christ Jesus to the nations (15:16); Epaphroditus was the Philippians' minister to Paul's need (Phil. 2:25); angels are God's ministers (Heb. 1:7); Christ serves as minister of the sanctuary (8:2). ¶ **3.** (*hupēretēs*; from *hupo*: under, and *eretēs*: rower) **Servant who has received a special service.** Ministers of the Word handed down their eyewitness report (Luke 1:2).

MINT (*hēduosmon*; from *hēdus*: sweet, pleasant, and *osmē*: odor) **Very aromatic herb that grows near water currents or in other humid places.** This word is used re paying tithes of mint vs. the weightier matters of justice, mercy, faith, and love of God (Matt. 23:23; Luke 11:42). ¶

MIRACLE 1. (*dunamis*; from *dunamai*: to be capable; lit.: power) **Work or deed whose cause is of a supernatural character.** Miracles manifested God's approval of Jesus (Acts 2:22). God worked them by Paul's hands (Acts 19:11). Performing miracles does not guarantee entrance into the kingdom of heaven (Matt. 7:22). The lawless one will work miracles (2 Thes. 2:9). Other refs.: Matt. 11:20, 21, 23; 13:54, 58; 14:2. **2.** (*sēmeion*; from *sēma*: mark) **Work or deed whose cause is of a supernatural character; sign, miraculous sign.** A miracle of healing was performed on a lame man (Acts 4:22). Other refs.: Luke 23:8; John 2:11, 23; 3:2.

MIRROR (*esoptron*; from *eisopsomai*: to look into, which is from *eis*: into, and *optomai*: to look) **Surface reflecting the images of objects, looking glass; glass, window.** Mirrors of antiquity were usually made of polished metal (see Ex. 38:8; Job 37:18). Figur., Christians now see in a mirror dimly (1 Cor. 13:12). The word of God is compared to a mirror reflecting man's natural condition (Jas. 1:23). ¶

MITE (*lepton*; from *leptos*: thin) **The smallest bronze coin, worth one eighth of a Roman penny; small copper coin, cent, penny.** A poor widow cast two mites into the temple treasury (Mark 12:42; Luke 21:2). Jesus spoke of paying the very last one (Luke 12:59). ¶

MITYLENE (*Mitulēnē*) **City of the island of Lesbos in the Aegean Sea to the west of Pergamum.** Paul came to Mitylene on his third missionary journey (Acts 20:14). ¶

MNASON (*Mnasōn*: remembering) **Man from Cyprus and an early disciple.** He accompanied Paul from Caesarea to Jerusalem; Paul was to lodge with him (Acts 21:16). ¶

MOLECH, MOLEK → MOLOCH

MOLOCH (*Moloch*: king, in Heb.) **Idol-god worshipped by the Ammonites, to whom human sacrifices were offered.** The Jews' forefathers took up Moloch's tabernacle and worshiped this false god (Acts 7:43). ¶

MONEY-CHANGER 1. (*kollubistēs*; from *kollubos*: small coin) **Person sitting at a table in the temple and exchanging currency.** Jesus overthrew the tables of the money-changers (Matt. 21:12; Mark 11:15; John 2:15). Other ref.: Luke 19:45 in some mss. ¶ **2.** (*kermatistēs*; from *kerma*: small coin of money) **See defin. of 1.** Ref.: John 2:14. ¶

MORNING STAR 1. (*astēr orthrinos*; from *orthros*: morning, dawn) **One of the titles of the Lord Jesus.** Christ is the "bright Morning Star" (Rev. 22:16); this title is used re His second coming. He will come later as the Sun of Righteousness for Israel and the world (see Mal. 4:2) and establish His millennial kingdom. Certain mss. have **2.** in Rev. 22:16. ¶ **2.** (*astēr prōinos*; from *prōi*: early in the morning) **See defin. of 1.** The morning star is promised to the overcomer in Thyatira (Rev. 2:28). Other ref.: Rev. 22:16; see **1.** ¶ **3.** (*phōsphoros*; from *phōs*: light, and *pherō*: to bring; lit.: light carrier) **Term designating the morning star that appears before the sunrise.** Christians do well to take heed to the prophetic word until the morning star rises in their hearts (2 Pet. 1:19). ¶

MOSES (*Mōseus*: drawn out (from the water), in Heb.) **Author of the Pentateuch, the first five books of the O.T.** Under the leadership of Moses, God delivered the Israelites from bondage in Egypt and led them through the Red Sea. He received the law of God and His commandments; he walked with Israel in the wilderness for forty years. See Acts 7:21–43; Heb. 11:23–29. His name is associated with the giving of the law, whereas grace and truth subsist through Jesus (John 1:17; 7:19; Rom. 10:5).

MOUNT OF OLIVES 1. (*Oros tōn Elaiōn*; mount: *oros*, olive: *elaia*) **Mountain east of Jerusalem.** Jesus went to the Mount of Olives before His final entrance into Jerusalem (Matt. 21:1; Mark 11:1; Luke 19:29, 37). He taught His disciples there (Matt. 24:3; Mark 13:3). After instituting the Supper, He went there (Matt. 26:30; Mark 14:26; Luke 22:39), as was His custom (Luke 21:37; John 8:1). **2.** (*Oros tou Elaiōnos*; mount: *oros*, olive tree: *elaiōn*) **See 1.** After Jesus' ascension, the disciples returned to Jerusalem, from the Mount of Olives (Acts 1:12). ¶

MYRA (*Mura*) **City of Lycia in Asia Minor.** Traveling to Italy, Paul landed in Myra (Acts 27:5). ¶

MYRIAD (*murias*; from *murios*: ten thousand) **Ten thousand, or a very large number.** This word is used re armies of angels (Heb. 12:22; Jude 14), angels, living creatures, elders (Rev. 5:11), mounted troops (9:16).

MYRRH (*smurna*) **Resinous gum extracted from a shrub native to Arabia and Ethiopia.** Myrrh flows spontaneously (liquid or pure myrrh; see Ex. 30:23) or is extracted by an incision in the bark. Fragrant and bitter, myrrh represents the sweet odor of Christ, the Man of Sorrows suffering in life and in death. Wise men offered myrrh to the child Jesus (Matt. 2:11). Nicodemus brought myrrh to prepare the body of Jesus for burial (John 19:39). The church of Smyrna (meaning "myrrh") was to suffer (Rev. 2:8; see v. 10). ¶

MYSIA (*Musia*: beach, region) **Region in northwestern Asia Minor.** On their second missionary journey, Paul and Silas came over against Mysia and passed it by (Acts 16:7, 8). ¶

MYSTERY (*mustērion*; from *mustēs*: person initiated to mysteries; lit.: that which is known by the initiated) **In the N.T., a mystery is a truth which was hidden, but is now revealed; also transl.: secret, secret thing.** This word is used re the church: "the mystery which had been hidden [. . .] but has now been made manifest" (Col. 1:26; see also Eph. 3:3, 4, 9; 5:32), the kingdom of God (Matt. 13:11; Mark 4:11; Luke 8:10), the blindness (or hardening) of Israel (Rom. 11:25), the resurrection of saints (1 Cor. 15:51), the gospel (Eph. 6:19), Christ the hope of glory (Col. 1:27), lawlessness (2 Thes. 2:7), godliness (1 Tim. 3:16).

MYSTERY OF LAWLESSNESS — The mystery of lawlessness in 2 Thes. 2:7 (see **MYSTERY** and **LAWLESSNESS**) corresponds to the wickedness of man, which is unrestrained and will reach a level of full development in the person of the antichrist.

MYTH → FABLE

N

NAAMAN (*Naiman*: pleasantness, in Heb.; other Greek spelling: *Neeman*) **Captain of the army of Syria.** He was a leper who was healed by Elisha (Luke 4:27; see 2 Kgs. 5). ¶

NAASSON → NAHSHON

NACHOR → NAHOR

NAGGAI (*Nangai*: shining, in Heb.) **Man of the O.T.** He is mentioned in the genealogy of Jesus (Luke 3:25). ¶

NAGGEE → NAGGAI

NAHOR (*Nachōr*: who snorts, in Heb.) **Man of the O.T.** He is mentioned in the genealogy of Jesus (Luke 3:34); he was the grandfather of Abraham (see Gen. 11:22–26). ¶

NAHSHON (*Naassōn*: diviner, in Heb.) **Man of the O.T.** He is mentioned in the genealogy of Jesus (Matt. 1:4; Luke 3:32); he was the grandfather of Boaz (see Ruth 4:20). ¶

NAHUM (*Naoum*: comfort, in Heb.) **Man of the O.T.** He is mentioned in the genealogy of Jesus (Luke 3:25). ¶

NAIN (*Nain*: beauty, in Heb.) **City of Galilee southeast of Nazareth.** Jesus resurrected a widow's only son in Nain (Luke 7:11). ¶

NAPHTALI (*Nephthalim*: my wrestling, in Heb.; see Gen. 30:8) **One of the twelve sons of Jacob and the tribe descended from him.** Capernaum is in its borders (Matt. 4:13, 15). Twelve thousand out of this tribe will be sealed (Rev. 7:6). ¶

NARCISSUS (*Narkissos*: from the same name as the flower) **Christian man of Rome.** Paul greets the Christians of his household (Rom. 16:11). ¶

NARD (*nardos*) **Perfume of a pleasant odor extracted from a herbaceous plant; it was very costly.** Mary of Bethany poured nard on Jesus' head and feet, anointing His body for burial (Mark 14:3; John 12:3). ¶

NATHAN (*Nathan*: (God) has given, in Heb.) **Man of the O.T.** He is mentioned in the genealogy of Jesus (Luke 3:31); he was one of David's sons. ¶

NATHANAEL (*Nathanaēl*: gift of God, in Heb.) **Disciple of Jesus.** Philip led him to Jesus; he recognized Jesus as the Son of God, the King of Israel (John 1:46–50). He was an Israelite of Cana in Galilee; Jesus, risen, manifested Himself to him at the Sea of Tiberias (21:2). ¶

NATION 1. (*genos*; from *ginomai*: to become) **Race, kinship.** Of Paul (Gal. 1:14). **2.** (*ethnos*) **Multitude, people, ethnic group; also transl.: Gentiles.** This word is used in the sing. re Israel (e.g., Luke 7:5; 23:2; John 11:51). It is used in the plur. re peoples other than Israel, usually pagan (Rom. 11:11), Gentile Christians (e.g., Rom. 16:4; Eph. 3:6), the unconverted in contrast to the church (Acts 14:2). God has made of one blood every nation of men (Acts 17:26). **3.** (one who is of the nations, one of the nations: *ethnikos*; from *ethnos*: see **2.**) **Person who belongs to a nation other than Israel.** Refs.: Matt. 6:7; 18:17. ¶ **4.** (as the nations: *ethnikōs*; from *ethnos*: see **2.**) **After the manner of**

those who do not belong to Israel. This word is used in contrast to after the manner of the Jews (Gal. 2:14). ¶ **5.** (one of another nation: *allophulos*; from *allos*: other, and *phulē*: tribe) **Stranger, foreigner.** It was unlawful for a Jew to associate with one of another nation (Acts 10:28). Other ref.: Acts 13:19 in some mss. ¶

NAZARENE (Nazarene, of Nazareth: *Nazarēnos*, *Nazōraios*; from the Heb. *netser*: branch; see Is. 11:1) **Inhabitant of Nazareth. This name also makes reference to a person who is consecrated to God (see Num. 6:1–21) with respect to the law of the Nazirite; see also Gen. 49:26 and Deut. 33:16.** This word is frequently used re Jesus (Matt. 2:23; 26:71; Mark 1:24; 10:47; 14:67; 16:6; Luke 4:34; 18:37; 24:19; John 18:5, 7; 19:19; Acts 2:22; 3:6; 4:10; 6:14; 22:8; 26:9). Paul was accused of being a leader of the sect of the Nazarenes, a derogatory term for Christians (Acts 24:5). ¶

NAZARETH (*Nazaret*) **City of Galilee.** Jesus lived there (Matt. 2:23; 4:13; 21:11; Mark 1:9; Luke 2:51; 4:16; Acts 10:38). Joseph and Mary were from there (Luke 1:26, see v. 27; 2:4, 39). Jews despised this city (John 1:45, 46). ¶

NEAPOLIS (*Neapolis*: new city) **Port of Macedonia, north of the Aegean Sea.** Paul entered Europe by way of this port of the city of Philippi (Acts 16:11). ¶

NEIGHBOR 1. (*geitōn*; from *gē*: country) **One who lives in the same region or the same country.** This word is used in the plur. (*geitones*) re those who might be invited for a meal (Luke 14:12) or called to rejoice over a recovered sheep (15:6) or coin (v. 9), those of a beggar (John 9:8). ¶ **2.** (*perioikos*; from *peri*: around, and *oikos*: house) **One who lives nearby.** This word is used re those of Elizabeth (Luke 1:58). ¶ **3.** (*plēsion*; from *pelas*: near) **Person who lives near another one.** Neighbors should be loved (Matt. 5:43). Jesus commanded anew (see Lev. 19:18) to love one's neighbor as oneself (Matt. 19:19; 22:39; Mark 12:31, 33; Luke 10:27; Rom. 13:9; Gal. 5:14; Jas. 2:8). A neighbor is one who shows mercy to another (Luke 10:29, 36). A neighbor should not be mistreated (Acts 7:27). Love does no wrong to a neighbor, but seeks to please and build him up (Rom. 13:10; 15:2). We should speak truth with a neighbor (Eph. 4:25), love him without partiality (Jas. 4:12). Under the new covenant with Israel, there will be no need for every man to teach his neighbor to know the Lord (Heb. 8:11). ¶

NEMESIS → JUSTICE

NEPHTALIM, NEPTHALIM → NAPHTALI

NEREUS (*Nēreus*: Lat. name of a god of the sea) **Christian man of Rome.** Paul sent greetings to him and his sister (Rom. 16:15). ¶

NERI (*Nēri*: lamp of Jehovah, in Heb.) **Man of the O.T.** He is mentioned in the genealogy of Jesus (Luke 3:27). ¶

NERO (*Nerōn*) **Roman emperor from A.D. 54 to 68.** Though not named in the N.T., he is the Caesar to whom Paul appealed (Acts 25:10, 11). Certain mss. have this name in a subscription, of no inspired authority, at the end of 2 Tim. 4. ¶

NEW BIRTH → BORN AGAIN (BE)

NEW CREATION (*kainos ktisis*; from *ktizō*: to create) **Creation that will succeed the present creation and will be eternal.** If anyone is in Christ, he is a new creation (2 Cor. 5:17). A Christian is a new creation (Gal. 6:15).

NICANOR (*Nikanōr*: conqueror, victorious) **Christian man of the N.T.** He was one of seven men chosen to serve in the church of Jerusalem (Acts 6:5). ¶

NICODEMUS (*Nikodēmos*: victorious in the midst of the people) **A Pharisee, member of the Sanhedrin and doctor of the law.** He came by night to

Jesus, who taught him that to enter the kingdom of God one must be born anew (John 3:1, 4, 9). He questioned other Pharisees who wished to seize Him without a hearing, contrary to the Law (7:50, see v. 51). With Joseph of Arimathea, he prepared Jesus' body for burial and laid it in the tomb (John 19:39, see vv. 40-42). ¶

NICOLAITAN (*Nikolaitēs*; from Nicolas: victorious over the people) **Follower of the doctrine of Nicolas.** The church of Ephesus hated their works (Rev. 2:6). The church of Pergamum was to repent of having some who held their doctrine (v. 15, see v. 16): a doctrine substantially the same as that of Balaam, tempting believers to eat idol sacrifices and to commit sexual immorality (see Rev. 2:14). ¶

NICOLAS (*Nikolaos*: victorious over the people) **Proselyte of Antioch.** He was one of seven men chosen to serve in the church of Jerusalem (Acts 6:5; see vv. 1–6). ¶

NICOPOLIS (*Nikopolis*: city of victory) **Prob. the city founded by Augustus in the region of Epirus in Greece.** Titus was to meet Paul there, where the apostle had decided to winter (Titus 3:12). ¶

NIGER (*Niger*: black, dark, in Lat.) **Christian man of Antioch.** This was the surname of Simeon, who was among the prophets and teachers in the church of Antioch (Acts 13:1). ¶

NINEVEH (*Nineuē*: dwelling of Nin) **Capital of the Assyrian Empire northeast of Israel.** Ref.: Luke 11:32 in some transl. ¶

NINEVITE (*Nineuitēs*) **Inhabitant of Nineveh.** Jonah was a sign, i.e., a testimony, to them, resulting in their repentance (Luke 11:30, 32). They will stand up at the judgment and condemn the generation of the Lord's time (Matt. 12:41). ¶

NOAH (*Nōe*: consolation, rest, in Heb.; see Gen. 5:28, 29) **Patriarch living at the time of the flood.** He is mentioned in the genealogy of Jesus (Luke 3:36). The coming of the Son of man shall be as his days: everyone went about their business before the flood (Matt. 24:37, 38; Luke 17:26, 27). He is mentioned among the persons of faith; he built an ark for the saving of his household, and by that ark, he condemned the world (Heb. 11:7). God waited with patience during his days, while the ark was being constructed (1 Pet. 3:20). He was a preacher of righteousness (2 Pet. 2:5). ¶

NYMPHAS (*Numphas*: bridegroom) **Christian man of Laodicea or Colossae; also transl.: Nympha (Christian woman).** Paul sent greetings to Nymphas and the church in his house (Col. 4:15). ¶

O

OBED (*Ōbēd*: who serves (God), in Heb.) **Man of the O.T.** He is mentioned in the genealogy of Jesus (Matt. 1:5; Luke 3:32); he was the son of Boaz and Ruth (see Ruth 4:13–22). ¶

OFFICER 1. (*praktōr*; from *prassō*: to do; lit.: agent, doer) **Justice officer, guard.** A judge might deliver a person to an officer; the officer might throw this person in prison (Luke 12:58). ¶ **2.** (*rhabdouchos*; from *rhabdos*: scepter, baton, and *echō*: to have, to hold) **Roman officer responsible to carry out the orders of the emperor and of the chief magistrates.** Officers were sent by and reported to magistrates (Acts 16:35, 38). ¶ **3.** (*hupēretēs*; from *hupo*: under, and *eretēs*: rower) **a. Servant, especially responsible for implementing decisions of the Sanhedrin or the synagogue; also transl.: guard, guard of the temple, official.** Peter stood and sat down with officers (Matt. 26:58; Mark 14:54; John 18:18). Officers struck Jesus (Mark 14:65; John 18:22). They were sent to arrest Jesus (John 7:32), but, impressed by His words, they did not do so (vv. 45, 46). Later, they accompanied Judas, arresting Jesus (John 18:3, 12) and cried out to crucify Jesus (19:6). Officers did not find the apostles in prison (Acts 5:22), but in the temple and brought them before the Sanhedrin (v. 26). **b. Subordinate officer, constable.** Ref.: Matt. 5:25, rather than *praktōr* (see **1.**).

OLIVE (*elaia*) **Fruit of the olive tree, of a greenish color and then blackish at maturity, smooth skinned; oil is extracted from the olive.** Olives cannot be produced by a fig tree (Jas. 3:12).

OLIVE TREE 1. (*elaia*) **Tree very widespread in Israel; the oil extracted from its fruit is used for food, lighting, fabrication of ointment or soap; the olive tree may live to 1,000 years, producing fruit throughout its entire life span.** God's grace grafted branches of the wild olive tree (the nations; see **2.**) into the good olive tree (Israel; see **3.**) (Rom. 11:17, 24). This word is used figur. of two witnesses (Rev. 11:4). **2.** (wild olive tree: *agrielaios*; from *agrios*: growing in the fields, and *elaia*: see **1.**) **Of, or belonging to the olive tree that grows naturally (i.e., not cultivated by man).** Refs.: Rom. 11:17, 24. ¶ **3.** (good olive tree: *kallielaios*; from *kallos*: beauty, and *elaia*: see **1.**) **Cultivated olive tree.** Ref.: Rom. 11:24. ¶

OLYMPAS (*Olumpas*; prob. from Olympus, the celestial dwelling place of pagan gods in Greece) **Christian man living in Rome.** Paul sends him greetings (Rom. 16:15). ¶

OMEGA (*Ō*) **Last letter of the Greek alphabet written "ω".** "The Alpha and the Omega" is a name of God and of Christ (Rev. 1:8, 11 in some mss.; 21:6; 22:13) affirming their eternal existence. ¶

ONESIMUS (*Onēsimos*: useful; from *oninēmi*: to be useful, to be beneficial) **Servant of Philemon.** He was formerly useless to Philemon (Phm. 10; see v. 11), from whom he fled. He met Paul in Rome, was converted, and was useful to Paul, who sent him back to his master, to be received as a brother in Christ. With Tychicus, he brought the letter to Philemon and the letter to the Colossians, in which Paul calls him the faithful and beloved brother who is one of them (Col. 4:9). ¶

ONESIPHORUS (*Onēsiphoros*: who brings a profit; from *onēsis*: benefit, profit, and *pherō*: to bring) **Christian man who most likely lived at Ephesus.** He visited and consoled the apostle Paul in prison at Rome; he rendered many services at Ephesus (2 Tim. 1:16; see vv. 17, 18); Paul greets his household (4:19). ¶

ORACLE 1. (*logion*; dimin. of *logos*: word, declaration, or from *logios*: orator) **Divine answer or affirmation; in a general sense: word of God transmitted by His servants.** The oracles of God refer to the Mosaic law (Acts 7:38). Other refs.: Rom. 3:2; Heb. 5:12; 1 Pet. 4:11. ¶ **2.** (to utter the oracles: *chrēmatizō*; from *chrēma*: matter, business) **To transmit a message, a warning from God.** Prophets uttered the oracles, transmitting the thoughts of God (Heb. 12:25).

OVEN (*klibanos*) **Device dug into the ground with clay walls where bread and cakes were baked; fire, furnace.** Field grass is thrown into the oven (Matt. 6:30; Luke 12:28). ¶

OVERSEER (*episkopos*; from *epi*: upon, and *skopos*: watchman) **Christian who watches over souls with authority and care. At the beginning overseers were chosen by the apostles or their delegates by virtue of their moral qualities. Also transl.: bishop.** Overseers were elders in a local church (Acts 20:28; see v. 17; Phil. 1:1), who met moral requirements (1 Tim. 3:2; Titus 1:7). Christ is the Overseer of the souls of Christians (1 Pet. 2:25). ¶

P

PAGAN → NATION

PALM, PALM TREE (*phoinix*) **Tree growing abundantly in parts of Israel, able to reach 65 feet (20 meters) in height.** The palm tree is an image of the righteous (see Ps. 92:12). Its branches were taken to hail Jesus, the supremely Righteous Man, as King of Israel (John 12:13). Palms branches are held by worshippers of God and the Lamb (Rev. 7:9). Jericho is the city of palm trees (see Deut. 34:3; 2 Chr. 28:15). ¶

PAMPHYLIA (*Pamphulia*: of every tribe, i.e., heterogeneous; from *pas*: all, and *phulē*: union of citizens, tribe) **Region in the south of Asia Minor.** Jews from Pamphylia were present in Jerusalem at Pentecost (Acts 2:10). Paul went there during his first missionary journey (Acts 13:13; 14:24); there Mark abandoned him (15:38). Paul passed near its coast during his fourth missionary journey (Acts 27:5). ¶

PAPER (*chartēs*; from *charassō*: to engrave, to inscribe) **Sheet made of fibers coming from the inside of the stem of the papyrus, a plant that grows in Egypt.** The apostle John wrote his second letter on paper (2 John 12). See **BOOK.** ¶

PAPHOS (*Paphos*: boiling, hot) **City situated in the west of Cyprus.** Paul met the proconsul Sergius Paulus and the magician Barjesus there during his first missionary journey (Acts 13:6, 13). ¶

PARABLE (*parabolē*; from *paraballō*: to compare, which is from *para*: beside, and *ballō*: to put, to throw) **Symbolic narrative drawn from contemporary life to illustrate more clearly a moral or spiritual lesson.** This word is used only in the synoptic Gospels (Matthew, Mark, and Luke). It is also transl. "image" (Heb. 9:9) and "in a figure" (11:19). Most of the Lord's parables, e.g., those in Matt. 13, teach truths re the kingdom of God. Speaking in parables, the Lord fulfilled an O.T. prophecy (Matt. 13:34, 35; comp. Ps. 78:2). Jesus spoke the word with many parables (Mark 4:33).

PARADISE (*paradeisos*) **Word of Asian origin designating the parks of kings and nobles of Persia; in the N.T., it designates a place of delights and heavenly happiness, where the redeemed rejoice in the presence of the Lord Jesus after their death.** The repentant thief was to be in paradise with Christ the same day (Luke 23:43). Paul was caught up into paradise (2 Cor. 12:4). The tree of life is in the paradise of God (Rev. 2:7). ¶

PARALYTIC (*paralutikos*; from *paraluō*: to be paralyzed, which is from *para*: beside, and *luō*: to loosen, to weaken) **Invalid who has lost the capacity for movement in a region of the body, particularly in the lower limbs.** Paralysis pictures man's inability to approach and serve God. Jesus healed many paralytics (Matt. 4:24; 8:6; 9:2, 6). Jesus forgave the sins of a paralytic brought by friends and healed him (Mark 2:3–5, 9, 10). ¶

PARALYZED (BE) (*paraluō*; from *para*: beside, and *luō*: to loosen, to weaken) **To suffer an incapacity for movement in a region of the body, particularly in the lower limbs.** Men brought a man who was paralyzed to Jesus (Luke 5:18) who forgave his sins and healed him (v. 24). This verb is used re many whom Philip healed (Acts 8:7), one whom Peter healed (9:33), and knees (Heb. 12:12). ¶

PARALYZED → PARALYTIC

PARCHMENT (*membrana*; Lat. word for: skin, tablets, parchment to write or to wrap a volume) **Animal skin used for writing manuscripts.** Paul asked Timothy to bring his parchments (2 Tim. 4:13). See **BOOK.** ¶

PARMENAS (*Parmenas*: steadfast) **Christian man of the N.T.** He was one of seven Christians chosen to serve in the church of Jerusalem (Acts 6:5). ¶

PARTHIAN (*Parthos*) **Inhabitant of Parthia in Asia, a country southeast of the Caspian Sea.** They conquered the Romans in 53 B.C. but were conquered by them in 39–38 B.C., which led to their decline. At Pentecost, Parthians heard the gospel in their own language (Acts 2:9; see v. 8). ¶

PASSOVER (*Pascha*; from the Heb. word *pesach*: to pass over, to spare) **The first of seven feasts of the Lord, celebrated in Israel on the fourteenth day of the first month of the Jewish calendar (see Lev. 23:4, 5; Deut. 16:1–8).** The Passover was first celebrated by Moses (Heb. 11:28; see Ex. 12), marking the beginning of Israel's history as a redeemed people. Israel's firstborns were spared by virtue of the lamb's blood, sprinkled on the door frames. This feast was celebrated during the Lord's time (Matt. 26:2; Mark 14:1; Luke 2:41; 22:1; John 2:13, 23; 6:4; 11:55; 12:1; 13:1; 18:39; 19:14) and thereafter (Acts 12:4). This word is used re the paschal lamb, sacrificed and eaten during this feast (Mark 14:12; Luke 22:7; John 18:28). Jesus ate the Passover with His disciples (Matt. 26:17–19; Mark 14:12, 14, 16; Luke 22:8, 11, 13); He greatly desired to eat this Passover with them before He suffered (Luke 22:15). This word is also used re Christ personally (1 Cor. 5:7): the paschal lamb represented Christ offering Himself as the atoning sacrifice and accomplishing redemption by shedding His blood (see 1 Pet. 1:18, 19). ¶

PATARA (*Patara*) **Seaport in Lycia.** Paul went there on his third missionary journey (Acts 21:1). ¶

PATMOS (*Patmos*) **Small rocky island in the south of the Aegean Sea, west of Miletus.** The apostle John was exiled on Patmos, where he wrote the book of Revelation after seeing a vision (Rev. 1:9). ¶

PATRIARCH (*patriarchēs*; from *patria*: family, race, and *archē*: beginning) **For a Jew, significant ancestor who was the founder of a family or a tribe.** This word is used re David (Acts 2:29), Jacob's sons (7:8, 9), and Abraham (Heb. 7:4). ¶

PATROBAS (*Patrobas*: who proceeds from the father, paternal) **Christian man of Rome.** Paul sends Patrobas greetings (Rom. 16:14). ¶

PAUL (*Paulos*; *paulus*, in Lat.: small, in small quantity) **Principal apostle of the Gentiles and author of several epistles of the N.T.** He was a Benjaminite, a citizen of Rome, a native of Tarsus, a Pharisee, and was taught by Gamaliel (Acts 22:3; see 5:34). Originally named Saul, witnesses at the stoning of Stephen laid their clothes at this young man's feet (see Acts 7:58). He violently persecuted the church, thinking to render service to God. Converted (about A.D. 36), he received the Holy Spirit when Ananias, a disciple in Damascus, laid hands on him. He then began to preach that Jesus is the Son of God (see Acts 9:20). His new Roman name, Paul, first appears after meeting the proconsul of Cyprus (Acts 13:9). Paul received his gospel and mission directly from heaven, having no need to be commissioned by brothers of Jerusalem; but did not act independently of the church already formed there. He introduced the church to teaching re its heavenly character. The truth of the church, Christ's body, was revealed to Paul; he taught that, in Christ Jesus, there is neither Jew nor Gentile. Though the question of ordinances of the law had been settled at Jerusalem, Paul endured much persecution from Jews and Judaizing teachers. He was truly the apostle of the nations, making several journeys to Asia and Europe. The book of Acts gives a partial account of his labors (2 Cor. 11:24–27). He was arrested at Jerusalem and sent to Caesarea for his safety, the object of assassination plots. He appealed to Caesar (Nero) and was sent to Rome as a prisoner. After two years of imprisonment (Acts 28:30, 31), he was no doubt liberated, as is implied by these final verses of Acts. He visited Palestine, Cyprus, Asia Minor, Macedonia, Achaia, and Crete. He had hoped to visit Spain (Rom. 15:24, 28). When he wrote the second epistle to Timothy, he was again a prisoner at Rome, expecting imminent death. According to history, he was beheaded by the sword, a form of execution usually reserved for a Roman citizen. (After Walter Biggar Scott.)

PAVEMENT (*lithostrōtos*; from *lithos*: stone, and *strōnnumi*: to overlay) **Place located in front of the courtroom (judgment seat) at Jerusalem; it was overlaid with mosaic paving and was used as a public tribunal.** Pilate presented Jesus to the people there, Gabbatha in Aram. (John 19:13). ¶

PEARL (*margaritēs*; *margarita*, in Lat.) **Solid body formed in a mollusk by the secretion of nacre around a foreign body (e.g., a grain of sand) which has been introduced in the shell.** Pearls are referred to as an adornment (1 Tim. 2:9; Rev. 17:4; 18:12, 16). The expr. "not to throw pearls before swine" means not to share precious truths of God's word indiscriminately (Matt. 7:6). The church is compared to a pearl of great price (Matt. 13:45, 46). Heavenly Jerusalem's twelve gates are twelve pearls, each gate a single pearl (Rev. 21:21). ¶

PENNY (*assarion*; from the Lat. *assarius*) **Roman copper coin worth about 1/16 of a Roman denarius; the denarius was equivalent to the salary of a laborer for a day; also transl.: *assaria*, cent, coin, copper, farthing.** Two sparrows were sold for a penny (Matt. 10:29), five sparrows for two pennies (Luke 12:6). ¶

PENTECOST (*Pentēkostē*; from *pentēkostos*: fiftieth, which is from *pente*: five) **Annual Jewish feast celebrated fifty days after the Feast of the Harvest of the firstfruits.** On that day, Israelites were to bring two wave-loaves baked with leaven as an offering to the Lord. See details in Lev. 23:15–21 and

Deut. 16:9–12. The church began to be formed on this day by the Holy Spirit descended from heaven (Acts 2:1). Paul planned to remain at Ephesus until that time (1 Cor. 16:8); he endeavored to reach Jerusalem then (Acts 20:16). ¶

PERDITION → DESTRUCTION

PERGA (*Pergē*: tower) **City of Pamphylia.** Paul announced the word of God there during his first missionary journey (Acts 13:13, 14; 14:25). ¶

PERGAMUM (*Pergamos*: citadel) **City of Mysia, in the northwest of Asia Minor; also written: Pergamos.** It is one of seven churches in Asia addressed by letter; Christians there had not denied the faith (Rev. 1:11; 2:12). ¶

PERSIS (*Persis*: woman of Persia) **Christian woman of Rome.** She labored much in the Lord (Rom. 16:12). ¶

PETER (*Petros*: a stone; in contrast with the rock: *petra* (Matt. 16:18; see 1 Cor. 3:11; 1 Pet. 2:3–8) **One of the twelve apostles.** Originally named Simon, son of John, Jesus also named him Cephas (Peter) (Luke 5:8; 6:14; John 1:40–42). A fisherman, he worked with James, John, and Andrew. Called by Jesus, they left everything and followed Him (Mark 1:16–17; see vv. 19, 20). Whenever Jesus chose a few disciples in certain circumstances, Peter is among them and named first; but no formalized authority is attributed to him. He is mentioned often in the Gospels; he was energetic and impulsive. When he refused to accept that Christ should suffer, Jesus rebuffed him as speaking on Satan's behalf (Matt. 16:23). In his self-confidence he denied his Lord, but sincerely repented. The Lord, resurrected, restored Peter and then entrusted him to shepherd and feed His lambs and sheep (John 21:15–17). Jesus gave him the keys of the kingdom of heaven (Matt. 16:19); when he preached to large crowds after the Holy Spirit came at Pentecost (see Acts 2:14–36), three thousand souls (primarily Jews of various nations) were saved and added to the church. By means of Peter, Cornelius, a Gentile, was converted (Acts 10). Thus, Peter opened the kingdom to both Jews and Gentiles. He was the apostle of the circumcision (Gal. 2:7). When he relapsed into Jewish prejudices, separating himself from Gentile Christians, Paul had to withstand him to the face (Gal. 2:11, 12–16). Peter wrote two epistles bearing his name, acknowledging that Paul's epistles treat some things that are hard to be understood (2 Pet. 3:15, 16). History says he was crucified at Rome: nailed, at his own request, upside down. Tradition says his wife also suffered with him. (After Walter Biggar Scott.)

PHALEK (*Phalek*: division, in Heb.; see Peleg, son of Eber: Gen. 11:16) **Man of the O.T.; also transl.: Phalec, Peleg.** He is mentioned in the genealogy of Jesus (Luke 3:35). ¶

PHANUEL (*Phanouēl*: face of God, in Heb.) **Israelite man of the tribe of Asher.** He was the father of Anna, a prophetess (Luke 2:36). ¶

PHARAOH (*Pharaō*: great house) **Title of the kings of Egypt.** God gave Joseph and his family favor in his sight (Acts 7:10, 13). The daughter of a later Pharaoh brought up Moses (Acts 7:21), but Moses refused to be called her son (Heb. 11:24). God showed His power by delivering the Israelites from Pharaoh's hand (Rom. 9:17). ¶

PHARES (*Phares*: breach, in Heb.; see Gen. 38:29) **Son of Judah and Tamar; also transl.: Perez.** He is mentioned in the genealogy of Jesus (Matt. 1:3; Luke 3:33). ¶

PHARISEE (*Pharisaios*; from an Aram. word signifying: to separate) **Member of a Jewish sect separated from the mass of the people on the principle of a life of superior holiness, devotion to God (e.g., fasting and long prayers) and knowledge of the law.** They are mentioned repeatedly in the Gospels and in Acts. They adhered to a form of godliness rather that to spiritual reality. Jesus reproached them for annulling God's commandment by their tradition (Matt. 15:1–9) and their hypocrisy (Matt. 23:23; Luke 18:9–14). They tried to tempt Jesus (e.g., Matt. 19:3) and to destroy Him (e.g., Matt. 12:14). Pharisees originated from a Jewish sect: the Hasidim (lit.: those who are godly), founded in the second century B.C. Paul was a Pharisee as to the law (Phil. 3:5).

PHENICIA → PHOENICIA

PHILADELPHIA (*Philadelpheia*: brotherly love) **City of Lydia in Asia Minor; it was built by the king of Pergamum, and several times more or less destroyed by earthquakes.** It is one of seven churches in Asia addressed by letter (Rev. 1:11; 3:7). Christians there kept the word of Christ's patience (see Rev. 3:8, 10). ¶

PHILEMON (*Philēmōn*: affectionate; from *phileō*: to love, which is from *philos*: dear, friend) **Christian man of the city of Colossae.** The church of Colossae met in his house (Phm. 1; see v. 2). Paul asked him to receive Onesimus, his runaway slave (see v. 17). His wife was probably Apphia and his son Archippus (see v. 2). Onesimus probably had been converted by means of Paul at Rome (see v. 10). ¶

PHILETUS (*Philētos*: beloved; from *phileō*: to love, which is from *philos*: dear, friend) **Man of the N.T.** He erred from the truth (2 Tim. 2:17), saying that the resurrection had already taken place (see v. 18). ¶

PHILIP (*Philippos*: lover of horses; from *philos*: friend, and *hippos*: horse) **a. One of the twelve apostles.** Refs.: Matt. 10:3; Mark 3:18; Luke 6:14; Acts 1:13. Jesus found and called him (John 1:43); he was from Bethsaida (v. 44). Philip told Nathanael about Jesus (John 1:45, see vv. 46, 48). Jesus tested Philip re feeding a large crowd (John 6:5, 7). Greeks came to Philip, wishing to see Jesus: he told Andrew of this (John 12:21, 22). He asked the Lord to show him the Father (John 14:8, 9). **b. Tetrarch of Ituraea and Trachonitis.** The word of God came to John the Baptist when he ruled (Luke 3:1). First husband of Herodias, his brother Herod married her unlawfully (Matt. 14:3, see v. 4;

Mark 6:17). **c. Christian man of Jerusalem.** Philip the Evangelist was one of seven Christians chosen to be occupied with service in the church of Jerusalem (Acts 6:5). He preached Christ in a city of Samaria, doing miracles (Acts 8:5, 6). Simon, a magician, believed his preaching, was baptized, and continued with him (Acts 8:12, 13, see v. 9), but was a hypocrite. Philip announced Jesus to the Ethiopian eunuch returning from Jerusalem, baptized him, and then the Spirit of the Lord caught Philip away. He preached in all cities from Azotus to Caesarea (Acts 8:26, 29–31, 34, 35, 38–40), where he lived (21:8) with his four daughters, who prophesied (see v. 9). ¶

PHILIPPI (*Philippoi*: belonging to Philip) **City of Macedonia bearing the name of Philip, the father of Alexander the Great; Caesar Augustus established a Roman colony there.** Paul sojourned there during his second missionary journey (Acts 16:12) and sailed from there on his third journey (20:6). He suffered and was mistreated there (1 Thes. 2:2): beaten publicly and imprisoned (see Acts 16:22–37). He wrote a letter to the church there (Phil. 1:1). ¶

PHILIPPIAN (*Philippēsios*) **Inhabitant of the city of Philippi, in Macedonia.** Paul wrote them a letter (see Phil. 1:1). They sent a gift to Paul (Phil. 4:15). ¶

PHILOLOGUS (*Philologos*: lover of words, who loves to talk) **Christian man of Rome.** Paul sends him greetings (Rom. 16:15). ¶

PHILOSOPHER (*philosophos*; from *philos*: friend, and *sophia*: wisdom) **One who devotes himself to philosophy, the study of wisdom.** Epicureans and Stoics were philosophers (Acts 17:18). ¶

PHILOSOPHY (*philosophia*; from *philos*: friend, and *sophia*: wisdom) **Search for wisdom and truth by intellectual efforts; in the N.T., the word has certainly a negative connotation.** Paul warns against philosophy (Col. 2:8); it is not after Christ. ¶

PHLEGON (*Phlegōn*: burning, zealous; from *phlegō*: to set fire, to light) **Christian man of Rome.** Paul sends him greetings (Rom. 16:14). ❡

PHOEBE (*Phoibē*: radiant; from *phoibos*: clear, brilliant) **Christian woman of Cenchrea.** Paul commends her to Christians of Rome; she helped many, incl. Paul (Rom. 16:1, see v. 2). ❡

PHOENICIA (*Phoinikē*: land of palm trees; from *phoinix*: palm tree) **Region of Israel along the Mediterranean Sea, northeast of Sidon.** Some Christians, fleeing persecution, reached it (Acts 11:19). Paul and Barnabas passed through it, recounting the conversion of Gentiles (Acts 15:3). Paul sailed to this region during his third missionary journey (Acts 21:2). ❡

PHOENIX (*Phoinix*: palm tree) **A harbor of the island of Crete; also transl.: Phenice, Phoenice.** Men sailing with Paul tried to reach this Mediterranean port during his fourth journey but failed (Acts 27:12; see vv. 13-44). ❡

PHRYGIA (*Phrugia*) **Region of central Asia Minor.** Jews of Phrygia were present in Jerusalem at Pentecost (Acts 2:10). Paul went through there during his second missionary journey (Acts 16:6) and strengthened all disciples there during his third journey (18:23). ❡

PHYGELUS (*Phugelos*: fugitive; akin to *phugē*: escape) **Christian man of Asia.** He turned away from Paul (2 Tim. 1:15). ❡

PILATE → PONTIUS PILATE

PILLAR (*stulos*; poss. from *istēmi*: to stand) **Vertical structure supporting the weight of a building, column; the word is used to indicate strength, stability, and authority.** In the church of Jerusalem, James, Cephas, and John were pillars (Gal. 2:9). This word is used re the truth and the church on earth

(1 Tim. 3:15), the Christian's firm, stable, permanent position in God's temple (Rev. 3:12), fire and an angel's feet (Rev. 10:1), divine holiness and righteousness (see Rev. 1:15). ❡

PISIDIA (*Pisidia*) **Region south of Phrygia, in Asia Minor.** Paul spoke in the synagogue of Antioch there (Acts 13:14) and passed through the region again on his first missionary journey (14:24). ❡

PONTIUS PILATE (*Pontios Pilatos*) **Governor of Judea.** He ruled from A.D. 26 to 36 (Luke 3:1). Chief priests and elders delivered Jesus to him, requiring His death (Matt. 27:2; Mark 15:1; Luke 23:1, 3; Acts 3:13; 13:28). Jews accused Jesus of perverting the Jewish nation, forbidding to give tribute to Caesar, and proclaiming Himself the king of the Jews; but Jesus did not defend Himself before Pilate. Jesus made the good confession before Pilate, maintaining the truth (1 Tim. 6:13). Pilate proposed to the crowd to release Jesus rather than Barabbas. After the crowd chose Barabbas, Pilate declared himself innocent of Jesus' blood, calling Him righteous. Pilate released Barabbas, had Jesus scourged and delivered Him up to be crucified (see Matt. 27:11–26; Mark 15:2–15; Luke 23:2–25; John 18:28 to 19:16; Acts 4:27). He placed a title on the cross reading: "Jesus the Nazarene, the king of the Jews" (see John 19:17–22). Pilate had Jesus' dead body delivered to Joseph of Arimathea; at their request, he charged chief priests and Pharisees to seal and guard the tomb (see Matt. 27:57–66; Mark 15:42–45; Luke 23:50–53; John 19:38). Tradition says Pilate was recalled to Rome, banished to Gaul, and committed suicide.

PONTUS 1. (*Pontos*: sea, from the name of the Black Sea, which borders this county) **Region in the northeast of Asia Minor.** Jews from there were present in Jerusalem at Pentecost (Acts 2:9). God's elects were scattered there and elsewhere (1 Pet. 1:1). ❡ **2.** (of Pontus, in Pontus: *Pontikos*) **Who inhabits this region.** Aquila and Priscilla were natives of there (Acts 18:2). ❡

PORCH 1. (*proaulion*; from *pro*: before, in front, and *aulē*: court, yard) **Exterior court between the door and the street, vestibule.** Peter went unto the porch of the high priest's palace (Mark 14:68). ¶ **2.** (*stoa*; poss. from *histēmi*: to stand up) **Covered gallery supported by columns, colonnade, covered colonnade.** The pool called Bethesda had five porches (John 5:2). Jesus walked in the temple at Jerusalem, in Solomon's porch (10:23): many gathered there when a lame man was healed in His name and when apostles worked signs and wonders (Acts 3:11; 5:12). ¶

POTTER (*kerameus*; from *keramos*: potter's clay) **One who makes vessels of clay.** The potter's field was bought for a burial place (Matt. 27:7, 10). The potter has authority over the clay: to make one vessel to honor and another to dishonor (Rom. 9:21). ¶

PRAETORIUM (*praitōrion*; from the Lat. *praetorium*) **Place where the praetor of the governor dispensed justice.** At Jerusalem, Jesus was taken there (Matt. 27:27; Mark 15:16; John 18:28, 33; 19:9). Paul was kept in Herod's Praetorium at Caesarea (Acts 23:35) and in the one at Rome where his bonds in Christ were known (Phil. 1:13). ¶

PRAYER 1. (*deēsis*; from *deomai*: to ask, to make known a need, which is the middle voice of *deō*: to lack, to need something) **Supplication addressed to God prompted by a need.** Anna served God with prayers (Luke 2:37); John's disciples made prayers (5:33). Christ offered up prayers with strong crying and tears (Heb. 5:7). **2.** (*enteuxis*; from *entunchanō*: to intercede, which is from *en*: in, and *tunchanō*: to obtain) **Request, intercession.** We should make prayers for all men (1 Tim. 2:1); every creature is sanctified by God's word and prayer (4:5). ¶ **3.** (*euchē*; from *euchomai*: to wish for, to pray) **Address to God.** The prayer of faith restores the sick (Jas. 5:15). Other refs. (vow): Acts 18:18; 21:23. ¶ **4.** (*proseuchē*; from *proseuchomai*: to pray, which is from *pros*: to, toward, and *euchomai*: see **3.**) **Spiritual communication of the Christian**

with God to ask, thank, praise, worship Him. The Lord spoke of prayer (Matt. 17:21; 21:13, 22; Mark 9:29; 11:17; Luke 19:46); He Himself spent time in prayer (Luke 6:12; 22:45). Believers were often in prayer (Acts 1:14; 2:42; 3:1; 6:4; 10:4, 31; 12:5; 16:13, 16). Paul was a man of prayer (Rom. 1:9 or 10; Eph. 1:16; 1 Thes. 1:2; Phm. 4) and he encouraged others to persevere in prayer (Rom. 12:12; 15:30; 1 Cor. 7:5; Eph. 6:18; Phil. 4:6; Col. 4:2; 1 Tim. 2:1; 5:5; Phm. 22), as did Peter (1 Pet. 3:7). Elijah prayed earnestly (lit. "with prayer") (Jas. 5:1). Other refs.: Col. 4:12; 1 Pet. 4:7; Rev. 5:8; 8:3, 4. ¶ **5.** (to make a prayer, to offer a prayer, to be praying, to pray: *proseuchomai*; from *pros*: toward, and *euchomai*: to pray) **See 4.** We should forgive when praying (Mark 11:25); scribes made long prayers (Mark 12:40; Luke 20:47). Jesus was praying (Luke 11:1). Peter was praying (Acts 11:5). Paul prayed (Phil. 1:9).

PREACH (to preach, to preach the gospel, to preach the glad tidings, to preach the good news: *euangelizō*; from *euangelos*: bringing good news, which is from *eu*: well, and *angellō*: to bring news, a message) **To announce, to communicate good news; most often it is concerning Jesus Christ, the Son of God.** This verb is used re Jesus, the gospel, about Jesus (Matt. 11:5; Luke 2:10; 4:18; 7:22; 20:1 in some mss.; Acts 5:42; 8:4, 35; 10:36; 11:20; 13:32; 14:15; 15:35; 17:18; Rom. 1:15; 10:15; 1 Cor. 15:1, 2; 2 Cor. 11:7; Gal. 1:11, 16, 23; Eph. 2:17; 3:8; 1 Pet. 1:12, 25), the birth of John the Baptist (Luke 1:19), the kingdom (Luke 4:43; 8:1; 16:16; Acts 8:12), the mystery of God (Rev. 10:7), the everlasting gospel (Rev. 14:6). John the Baptist preached to the people (Luke 3:18); the apostles preached the gospel (Luke 9:6). Peter and John preached the word of the Lord (Acts 8:25), as did Philip (v. 40), Paul, Barnabas, and others (Acts 14:7, 21; 16:10). Paul, in particular, was called to preach the gospel (Rom. 15:20; 1 Cor. 1:17; 9:16, 18; 2 Cor. 10:16; Gal. 1:8; 4:13).

PREDESTINATE → PREDESTINE

PREDESTINE (*proorizō*; from *pro*: before, and *horizō*: to determine, to limit) **To designate, to determine in advance; also transl.: to predestinate.**

Predestination accompanies election, defining that for which Christians are set apart in God's plans. The redeemed forming the church are predestined to be conformed to the image of God's Son (Rom. 8:29, 30), for adoption through Jesus Christ to God Himself (Eph. 1:5), to the praise of His glory (v. 11; see v. 12). God predestined His wisdom before the ages to the glory of Christians (1 Cor. 2:7). Other ref.: Acts 4:28 (to determine before). ¶

PREPARATION DAY (Preparation, Preparation Day: *Paraskeuē*; from *paraskeuazō*: to prepare, which is from *para*: for, and *skeuazō*: to prepare) **Day preceding a Sabbath, i.e., a Friday.** On the following day of the Preparation, Pilate was asked to secure Jesus' tomb (Matt. 27:62). Jesus was put to death on this day (Mark 15:42; Luke 23:54; John 19:14, 31, 42). ¶

PRICE (*timē*; from *tiō*: to revere, to pay honor) **Value of a thing, what one pays to obtain it; also transl.: money, proceeds, value.** This word is used re blood (Matt. 27:6), Him who was priced (v. 9), property sold by early Christians (Acts 4:34). Ananias kept back part of the price from the sale of his land (Acts 5:2, 3); Abraham bought a tomb for a sum of money (lit.: for a price of silver) (7:16). A high price was found for the books of magic that were burned (Acts 19:19). Christians have been bought with a price (1 Cor. 6:20; 7:23). Christ, as the head of the corner, has preciousness (or: price) for believers (1 Pet. 2:7).

PRIEST 1. (*hiereus*; from *hieros*: holy, sacred) **Person who exercised priesthood (see PRIESTHOOD) in Israel; the term applies also to Christ and to Christians.** There were priests in the Lord's time (e.g., Matt. 8:4; Mark 1:44; Acts 4:1) and previously (Heb. 7:14, 21, 23; 9:6). Jesus Christ is the great priest over the house of God (Heb. 10:21), a priest forever per the order of Melchizedek (Heb. 5:6; 7:15, 17). He has made Christians priests for His God and Father (Rev. 1:6), as likewise the redeemed of all dispensations (5:10). Other refs.: Matt. 12:4, 5; Mark 2:26; Luke 1:5; 5:14; 6:4; 10:31; 17:14; John 1:19; Acts 4:1; 6:7; 14:13 (priest of Zeus); Heb. 7:1, 3, 11; 8:4; 10:11; Rev. 20:6. ¶

2. (chief priest: *archiereus*; from *archē*: chief, and *hiereus*: see **1.**) **Principal person among those who exercised the priesthood in Israel.** Chief priests were a class of priests heading the larger group of priests (e.g., Matt. 2:4; Acts 4:23); they delivered Jesus to be condemned to death and crucified Him (Luke 24:20). **3.** (to execute the priest's office, to fulfill priestly service, to serve as priest, to perform priestly service, to serve as priest: *hierateuō*; from *hiereus*: priest) **To accomplish the functions of a priest in Israel; see 1.**) Zacharias fulfilled his priestly service before God (Luke 1:8). ¶

PRIESTHOOD 1. (*hierateia*; from *hierateuō*: to officiate as a priest, which is from *hiereus*: priest, which is from *hieros*: holy, sacred) **Priestly functions consisting essentially in offering the sacrifices prescribed by God under the law, interceding for the people and carrying out the divine service of the tabernacle, then later of the temple; also transl.: priest's office, priestly office)** It was a custom of the priesthood to choose one priest to enter the temple and burn incense (Luke 1:9). Those of Levi's sons who received the priesthood are commanded to take tithes from the people (Heb. 7:5). ¶ **2.** (*hierateuma*; from *hierateuō*: to officiate as a priest, which is from *hiereus*: see **1.**) **Body or order of priests exercising priestly functions; see 1.** Christians constitute a holy priesthood (1 Pet. 2:5) offering spiritual sacrifices to God; they are a royal priesthood, in testimony before the world (v. 9). ¶ **3.** (*hierōsunē*; from *hieros*: holy, sacred) **See 1.** The priesthood was a Levitical one, reserved for the descendants of Aaron, the sons of Levi (Heb. 7:11). With Jesus' rise as priest after the order of Melchizedek, the priesthood changed (Heb. 7:12); He holds His priesthood permanently (v. 24). Other ref.: Heb. 7:14 in some mss. ¶ **4.** (high priest: *archiereus*; from *archē*: chief, and *hiereus*: see **1.**) **Principal person among those who exercised the priesthood in Israel.** Under the high priesthood (lit.: the high priest) of Annas and Caiaphas, God's word came to Zacharias' son John (Luke 3:2).

PRINCIPALITY (*archē*) **Dignitary exercising a certain authority; also transl.: dominion, power, rule, ruler.** This word is used re spiritual powers, good (Eph. 1:21; 3:10) or evil (Rom. 8:38; 1 Cor. 15:24; Eph. 6:12; Col. 2:15), of an invisible world. Principalities were created in, by, and for God's dear Son (Col. 1:16); Christ is the head of all rule and authority (2:10). This word is also used re civic rulers on earth: Christians are to be in subjection to principalities (Titus 3:1).

PRISCA, PRISCILLA (*Priska*, *Priskilla*: ancient, virtuous [*priscus*, in Lat.]) **Christian woman of Jewish origin.** She was Aquila's wife. She is called Prisca (2 Tim. 4:19, dimin. of Priscilla) and Priscilla (Acts 18:2, 18, 26; Rom. 16:3; 1 Cor. 16:19). See **AQUILA.** ¶

PROCHORUS (*Prochoros*: who leads the chorus or praise; from *pro*: before, and *choros*: dancing) **Christian man of the N.T.** He was one of seven men chosen to serve in the church at Jerusalem (Acts 6:5). ¶

PROCONSUL 1. (*anthupatos*; from *anti*: in place of, and *hupatos*: consul, which is from *huper*: over, above) **Originally, one invested with full military power, who acted in place of the consul to govern a Roman province; in N.T. times, one who governed a settled senatorial Roman province.** Sergius Paulus was the proconsul of Cyprus (Acts 13:7, 8, 12). There were proconsuls at Ephesus (19:38). ¶ **2.** (to be proconsul: *anthupateuō*; from *anthupatos*: see **1.**) **To act in place of the consul.** Gallio was proconsul of Achaia (Acts 18:12). ¶

PROCORUS → PROCHORUS

PROPHECY (*prophēteia*; from *prophēteuō*: to prophesy, which is from *prophētēs*: prophet) **a. Prediction of future events.** Many O.T. prophecies have been fulfilled, e.g., that of Isaiah re the Jewish people's condition at Jesus' coming (Matt. 13:14). No prophecy of Scripture is explained by its own particular meaning (2 Pet. 1:20) nor does it come by man's will (v. 21). Revelation is the N.T. book that unfolds the most future events after Christ's return (chapters 4–22) and church history up to that moment (chapters 2 and 3). The expr.

"the words of the prophecy" occurs five times (Rev. 1:3; 22:7, 10, 18, 19); the spirit of prophecy is the testimony of Jesus (19:10); no rain will fall during the days of the prophecy of the two witnesses (11:6). **b. Presentation of the mind of God.** Prophecy is a gift of grace (Rom. 12:6) given by the Spirit (1 Cor. 12:10; see vv. 8, 9) to be exercised in love (13:2); prophecies will be done away (13. 8). Its purpose is edification (1 Cor. 14:6) and it benefits believers (v. 22). Prophecies are not to be lightly esteemed (1 Thes. 5:20). Preceding prophecies were made re Timothy (1 Tim. 1:18); he had received a gift of grace by prophecy (4:14). ¶

PROPITIATION 1. (*hilasmos*; from *hilaskomai*: to be propitious, to be gracious, which is from *hilaos*: favorable, propitious) **Among the ancient pagans, to make propitiation meant to propitiate the gods, to appease them. In the word of God, we find that He is propitiated, not by what man on his own initiative can bring to Him, but by the expiatory sacrifice of Christ at Calvary.** Giving His life as the sacrifice for sin, Jesus Christ accomplished a work that allows God to receive the sinner in grace. Christ is the propitiation for our sins (1 John 2:2; 4:10). ¶ **2.** (to make propitiation: *hilaskomai*; see **1.**) **See defin. in 1.** As high priest, Jesus made propitiation for the people's sins (Heb. 2:17). Other refs.: Luke 18:13 (to be merciful). ¶ **3.** See **MERCY SEAT**.

PROSELYTE (*prosēlutos*; from *proserchomai*: to approach, to come near, which is from: *pros*: to, and *erchomai*: to go, to come) **Stranger from among the Gentiles who adhered to Judaism; also transl.: convert.** Hypocritical scribes and Pharisees made a proselyte adhering to their sect (Matt. 23:15). Proselytes were present on the day of Pentecost (Acts 2:10). Nicholas was a proselyte of Antioch (Acts 6:5). Many devout proselytes followed Paul and Barnabas (Acts 13:43). ¶

PROSTITUTE (*pornē*; from *pernēmi*: to sell) **One who engages in sexual relations for money.** Rahab was a prostitute (Heb. 11:31; Jas. 2:25) and figur. Babylon the great (Rev. 17:1, 5, 15, 16; 19:2). Other refs.: Matt. 21:31, 32; Luke 15:30; 1 Cor. 6:15, 16. ¶

PTOLEMAIS (*Ptolemais*) **City in northern Israel on the Mediterranean Sea.** During his third missionary journey, Paul greeted brothers from there (Acts 21:7). ¶

PUBLICAN (chief among the publicans: *architelōnēs*; from *archō*: to begin, to command, which is from *archē*: beginning, and *telōnēs*: tax collector) **Person in charge of those responsible to collect taxes.** Zaccheus was the chief among the publicans (Luke 19:2). ¶

PUBLIUS (*Poplios*; Roman name: Publius) **Chief man of the island of Malta.** He lodged Paul and his shipwrecked companions. Paul healed his fever-stricken father (Acts 28:7, 8). ¶

PUDENS (*Poudēs*; *pudens*, in Lat.: honest, modest) **Christian man of Rome.** Paul sent his greetings to Timothy (2 Tim. 4:21). ¶

PURPLE (adj.) (*porphurous*; from *porphura*: purple dye or garment) **Dyed purple.** Used re a robe put on Jesus in mockery (John 19:2, 5). Babylon was clothed with purple (Rev. 18:16). Other ref.: Rev. 17:4 in some mss. ¶

PURPLE (noun) **1.** (*porphura*) **The color purple was the imperial color; the bright red-blue dye was obtained from mollusks and used to dye fabrics.** Jesus was clothed with purple (i.e., a purple garment) in mockery (Mark 15:17), then took it off Him (v. 20). A rich man (Luke 16:19) and Babylon the great (Rev. 17:4) are clothed in purple. Other ref.: Rev. 18:12. ¶ **2.** (seller of purple, dealer in purple: *porphuropōlis*; from *porphura*: see **1.**, and *pōleō*: to sell) **One who sells objects dyed purple.** Lydia, an early European convert, was a seller of purple (Acts 16:14). ¶

PUTEOLI (*Potioloi*: sulphurous wells or springs) **Port of Italy near Naples.** Paul stayed there with brothers for seven days, while journeying to Rome (Acts 28:13). ¶

PYRRHUS (*Purros*: red like fire; from *pur*: fire) **Father of Sopater.** Sopater of Berea was his son (Acts 20:4). ¶

PYTHON (*Puthōn*; from *Puthō*: region where Delphi, an ancient Greek city, was situated) **In Greek mythology, it was a serpent or dragon that guarded the oracle of Delphi and was killed by Apollo; also transl.: divination.** A slave girl having a spirit of Python met Paul at Philippi (Acts 16:16); he delivered her in the name of Jesus Christ. ¶

Q

QUADRANS (*kodrantēs*; from Lat. *quadrans*: quarter of an *assarion*) **Small coin worth two mites or 1/64 of a denarius; also transl.: cent, farthing, penny.** A man was obliged to remain in prison until he had paid the last quadrans (Matt. 5:26); in some mss.: Luke 12:59. Two mites (or: small copper coins) make a quadrans (Mark 12:42). ¶

QUARTUS (*Kouartos*: fourth, in Lat.) **Christian man living at Corinth.** He sent greetings to the Christians of Rome (Rom. 16:23). ¶

QUATERNION (*tetradion*; from *tessares*: four) **Group of four soldiers, squad.** Herod delivered Peter to four quaternions of soldiers (Acts 12:4). ¶

QUICKENING → LIFE (TO GIVE)

QUIRINIUS (*Kurēnios*; *Quirinus* (not *Quirinius*) was the name given to Romulus, the founder of Rome, after his death) **Governor of Syria.** The census under Caesar Augustus was made when he was governor (Luke 2:2). ¶

R

RABBI 1. (*Rhabbi*; from the Heb. *rab*: elder, master) **Aram. word designating a master who teaches, a doctor of the law among the Jews.** The scribes and the Pharisees loved to be called Rabbi, Rabbi (Matt. 23:7); Jesus said they were not to be called rabbi (v. 8). Jesus was called Rabbi by disciples (Matt. 26:25, 49; Mark 9:5; 11:21; 14:45; John 1:38, 49; 4:31; 6:25; 9:2; 11:8), by Nicodemus (John 3:2). John the Baptist was also called Rabbi (John 3:26). ¶ **2.** See **RABBONI**.

RABBONI (*Rhabboni*; intens. form of *Rhabbi*: master) **Aram. word signifying "my great master" and indicating respect.** Jesus was called Rabboni by the blind Bartimaeus (Mark 10:51) and by Mary Magdalene (John 20:16). ¶

RACA (*rhaka*) **Aram. word of contempt meaning stupid, worthless.** One would be guilty of saying it to one's brother (Matt. 5:22). ¶

RACHAB → RAHAB

RACHEL (*Rhachēl*: ewe or sheep, in Heb.) **Wife of Jacob (see Gen. 29:9–20, 28).** Rachel weeping for her children (Matt. 2:18) is related to the massacre of infants in Bethlehem. See Jer. 31:15, a prophecy re the persecuted diaspora. ¶

RAGAU → REU

RAHAB 1. (*Rhaab*: proud, in Heb.) **Prostitute of Jericho who received the Israelite spies and hid them.** By faith, she did not perish with unbelievers (Heb.

11:31; see Josh. 6). She was justified by her works (Jas. 2:25). ¶ **2.** (*Rhachab*) **Same as 1.** She was Boaz's mother and David's great-grandmother; one of four O.T. women who are mentioned in Jesus' genealogy (Matt. 1:5). ¶

RAMAH (*Rhama*: elevated place, in Heb.) **Locality north of Jerusalem.** Lamentation was heard there (Matt. 2:18) re the massacre of Bethlehem infants under Herod (see O.T. prophecy: Jer. 31:15). ¶

RANSOM 1. (*lutron*; from *luō*: to unbind) **Price paid to liberate a captive person.** The Son of Man gave Himself a ransom for many (Matt. 20:28; Mark 10:45). ¶ **2.** (*antilutron*; from *anti*: instead of, in return, and *lutron*: see **1.**) **Same meaning as 1., with the idea of exchange.** Christ Jesus gave Himself a ransom for all (1 Tim. 2:6). ¶ **3.** See **REDEMPTION**.

RAPTURE → TRANSLATION

RAVEN (*korax*; *corvus*, in Lat.) **Omnivorous bird, which feeds habitually on dead animals; it is frequently seen in Israel.** God feeds the ravens (Luke 12:24). ¶

REBECCA → REBEKAH

REBEKAH (*Rhebekka*: attaching, fascinating by beauty, in Heb.; see Gen. 24:15) **Wife of Isaac.** She bore Jacob and Esau (Rom. 9:10; see vv. 11–13). ¶

RECONCILIATION 1. (*katallagē*; from *katalassō*: to reconcile, which is from *kata*: intens., and *allassō*: to change; lit.: to change mutually) **Restoration of relations between persons in disagreement.** Christians have received the reconciliation through the Lord Jesus Christ (Rom. 5:11) The casting away of the Jews brings reconciliation to the world (Rom. 11:15). Christians have the service of addressing the word of reconciliation to unbelievers (2 Cor. 5:18, 19). ¶ **2.** See **PROPITIATION**.

REDEMPTION 1. (*lutrōsis*; from *lutroō*: to release after receipt of a ransom, which is from *lutron*: ransom, i.e., the price paid for the deliverance of someone, which is from *luō*: to loosen, to unbind) **Act of freeing after payment of a ransom, deliverance.** Redemption was accomplished by God for His people (Luke 1:68); some people looked for redemption in Jerusalem (2:38). Christ has obtained an eternal redemption (Heb. 9:12). ¶ **2.** (*apolutrōsis*; from *apolutroō*: to let go after payment of a ransom, which is from *apo*: from, and *lutroō*: see **1.**) **Repurchase at the price of a ransom, followed by deliverance.** The redemption of Jews will draw near during the great tribulation (Luke 21:28). The redemption of Christians, formerly slaves of sin, is eternal and has been obtained by the blood of Christ (Rom. 3:24; 1 Cor. 1:30; Eph. 1:7; Col. 1:14). The future day of redemption concerns deliverance of the Christian's body at the Lord's coming (Rom. 8:23; Eph. 4:30) and the inheritance already redeemed but not yet delivered from the enemy (Eph. 1:14). Christ paid the redemption for transgressions committed under the covenant of the law (Heb. 9:15). Other ref.: Heb. 11:35. ¶

REED (*kalamos*) **Aquatic plant found in marshes or near rivers; its height may exceed 10 feet (3 meters); the stems are hollow and consequently fragile and swayed easily by the wind.** A reed was shaken by the wind (Matt. 11:7; Luke 7:24). Jesus would not break a bruised reed, i.e., the nation of Israel under oppression (Matt. 12:20). Mockers put a reed in Jesus' right hand, then beat Him on the head with it (Matt. 27:29, 30; Mark 15:19). A vinegar-filled sponge was fixed on a reed and presented to the Lord on the cross (Matt. 27:48; Mark 15:36). The reed is used symbolically as a measuring stick in Rev. 11:1; 21:15, 16. Other refs.: 3 John 1:13. ¶

REFORMATION (*diorthōsis*; from *diorthoō*: to correct, to modify) **Rectification, setting things right.** By His coming into the world and His expiatory sacrifice, Jesus Christ has restored things; this is the time of reformation (Heb. 9:10). Christ established a new order of things, having obtained an eternal redemption (see Heb. 9:9–12). ¶

REGENERATION (*palingenesia*; from *palin*: anew, and *genesis*: generation) **Establishment of a new order of things in comparison to a former one.** God saved Christians by the washing of regeneration (Titus 3:5). This word is used re the restoration of all things, during Christ's future reign (Matt. 19:28). ¶

REGISTRATION → CENSUS

REGRET 1. (*metamelomai*; from *meta*: denoting change, and *melō*: to be preoccupied, to repent) **Change of mind on a given subject.** Paul did not regret having grieved the Corinthians in his first letter, even if he had regretted it previously (2 Cor. 7:8). **2.** (never to be regretted: *ametamelētos*; from *a*: neg., and *metamelomai*: see **1.**) **Concerning which one is not inclined to change one's mind, irrevocable.** Repentance to salvation is never to be regretted (2 Cor. 7:10). Other ref.: Rom. 11:29. ¶

REHOBOAM (*Rhoboam*: who enlarges the people, in Heb.) **Son of Solomon (see 1 Kgs. 11:43; 14:21).** He is mentioned in the genealogy of Jesus (Matt. 1:7a, b). The kingdom of Israel was divided in two during his reign; only Judah and Benjamin followed him (see 1 Kgs. 12:16–24). The other ten tribes established Jeroboam king of Israel (see 1 Kgs. 12:20). ¶

REINS (*nephros*; used in the plur.) **Kidneys, the double organ of the body which purifies the blood; it symbolizes the inward life of man, fathomed by God.** The reins correspond to the sentiments, the thoughts, the will; the Lord searches them (Rev. 2:23; see Ps. 7:9; 26:2; Jer. 17:10). ¶

RELIGIOUS 1. (*thrēskos*) **Which concerns Christian service in its external expression.** Someone might in vain think himself to be religious (Jas. 1:26). ¶ **2.** (very religious: *deisidaimonesteros*; compar. of *deisidaimōn*: religious, from *deidō*: to fear, and *daimōn*: supernatural spirit) **Superstitious, devoting oneself to the cult of demons.** The men of Athens were very religious (Acts 17:22). ¶

REMISSION (*aphesis*; from *aphiēmi*: to send forth, to let go, which is from *apo*: from, and *hiēmi*: to send) **Forgiveness of sins, which necessitated the sacrifice of Christ on the cross where He bore our sins and was made sin for us.** This word is used in the expr. "remission of sins" (Matt. 26:28; Mark 1:4; Luke 1:77; 3:3; 24:47; Acts 2:38; 5:31; 10:43; 13:38; 26:18; Col. 1:14; Heb. 10:18) and "forgiveness (or: remission) of offences" (Eph. 1:7). Without blood-shedding, there is no remission (Heb. 9:22). Other refs: Mark 3:29; Luke 4:18. ¶

REMNANT 1. (*leimma*; from *leipō*: to leave) **Smaller number of persons remaining from a larger group.** A remnant of Israel is saved at the present time, per the election of grace (Rom. 11:5). ¶ **2.** (*kataleimma*; from *kata*: intens., and *leimma*: see **1.**) **A small remainder; see 1.** This word is used re a faithful few in Israel that will be saved (Rom. 9:27, see Is. 10:22); other mss.: *hupoleimma*. ¶ **3.** (*loipos*; from *leipō*: to leave) **Small group of faithful believers in the midst of the people of Israel, whereas most have turned away from God.** Satan will make war against this remnant (Rev. 12:17). **4.** (the remnant: *oi kataloipoi*: plur. of *kataloipos*; from *kataleipō*: to leave behind; lit.: those who remain, the rest) **A small group of faithful believers, a residue, the rest.** The remnant of men may seek the Lord (Acts 15:17). ¶

REMORSE (to feel, to be filled with, to be seized with remorse: *metamelomai*; from *meta*: concerning, and *melō*: to be preoccupied) **Agonizing regret, with a sense of a guilty conscience.** Judas was filled of remorse after he delivered Jesus up (Matt. 27:3).

REMPHAN → ROMPHA

REPENTANCE (*metanoia*; from *metanoeō*: to repent, which is from *meta*: denoting change, and *noeō*: to perceive, to think, which is from *nous*: mind, understanding; lit.: change of mind) **Change of heart and mind, turning toward a better way; deep regret for a past action or course of action.**

Repentance is toward God (Acts 20:21), leading the sinner to pass the same judgment as God re his state of sin and the faults he has committed. The sinner can then turn to God, imploring His grace, and God grants him salvation in Christ. God's goodness leads the sinner to repentance (Rom. 2:4). The Lord is willing that all should come to repentance (2 Pet. 3:9). John baptized Israelites with water for repentance (Matt. 3:11; Mark 1:4; Luke 3:3; Acts 13:24), in view of receiving Christ (Acts 19:4); he told them to produce fruit in keeping with repentance (Matt. 3:8; Luke 3:8). God gave repentance to Israel and the nations (Acts 5:31; 11:18). Paul said to do works worthy of repentance (Acts 26:20), which the Corinthians did (2 Cor. 7:9, 10).

REPHAN → ROMPHA

RESPECT OF PERSONS (*prosōpolē(m)psia*; from *prosōpon*: face, person, and *lambanō*: to take) **Favoritism, preference; also transl.: acceptance of persons, partiality.** With God, there is no respect of persons (Rom. 2:11; Eph. 6:9; Col. 3:25); it should not characterize believers (Jas. 2:1). ¶

RESTORING (*apokatastasis*; from *apokathistēmi*: to restore, which is from *apo*: anew, and *kathistēmi*: to constitute, which is from *kata*: down, and *histēmi*: to stand) **Reinstatement of a thing or person to its previous state.** The restoring of all things (Acts 3:21) is a time when Jesus Christ will reinstate all per God's mind. ¶

RESURRECTION 1. (*anastasis*; from *anistēmi*: to stand up, which is from *ana*: again, and *histēmi*: to stand) **Return to life of a person who has died.** Jesus spoke about resurrection (Matt. 22:30, 31; Luke 14:14; 20:35, 36), especially that of life and that of judgment (John 5:29). Lazarus would rise again in the resurrection (John 11:24). Jesus Himself is the resurrection (John 11:25). Sadducees denied the resurrection (Matt. 22:23, 28; Mark 12:18, 23; Luke 20:27, 33; Acts 23:8), as did some Corinthians (1 Cor. 15:12, 13). Hymenaeus and Philetus said it had already taken place (2 Tim. 2:18). Jesus' resurrection (Acts

1:22; 2:31; 4:33; 26:23; Rom. 6:5; Phil. 3:10; 1 Pet. 1:3; 3:21) is at the foundation of Christian faith. Apostles announced the resurrection from among the dead, i.e., of Christians at the Lord's coming (Acts 4:2; 17:18), and the resurrection of the dead (Acts 17:32; 23:6; 24:21; 1 Cor. 15:42; Heb. 6:2; 11:35). There will be a resurrection of the just and of the unjust (Acts 24:15; Rev. 20:5, 6; see Rev. 20:13). Resurrection came by man, i.e., Jesus Christ (1 Cor. 15:21). Jesus is marked out Son of God by the resurrection of the dead (Rom. 1:4). Other ref.: Luke 2:34. ¶ **2.** (*egersis*; from *egeirō*: to wake up) **See defin. in 1.** After the resurrection of Jesus, risen saints appeared to many (Matt. 27:53). ¶ **3.** (*exanastasis*; from *ek*: out, and *anastasis*: resurrection) **Return to life of an O.T. believer or a Christian who has died.** Paul sought to arrive at the resurrection from among the dead (Phil. 3:11). ¶

REU (*Rhagau*: friend, in Heb.; Reu in Gen. 11:18, 20) **Man of the O.T.** He is mentioned in the genealogy of Jesus (Luke 3:35). ¶

REUBEN (*Rhoubēn*: see, a son!, in Heb.; see Gen. 29:32) **One of the twelve sons of Jacob and the tribe descended from him.** Twelve thousand out of this tribe will be sealed (Rev. 7:5). ¶

REVELATION 1. (*apokalupsis*; from *apokaluptō*: to reveal, which is from *apo*: out of, and *kaluptō*: to cover, to hide) **Disclosure of that which was hidden; also transl.: appearance, appearing, manifestation, revealing.** This word is used re the manifestation of Jesus Christ at His first (Luke 2:32) and second coming (1 Cor. 1:7; 2 Thes. 1:7; 1 Pet. 1:7, 13; 4:13), God's righteous judgment (Rom. 2:5), the sons of God (Rom. 8:19), the mystery that has now been made manifest (Rom. 16:25), speaking by revelation (1 Cor. 14:6, 26), the spirit of wisdom and of revelation (Eph. 1:17), the revelation of Jesus Christ that God gave Him to show the things that must soon take place (Rev. 1:1). Other refs.: 2 Cor. 12:1, 7; Gal. 1:12; 2:2; Eph. 3:3. ¶ **2.** (to be, to make, to come a revelation: *apokaluptō*; see **1.**) **To manifest something formerly hidden.** A revelation may be made to someone seated in the church (1 Cor. 14:30).

REWARD (noun) **1.** (*antapodosis*; from *antapodidōmi*: to repay, to requite, which is from *anti*: in turn, and *apodidōmi*: to give, to pay, which is from *apo*: from, and *didōmi*: to give) **Recompense, compensation.** The Christian will receive the reward of the inheritance (Col. 3:24). ¶ **2.** (*misthos*; lit.: salary, wages) **a. Remuneration, recompense.** The faithful will receive a reward from God (Matt. 5:12; 10:41, 42; Mark 9:41; Luke 6:23, 35; 1 Cor. 3:8, 14; Rev. 11:18; 22:12). **b. Retribution.** The unrighteous receives the reward (i.e., punishment) of unrighteousness (2 Pet. 2:13). **3.** (*misthapodosia*; from *misthos*: see, and *apodidōmi*: see **1.**) **Remuneration, recompense.** The Christian's confidence has great reward (Heb. 10:35). Moses looked to the reward (Heb. 11:26).

REWARD (verb) (*apodidōmi*; from *apo*: from, and *didōmi*: to give) **To give in return, to reimburse.** God the Father will reward one who does alms (Matt. 6:4), prays to Him (v. 6), and fasts in secret (v. 18).

REWARDER (*misthapodotēs*; from *misthos*: remuneration, reward, and *apodidōmi*: to render, which is from *apo*: from, and *didōmi*: to give) **One who gives a salary, a recompense, or a reward.** God is the rewarder of those who seek Him (Heb. 11:6). ¶

RHEGIUM (*Rhēgion*: breach) **Maritime city situated at the southwest extremity of Italy.** Paul, a prisoner going to Rome, stayed there for one day on his fourth journey (Acts 28:13). It is now called Rheggio, the capital of Calabria. ¶

RHESA (*Rhēsa*: Jehovah has healed; others: head) **Israelite man, son or descendant of Zerubbabel.** He is mentioned in the genealogy of Jesus (Luke 3:27). ¶

RHODA (*Rhodē*: rose) **Servant girl of Mary, the mother of John who was surnamed Mark.** She recognized Peter's voice, when he knocked at the door (Acts 12:13; see vv. 14–16). ¶

RHODES (*Rhodos*: rose) **Island of the Mediterranean Sea southwest of Asia Minor.** Paul came there on his third journey (Acts 21:1). ¶

ROBOAM → REHOBOAM

ROMAN 1. (*Rhōmaios*; from *Rhōmē*: Rome) **a. Inhabitant of the city of Rome.** At Pentecost, visitors from Rome (Romans sojourning) were present in Jerusalem (Acts 2:10). **b. Citizen of the Roman Empire, enjoying the privileges which were reserved for this title.** Jewish leaders feared Romans, perceiving Jesus as a political threat, would take away their place and nation (John 11:48). This word is used re citizens of Philippi (Acts 16:21), and Paul and Silas (vv. 37, 38). Paul was delivered to Romans by Jews at Jerusalem (Acts 28:17); being one by birth, Paul escaped scourging (22:25–27, 29; 23:27) and was entitled to fair trial (25:16), wherefore he appealed to Caesar (see vv. 10–12). ¶ **2.** (*Rhōmaikos*; from *Rhōmaios*: see **1.**) **In Roman (language), i.e., in Latin.** The inscription written over Jesus' cross was written in Greek, Roman, and Hebrew letters (Luke 23:38). ¶

ROME (*Rhōmē*) **Rome was the capital of Italy and the Roman Empire.** Claudius ordered all Jews to leave Rome (Acts 18:2). Paul purposed to see Rome (Acts 19:21). He was to testify of the Lord at Rome (Acts 23:11); he went there as a prisoner during his fourth journey (28:14, 16). In Rome, Onesiphorus sought and found him (2 Tim. 1:17). Paul wrote a letter to the Christians of Rome (Rom. 1:7), in which he said he was ready to preach the gospel to them (v. 15). ¶

ROMPHA (*Rhemphan*; prob. a name of the god Saturn or Moloch (*Kiyyun,* in Heb.) **Egyptian idol.** Israelites worshiped him in the desert (Acts 7:43), taking up his emblematic star (see Amos 5:25, 26). ¶

RUE (*pēganon*) **Plant with heavily scented yellow flowers; it is used as an infusion, to season black olives and for medical purposes.** Pharisees paid tithes of rue (Luke 11:42). ¶

RUFUS (*Rhouphos*: red, redheaded; *rufus*, in Lat.: red) **Son of Simon of Cyrene.** His father Simon carried Jesus' cross (Mark 15:21). It is perhaps the same Rufus at Rome whom Paul greeted (Rom. 16:13). ¶

RUTH (*Rhouth*: friend, in Heb.) **Moabite woman who married Boaz.** See Ruth 1:4; 4:13. She is one of four women, in addition to Mary, mentioned in the genealogy of Jesus (Matt. 1:5). ¶

S

SABACHTHANI (*sabachthani*) **Aram. term that means "you have forsaken me".** This word is used by Jesus on the cross, crying out to His God (Matt. 27:46; Mark 15:34; see Ps. 22:2) ¶

SABAOTH (*Sabaōth*; from the Heb. *tsaba*: crowd of people) **Multitude of people, troops assembled for combat; lit. in Heb.: of hosts.** The Lord of Sabaoth is the Lord particularly of armies of angels (Rom. 9:29; Jas. 5:4). ¶

SABBATH 1. (*sabbaton*; from the Heb. *shabbath*: rest) **Seventh and last day of the week, day of rest prescribed by the Lord for His people, in relation to the rest of God after creation (see Ex. 20:8–11; 31:17) and to redemption (see Deut. 5:12–15).** This word is used frequently in the Gospels (e.g., Luke 4:16) and in Acts (e.g., 13:14). Christians are not to be judged re observance of Sabbaths (Col. 2:16), which are replaced by the Lord's Day, the first day of the week. Jesus, the Son of man, is Lord of the Sabbath (Matt. 12:8; Mark 2:28; Luke 6:5). **2.** (day before the Sabbath: *prosabbaton*; from *pro*: before, and *sabbaton*: see **1.**) **Eve of the Sabbath.** The Preparation day was the day before the Sabbath (Mark 15:42). ¶

SABBATH DAY'S JOURNEY (*sabbatou hodos*) **Measure of distance of approx. 3/4 of a mile (1,100 meters); the scribes allowed the Jews to travel only that distance on the day of the Sabbath.** The Mount of Olives is a Sabbath day's journey from Jerusalem (Acts 1:12).

SABBATH REST (*sabbatismos*; from *sabbatizō*: to observe the Sabbath, which is from *sabbaton*: Sabbath) **Cessation of activities on the Sabbath day.** A Sabbath rest remains for God's people (Heb. 4:9). ¶

SACKCLOTH (*sakkos*; from the Heb. *sak*: cloth used for making sacks) **Rough clothing.** A sackcloth was worn directly on the skin, expressing repentance (Matt. 11:21; Luke 10:13). The sun became as hair sackcloth (Rev. 6:12). Two witnesses will prophesy 1260 days, clothed in sackcloth (Rev. 11:3). ¶

SADDUCEE (*Saddoukaios*; prob. from *Sadōk*: Sadoc, i.e., Zadok; see 1 Kgs. 2:35) **Member of a Jewish sect; the Sadducees came from a political sect that promoted the Hellenization of Judaism, extolling the advantages of Greek life and culture.** John the Baptist challenged the Sadducees re repentance (Matt. 3:7). They tempted Jesus re a sign from heaven (Matt. 16:1); Jesus said to be on guard vs. their leaven (v. 6) and their doctrine (vv. 11, 12). They said there is no resurrection, nor angel, nor spirit (Matt. 22:23, 34; Mark 12:18; Luke 20:27; Acts 23:8). They opposed the apostles (Acts 4:1; 5:17), incl. Paul (23:6, 7). ¶

SADOK → ZADOK

SAIL (noun) **1.** (*skeuos*) **Ship's equipment used to harness the wind.** Mariners struck sail (Acts 27:17). **2.** (to set sail, to make sail: *anagō*; from *ana*: up, and *agō*: to go) **To take to open water, to navigate; also transl.: to launch, to put to sea, to sail, to depart, to loose.** Paul and his companions set sail (Acts 27:2, 4; 28:11). Other refs.: Acts 27:12, 21.

SALAMIS (*Salamis*) **City on the southeast of Cyprus.** Barnabas and Paul announced the word of God in synagogues there (Acts 13:5). ¶

SALATHIEL → SHEALTIEL

SALEM (*Salēm*: peace, in Heb.) **This name refers to Jerusalem.** See Ps. 76:2. Melchizedek was king of Salem (Heb. 7:1, 2). ¶

SALIM (*Saleim*: completed, in Aram.) **Place near Aenon.** John baptized in Aenon, near Salim (John 3:23). ¶

SALMON (*Salmōn*: investiture, in Heb.) **Man of the O.T., husband of Rahab and father of Boaz.** He is mentioned in the genealogy of Jesus (Matt. 1:4, 5; Luke 3:32). ¶

SALMONE (*Salmōnē*: clothing) **Promontory of eastern Crete.** Paul sailed under Crete opposite this place (Acts 27:7). ¶

SALOME (*Salōmē*: peaceful, in Heb.) **One of the women who followed and served Jesus in Galilee.** She was present at the crucifixion (Mark 15:40); she bought sweet spices to anoint Jesus' body (16:1). ¶

SALVATION 1. (*sōtēria*; from *sōtēr*: liberator, savior) **a. Eternal redemption of a sinful person, obtained by repentance and faith in the perfect sacrifice of Jesus Christ at the cross.** This salvation is: so great (Heb. 2:3), ascribed to God (Rev. 7:10). Jesus Christ alone procures salvation (Acts 4:12); believers obtain it through Him (1 Thes. 5:9). Christ is its author (Heb. 2:9, 10). God chose Christians from the beginning for it (2 Thes. 2:13). It is of the Jews (John 4:22; 1 Pet. 1:10); the Lord sprang from the Jews; He and His salvation were offered to them (Luke 1:77; 19:9; Rom. 10:1), then to Gentiles (Acts 13:26, 47; 16:17; Rom. 11:11; 2 Tim. 2:10). Grace that brings salvation has appeared to all men (Titus 2:11 (*sōtērios* see **3.**); 2 Cor. 6:2). The gospel is the power of God to salvation (Rom. 1:16; Eph. 1:13); with the mouth confession is made to salvation (Rom. 10:10). The salvation of their souls (1 Pet. 1:9) is a present reality for Christians (Phil. 1:28; see 1 Cor. 1:18). Their future salvation, when bodies of Christians will be transformed, is ready to be revealed (1 Pet. 1:5); they will inherit salvation (Heb. 1:14); it is nearer than when they first believed (Rom. 13:11). Christ will appear for salvation to those who wait for Him (Heb. 9:28). Presently, Christian salvation is continual deliverance from the servitude of sin (Phil. 2:12; 1 Pet. 2:2 in some mss.). Sorrow according to God works repentance leading to salvation (2 Cor. 7:10). It may also designate temporal deliverance (Phil. 1:19). The hope of salvation is presented as a helmet (1 Thes. 5:8); the day of salvation is now (2 Cor. 6:2). Paul's affliction was for the Corinthians' salvation (2 Cor. 1:6). God's word can make a person wise to salvation (2 Tim. 3:15). The Lord's patience is salvation (2 Pet. 3:15). Jude mentions the common salvation (Jude 3). Better things are connected to salvation (Heb. 6:9). This word is used re victory over Satan and Babylon (Rev. 12:10; 19:1). **b. Deliverance, liberation.** Zacharias speaks of a horn of salvation in the house of David (Luke 1:69), that they should be saved (lit.: a salvation) from their enemies (v. 71). God would deliver Joseph's brothers (lit.: give them salvation) by Joseph (Acts 7:25). Other ref.: 1 Thes. 5:8. **2.** (*sōtērion*; from *sōter*: savior, liberator) **See a. in 1.** Salvation is of God (Luke 2:30; 3:6). It is offered to Gentiles (Acts 28:28). Christians have a helmet of salvation (Eph. 6:17: *sōtērion*; 1 Thes. 5:8: *sōtēria*). ¶ **3.** (that brings salvation: *sōtērios*; from *sōter*: savior, liberator) **Which saves; see a. in 1.** God's grace that brings salvation has appeared to all men (Titus 2:11). ¶

SAMARIA (*Samareia*: watch-post, in Heb.) **Region of central Israel.** Going south up to Jerusalem, Jesus went through its midst (Luke 17:11); going north to Galilee He passed through it (John 4:4, 5, 7). The disciples were to be Jesus' witnesses there (Acts 1:8); persecuted Christians were scattered there (8:1); Philip preached Christ there (v. 5); Simon the magician beguiled that nation (v. 9); Samaria received God's word (v. 14); then the early church there had peace (9:31). Paul and Barnabas passed through it, going to Jerusalem (Acts 15:3). ¶

SAMARITAN (*Samaritēs*; *Samaritis* in John 4:9) **Inhabitant of the district of Samaria, in central Israel.** They were not of pure Jewish race; they practiced a mixed religion (see 2 Kgs. 17:24–41). At first, Jesus did not send the apostles to preach in their cities (Matt. 10:5). Later He sent messengers to one of their villages (Luke 9:52). The parable of the "Good Samaritan" (Luke 10:33; see vv. 30–37) illustrates God's mercy toward the sinner. Jesus asked to drink of a Samaritan (*Samaritis*) woman (John 4:9). Many Samaritans believed on Jesus because of her word; He stayed there with them for two days (John 4:39, 40). Jews called Jesus a Samaritan in disrespect (John 8:48). A Samaritan, one of ten lepers healed by Jesus, returned to thank Him (Luke 17:16). Peter and John preached the gospel in many of their villages (Acts 8:25). ❡

SAMOS (*Samos*: height) **Island of the Aegean Sea southwest of Asia Minor, near Ephesus.** Paul sailed over to it (Acts 20:15). ❡

SAMOTHRACE (*Samothrakē*: height of Thrace) **Island in the northeast part of the Aegean Sea.** Paul sailed to it (Acts 16:11). ❡

SAMSON (*Sampsōn*: like the sun, in Heb.) **One of the judges of the O.T.** He delivered Israel from the Philistines (see Judges 13–16). According to his Nazirite vow, he was not to cut his hair, the secret of his great strength. He is cited among O.T. men of faith (Heb. 11:32). ❡

SAMUEL (*Samouēl*: heard of God, God has answered, in Heb.) **One of the major prophets of the O.T.** He was the first prophet (Acts 3:24) to replace judges in Israel at beginning of kingship (13:20). He is cited among O.T. men of faith (Heb. 11:32). ❡

SANCTUARY (*hagion*; from *hagios*: holy, which is from *hagos*: religious respect, reverence toward God; same root as *hagnos*: pure) **Dwelling place of God on the earth in the O.T.** The first covenant had an earthly sanctuary, i.e., a tabernacle in the wilderness (Heb. 9:1; see Ex. 25–31), picturing the heavenly sanctuary into which Jesus, the high priest, has entered (see Heb. 9:24). Heb. 9 describes the sanctuary (*hagion*) in the wilderness as a whole (v. 1), the outer part (*hagion*), i.e., the court with its contents (v. 2), and the inner part, i.e., the

Holy of Holies (Holiest of all, Most Holy Place) (*hagia hagiōn*) (v. 3). Christians have boldness to enter the Holy of Holies (the Holiest) (*hagion*) by the blood of Jesus (Heb. 10:19), who is Minister of the sanctuary (8:2). Other refs.: Heb. 9:8, 12, 24, 25; 13:11. ¶

SANHEDRIN (*sunedrion*; from *sun*: together, and *hezomai*: to sit; *hedra* is a seat, and *sunedros* is a member of an assembly) **Supreme judicial council of the Jewish nation, situated in Jerusalem; also transl.: council, court, supreme court.** It was composed of seventy members: chosen chief priests and elders of the Jews; the high priest presided over it (Matt. 5:22; 10:17; 26:59; Mark 13:9; 14:55; 15:1; Luke 22:66; John 11:47; Acts 4:15; 5:21, 27, 34, 41; 6:12, 15; 22:30; 23:1, 6, 15, 20, 28; 24:20). It was not authorized to impose the death penalty, which was the Roman governor's prerogative (see John 18:31). Originally, Moses chose seventy men, elders of Israel, to assist in judicial matters (see Num. 11:16). ¶

SAPPHIRA (*Sapphira*: beautiful, in Aram.) **Woman of the early church.** She was Ananias' wife (Acts 5:1). Both lied to the Holy Spirit, bringing judgment of death instantly on themselves (see Acts 5:1–11). ¶

SARAH (*Sarra*: princess, in Heb.) **Wife of Abraham.** Although she was aged and sterile (Rom. 4:19), God promised she would have a son (9:9), which she believed (Heb. 11:11). She obeyed her husband (1 Pet. 3:6). ¶

SARDIS (*Sardeis*) **Principal city of Lydia in Asia Minor.** It is one of seven churches addressed (Rev. 1:11). Sardis is both reproached (Rev. 3:1) and commended (v. 4). ¶

SARDIUS 1. (*sardinos*) **Precious stone found in the region of Sardis; it is a variety of chalcedony having a red color.** The One seated on the throne appeared like a sardius stone (Rev. 4:3; *sardios* in some mss.). ¶ **2.** (*sardios*)

Precious stone of red or reddish-yellow color. Sardius adorns the new Jerusalem's sixth foundation (Rev. 21:20). Also Rev. 4:3 in some mss. ¶

SARDONYX (*sardonux*) **Precious stone, of various colors showing white or light brown stripes.** It adorns the heavenly Jerusalem's fifth foundation (Rev. 21:20). ¶

SAREPTA → ZAREPHATH

SARON → SHARON

SATAN 1. (*Satanas*: adversary, in Heb.) **The adversary of God, Christ, Christians, and humanity in general.** Satan tempted Jesus (Mark 1:13), who told him to depart (Matt. 4:10; Luke 4:8 in some mss.). If Satan casts out Satan, he is divided vs. himself (Matt. 12:26; Mark 3:23, 26; Luke 11:18). Jesus perceived Satan behind Peter's words (Matt. 16:23; Mark 8:33). Satan takes away God's word sown in certain hearts (Mark 4:15). Jesus saw him fall from Heaven (Luke 10:18); Satan bound a woman with a spirit of infirmity (Luke 13:16). He entered into Judas Iscariot (Luke 22:3; John 13:27). He wanted to sift the apostles (Luke 22:31). He filled Ananias' heart (Acts 5:3); Gentiles might turn from his power to God (Acts 26:18). God will bruise him under Christians' feet (Rom. 16:20). A sexually immoral man was to be delivered to Satan (1 Cor. 5:5). Satan might tempt spouses due to their lack of self-control (1 Cor. 7:5). Forgiving others frustrates his schemes (2 Cor. 2:11); he transforms himself into an angel of light (v. 14). He hindered Paul from going to the Thessalonians (1 Thes. 2:18). The lawless one's coming is per Satan's working (2 Thes. 2:9, 10). Two blasphemers were delivered to him (1 Tim. 1:20); some turned aside after him (5:15). Satan is mentioned re a synagogue (Rev. 2:9; 3:9), a throne where he dwells (2:13), his depths (v. 24). He is also termed the great dragon, that old serpent, the devil (Rev. 12:9); he will be bound for a thousand years (20:2), then released (v. 7), and ultimately cast into the lake of fire and brimstone (see v. 10). ¶ **2.** (*Satan*: adversary, in Heb.) **See 1.** Paul's thorn in the flesh was a messenger of Satan (2 Cor. 12:7). ¶

SAUL 1. (*Saoul*: asked, desired, in Heb.) **a. Hebrew name of the apostle Paul up to his conversion.** Jesus addressed him by this name (Acts 9:4; 22:7; 26:14), as did Ananias (9:17; 22:13). **b. First king whom God gave to His people Israel (see 1 Sam. 10:1)** This Saul reigned for forty years (Acts 13:21). ¶ **2.** (*Saulos*: asked, desired, in Heb.) **Greek name of the apostle Paul until sent forth by the Holy Spirit.** Stephen's persecutors laid their clothes at his feet (Acts 7:58), with his consent to Stephen's death (8:1). Saul ravaged the church (Acts 8:3), breathing out threats and slaughter vs. disciples (9:1), but the Lord stopped him on the road to Damascus (vv. 8, 11). He stayed with disciples at Damascus (Acts 9:19), demonstrating to Jews that Jesus was the Christ (v. 22). He learned of the Jews' plot vs. himself (Acts 9:23, 24) and went to Jerusalem (v. 26). Later, Barnabas went to Tarsus to seek him (Acts 11:25); he delivered relief from brothers in Antioch to those in Judea (v. 30). He returned from Jerusalem (Acts 12:25) to Antioch, where he was among the prophets and teachers (13:1). The Holy Spirit set him for the Lord's work (Acts 13:2). Sergius Paulus desired him to speak God's word (Acts 13:7); he withstood Elymas, the sorcerer (v. 9). ¶

SAVIOR (*Sōtēr*; from *sōzō*: to deliver, to save) **He who brings salvation, deliverance; liberator.** This word is used re God (Luke 1:47; 1 Tim. 1:1; 2:3; 4:10; Tit. 1:3; 2:10; 3:4; Jude 25). It is also used re the Lord Jesus (Luke 2:11; Acts 5:31; Phil. 3:20), who is the Savior of the world (John 4:42; 1 John 4:14), of Israel (Acts 13:23), and of the members of the church (Phil. 3:20; 2 Tim. 1:10). He is both God and Savior (Titus 2:13; 2 Pet. 1:1).

SCARLET (*kokkinos*; from *kokkos*: cochineal insect, grain, as the grain-shape of the eggs of the insect) **Bright red color obtained from the cochineal.** This word is used re a robe (Matt. 27:28), wool (Heb. 9:19), a beast (Rev. 17:3), a color (17:4; 18:12, 16). ¶

SCEVA (*Skeuas*: fitted) **Jewish high priest.** His seven sons were exorcists (Acts 19:14; see vv. 13–18). ¶

SCORPION (*skorpios*) **Animal inhabiting hot countries, bearing a venomous stinger.** The sting of the scorpion is painful and may be fatal. Refs.: Luke 10:19; 11:12; Rev. 9:3, 5, 10. ¶

SCRIBE (*grammateus*; from *gramma*: letter, written document, which is from *graphō*: to write) **The scribes studied the law and taught it to the Jewish people; also transl.: teacher of the law.** Scribes acted as jurists (see Ezra 7:6; Neh. 8:2, 13). They are often associated with Pharisees (e.g., Matt. 12:38), elders (e.g., 26:57), and chief priests (e.g., Luke 20:1) in hatred of Jesus. The Lord calls them hypocrites and blind guides (Matt. 23:13–34). This word is mainly used in the Gospels.

SCYTHIAN (*Skuthēs*) **Inhabitant of a region north of the Black Sea.** It designated a barbaric, uncultured person (Col. 3:11). ¶

SEA OF GLASS (sea: *thalassa*; of glass: *hualinos*; from *huō*: to rain, with the notion of rain's transparency) **Symbol of definitive, unchangeable purity, worthy of the glory of God.** The O.T. sea of brass (or: laver of bronze; see Ex. 30:17–21; 38:8) was used to purify priests. The N.T. sea of glass pictures the character of heavenly saints re God's judgment throne (Rev. 4:6); the sea of glass mixed with fire (15:2) relates to those overcoming the beast through the fire of martyrdom. ¶

SEAL (noun) (*sphragis*; comp. *phrassō*: to close up, to silence by authenticating) **Impressed mark, most frequently on a letter, allowing it to be stamped with a signet; the seal certifies the ownership of the document on which it is affixed.** This word is used re the righteousness of faith (Rom. 4:11), Paul's apostleship (1 Cor. 9:2), God's firm foundation (2 Tim. 2:19). The book in the right hand of the One seated on the throne had seven seals (Rev. 5:1, 2, 5, 9; 6:1, 3, 5, 7, 9, 12; 8:1). A seal is a distinct mark certifying ownership: an angel had the seal of the living God (Rev. 7:2); some did not have God's seal on their foreheads (9:4). ¶

SEAL (verb) **1.** (*sphragizō*; from *sphragis*: seal) **To affix a seal; to attest, to certify; also transl.: to make sure, to mark with a seal.** This word is used re attesting security (Matt. 27:66: sealing the stone of a tomb; Rev. 20:3: sealing the abyss over Satan), solemnly declaring (John 3:33: sealing that God is true), identifying particularly (6:27: the Son of man by the Father; Rev. 7:3: God's servants; vv. 4, 5, 8: believers from among Israel's tribes), safely delivering (Rom. 15:28; a gift of liberality as fruit), concealing the meaning (Rev. 10:4: of things uttered; 22:10: of sayings). God has sealed Christians (2 Cor. 1:22) with the Holy Spirit (Eph. 1:13: certifying that they belong to Him) for the day of redemption (4:30). Other ref.: 2 Cor. 11:10 in some mss. ¶ **2.** (*katasphragizō*; from *kata*: intens., and *sphragizō*: see **1.**) **Stronger term than the preceding one.** John saw a book sealed with seven seals (Rev. 5:1). ¶

SECT (*hairesis*; from *haireō*: to choose, to take; lit.: choice of a particular doctrine; from which: heresy) **A sect is characterized by the adherence of its members to a particular doctrine under the instigation and direction of a false teacher; also transl.: difference, division, faction, heresy, party, school of opinion.** There were sects of the Sadducees (Acts 5:17), the Pharisees (15:5; 26:5), and the Nazarenes (24:5). Heresies are a work of the flesh (Gal. 5:20). Jews called Christianity a sect (Acts 24:14; 28:22). Sects must exist among Christians to make those approved evident (1 Cor. 11:19). False teachers would introduce destructive heresies (2 Pet. 2:1). ¶

SECUNDUS (*Sekoundos*; *secundus*, in Lat.: second, happy, prosperous) **Christian Macedonian of Thessalonica.** He accompanied Paul into Asia (Acts 20:4). ¶

SELEUCIA (*Seleukeia*) **City of Syria near Antioch and port of the Mediterranean Sea.** Paul and Barnabas went there during their first missionary journey (Acts 13:4). ¶

SEM → SHEM

SEMEI → SEMEIN

SEMEIN (*Semein*: renowned, in Heb.) **Man of the O.T.** He is mentioned in the genealogy of Jesus (Luke 3:26). ¶

SERAPHIM (in Heb.: *seraph*; lit.: burning) **Angels proclaiming the holiness and glory of God.** Seraphim are mentioned only in the O.T. (Is. 6:2, 6). Comp.: **CHERUBIM.** ¶

SERGIUS PAULUS (*Sergios Paulos*) **Proconsul of Cyprus.** He called for Barnabas and Saul. He wanted to hear the word of God (Acts 13:7); he believed, astonished at the doctrine of the Lord (see vv. 8–12). ¶

SERPENT (*ophis*) **Prudent and cunning reptile, many species of which have good to excellent eyesight; also transl.: snake.** Jesus says to be prudent like serpents (Matt. 10:16). Moses lifted up the bronze serpent in the desert (John 3:14); some tempted the Lord and were destroyed by serpents (1 Cor. 10:9; see Num. 21:9). The devil is called the serpent (Rev. 12:9, 14, 15; 20:2); he, the ancient serpent, deceived Eve (2 Cor. 11:3). The word is used lit. (Matt. 7:10; Mark 16:18; Luke 10:19; 11:11) and figur. (Matt. 23:33; Rev. 9:19). ¶

SERUCH → SERUG

SERUG (*Sarouch*: branch, in Heb.) **Man of the O.T.** He is mentioned in the genealogy of Jesus (Luke 3:35). He was Abraham's ancestor (see Gen. 11:20–23). ¶

SERVANT (fem.) (*diakonos*) **One who accomplishes a service (e.g., received from the Lord).** Phoebe was a servant of the church at Cenchrea (Rom. 16:1).

SERVANT 1. (*diakonos*) **Person who accomplishes a service, with emphasis on his or her work; also transl.: attendant, deacon, minister, ministering**

servant. This word designates one who has received a service from the Lord (John 12:26; 1 Cor. 3:5; 2 Cor. 6:4; Eph. 3:7; 6:21; Phil. 1:1; Col. 1:7, 23, 25; 4:7; 1 Thes. 3:2 in some mss.; 1 Tim. 3:8, 12; 4:6). The ruler is God's servant to do good to Christians; he is God's servant to bring wrath on wrongdoers (Rom. 13:4). Christ became a servant of the circumcision (Rom. 15:8). The word is used re a person who serves another of higher rank (Matt. 20:26; 22:13; 23:11; Mark 9:35; John 2:5, 9). **2.** (*doulos*) **Slave or bondservant, i.e., a person dominated by another one through birth, purchase, conquest; household servant, with emphasis on the relationship to his master.** A servant could be one who is a slave possessed by his master (e.g., Matt. 8:9; Eph. 6:8). A believer who desires to be first should be a servant of all (Matt. 20:27; Mark 10:44). Simeon called himself the Lord's servant (Luke 2:29). Whoever commits sin is a slave of sin (John 8:34); before conversion, Christians were slaves of sin (Rom. 6:17, 20). God would pour out of His Spirit on His bondmen and bondwomen (Acts 2:18). Christ took the form of a servant (Phil. 2:7). **3.** (servant, ministering servant: *therapōn*; from which *therapeuō*: to serve, to heal) **Person who attends to service, with emphasis on the freedom of the service, dignity of the office, and personal relationship to the one served.** Moses was faithful as a ministering servant (Heb. 3:5). ¶ **4.** (hired servant: *misthios*; from *misthos*: reward, salary) **Person who works for a salary, worker; also transl.: hired man.** The prodigal remembered his father's well-fed hired servants (Luke 15:17); he intended to ask his father to treat him like a hired servant (v. 19). Other ref.: Luke 15:21 in some mss. ¶ **5.** (household servant, servant: *oiketēs*; from *oikos*: house) **Domestic, often a slave; with emphasis on the privileged place in the family household.** No servant can serve two masters (Luke 16:13). Cornelius sent two household servants to Joppa (Acts 10:7). We are not to judge another's servant (Rom. 14:4). Servants must submit to their masters (1 Pet. 2:18). ¶ **6.** (*pais*; lit.: child) **Lit.: boy, young man; with emphasis on a personal relationship with the master.** This word may designate an attendant, one who renders service, and even a slave (Matt. 8:6, 8, 13; 14:2; Luke 7:7; 12:45; 15:26). It is used re Jesus (Matt. 12:18; Acts 3:13, 26;

4:27, 30), Israel (Luke 1:54), David (Luke 1:69; Acts 4:25). **7.** (*hupēretēs*; from *hupo*: under, and *ēretēs*: rower) **Minister, attendant having a special service, emphasizing assistance to his superior.** This word is used re John Mark (Acts 13:5), Paul (26:16), Paul and Sosthenes (1 Cor. 4:1). In John 18:36, the Lord's servants are prob. angels.

SETH (*Sēth*: compensation, in Heb.) **Third son of Adam.** He is mentioned in the genealogy of Jesus (Luke 3:38). See Gen. 4:25. ¶

SEXUAL IMMORALITY (*porneia*; to commit sexual immorality: *porneuō*; from *pornos*: male prostitute, which is from *pernaō*: to sell) **Sexual relations outside the bonds of marriage; also transl.: fornication.** These words are used re committing adultery (Matt. 5:32; 19:9), birth (John 8:41), the Corinthians (1 Cor. 5:1), each man having his own wife and each woman having her own husband (1 Cor. 7:2). Sexual immorality is expressly forbidden by God (Acts 15:20, 29; 21:25; 1 Cor. 6:18; 10:8; Eph. 5:3; 1 Thes. 4:3). The term *porneia* also describes figur. worldly unbelievers (Rev. 14:8; 17:2, 4; 18:3, 9; 19:2).

SHARON (*Sarōn*: plain, in Heb.) **District of Samaria north of Joppa, near the Mediterranean Sea.** When all who lived there saw Aeneas (formerly paralyzed) healed, they turned to the Lord (Acts 9:35). ¶

SHEALTIEL (*Salathiēl*: I asked God, in Heb.) **Man of the O.T. (see 1 Chr. 3:17).** He is mentioned in the two genealogies of Jesus Christ (Matt. 1:12; Luke 3:27). ¶

SHECHEM (*Suchem*: shoulder, in Heb.) **a. Place in Canaan.** Jacob and the patriarchs were carried back there (Acts 7:16) **b. Man of the O.T.** Abraham bought a tomb from Shechem and his brothers (Acts 7:16; see also Gen. 34:1–31). ¶

SHELAH (*Sala*: sprout, in Heb.) **Man of the O.T.** He is mentioned in the genealogy of Jesus (Luke 3:35). ¶

SHEM (*Sēm*: name, renown, in Heb.) **One of Noah's sons.** He is mentioned in the genealogy of Jesus (Luke 3:36). He and his brother Japheth showed respect to their father, who became drunk after the flood; Noah blessed them (see Gen. 9:20–27). ¶

SHEPHERD (noun) **1.** (*poimēn*) **a. Person who takes care of sheep.** Refs.: Matt. 9:36; 25:32; Mark 6:34; Luke 2:8, 15, 18, 20; John 10:2. Figur., Jesus is the shepherd of the sheep, i.e., of believers (Matt. 26:31; Mark 14:27; John 10:16; 1 Pet. 2:25). He is the good Shepherd (John 10:11, 14); a hired hand is not the shepherd (v. 12). **b. One who watches out for the welfare of souls.** Jesus is the great Shepherd of the sheep (Heb. 13:20). He gave shepherds to perfectly equip the saints (Eph. 4:11). Other ref.: Jude 12 (added in some transl.). ¶ **2.** (Chief Shepherd: *Archipoimēn*; from *archē*: chief, and *poimēn*: see **1.**) **The Chief Shepherd, Jesus Christ Himself.** Elders who shepherd God's flock well will receive the crown of glory when the Chief Shepherd appears (1 Pet. 5:4). ¶

SHEPHERD (verb) (*poimainō*; from *poimēn*: shepherd) **a. In a lit. sense: to guide, guard, and otherwise take care of the flock, as well as lead it to nourishment; also transl.: to feed, to tend, to look after.** Refs.: Luke 17:7; 1 Cor. 9:7. **b. In a spiritual sense: to act as a shepherd taking care of souls, i.e., ensuring they have good food, guiding them in the right way, and taking care of those who are weak and sick; this verb also means to rule, to govern; also transl.: to feed, to tend, to look after, to rule, to be shepherd.** A leader coming out of Bethlehem would shepherd Israel (Matt. 2:6). Peter was to shepherd Jesus' sheep (John 21:16). The Holy Spirit set elders to shepherd the church of God (Acts 20:28); they are to shepherd God's flock (1 Pet. 5:2). The overcomer will shepherd the nations with a rod of iron (Rev. 2:27); the

Lamb will shepherd those coming out of the great tribulation (7:17). The Lord Jesus will shepherd the nations with a rod of iron (Rev. 12:5; 19:15). Other ref.: Jude 12. ¶

SIDON 1. (*Sidōn*: fishing, in Heb.) **Phoenician port city on the Mediterranean Sea.** Sidon is favorably contrasted to the unrepentant cities of Galilee (Matt. 11:21, 22; Luke 10:13, 14). Jesus withdrew to the region of Sidon (Matt. 15:21; Mark 7:24, 31). Many people of this region came to Him (Mark 3:8; Luke 6:17). Paul landed at Sidon (Acts 27:3). Other ref.: Luke 4:26 in some mss. ¶ **2.** (of Sidon: *Sidōnios*; see **1.**) **Region of Sidon.** Zarephath is in the land of Sidon (Luke 4:26 in some mss.). Herod was very angry with the people of Sidon (Acts 12:20). See also 1 Kgs. 16:31. ¶

SILAS (*Silas*; dimin. of Silvanus) **Christian man of Jerusalem.** The church of Jerusalem chose him to accompany Paul and Barnabas to Antioch, communicating decisions re questions of Jewish law (Acts 15:22, 27, 32; v. 34 in some mss.). He accompanied Paul to Syria, Cilicia, Thessalonica, and Berea (Acts 15:40; 17:4, 10, 14, 15). Imprisoned at Philippi, he and Paul were miraculously freed (Acts 16:19, 25, 29). He rejoined Paul at Corinth (Acts 18:5). See **SILVANUS.** ¶

SILOAM (*Silōam*: sent) **Pool of water at Jerusalem, fed by the spring of Gihon.** See 2 Chr. 32:3, 4; Neh. 3:15; Is. 8:6. A tower there fell, killing eighteen people (Luke 13:4). Jesus sent a blind man to wash himself in the pool of Siloam (John 9:7, 11). ¶

SILVANUS (*Silouanos*; from *silva*: forest, in Lat.) **Christian man of Jerusalem.** Paul, Silvanus, and Timothy preached the Son of God, Jesus Christ (2 Cor. 1:19); these three addressed the church of Thessalonica (1 Thes. 1:1; 2 Thes. 1:1). Peter wrote his first letter by Silvanus, prob. the same believer (1 Pet. 5:12). See **SILAS.** ¶

SILVER 1. (*arguros*; from *argos*: bright, shining) **Precious metal following gold in the scale of values.** This word is used by Jesus (Matt. 10:9), Paul (Acts 17:29; 1 Cor. 3:12), James (Jas. 5:3), and an angel (Rev. 18:12). ¶ **2.** (silver, of silver: *argureos*; from *arguros*: see **1.**; also spelled: *argurous*) **Which is made in silver.** Demetrius made silver temples (Acts 19:24). In a great house (i.e., Christendom), there are vessels of silver (2 Tim. 2:20). Men will not stop worshipping idols of silver (Rev. 9:20). ¶ **3.** (money, silver, silver coin, piece of silver: *argurion*; from *arguros*: see **1.**) **Coins of silver used to buy or sell.** Refs.: Matt. 25:18, 27; 26:15; 27:3, 5, 6, 9; 28:12, 15; Mark 14:11; Luke 9:3; 19:15, 23; 22:5; Acts 3:6; 7:16; 8:20; 19:19; 20:33; 1 Pet. 1:18. ¶

SIMEON (*Sumeōn*: hearing, in Heb.; see Gen. 29:33) **a. Son of Jacob and name of one of the twelve tribes descended from him.** Twelve thousand from this tribe of Simeon will be sealed (Rev. 7:7). **b. Just and devout man living at Jerusalem.** He took the child Jesus in his arms and blessed Joseph and Mary (Luke 2:25, 34). **c. Anther form of the name of Simon Peter.** Refs.: Acts 15:14; 2 Pet. 1:1. **d. Man of the O.T.** He is mentioned in the genealogy of Jesus (Luke 3:30). **e. Christian man of Antioch.** See **NIGER**. ¶

SIMON (*Simōn*: hearing, in Heb.) **a. One of the twelve apostles called Peter.** Andrew spoke to his brother Simon Peter re Jesus (John 1:41, 42) and brought him to Jesus (v. 42). Jesus saw and called him (Matt. 4:18; Mark 1:16). Simon's name is listed first among the apostles (Matt. 10:2; Mark 3:16; Luke 6:14; 22:31; John 21:2). He said that Jesus is the Christ, the Son of the living God (Matt. 16:16, 17), who has the words of eternal life (John 6:68). Jesus healed Simon's mother-in-law (Mark 1:29, 30; Luke 4:38). Simon Peter cut off Malchus' ear with his sword (John 18:10); he denied Jesus (vv. 15, 25), but Jesus restored him (21:15–17). See **PETER**. **b. Another of the twelve apostles.** Simon the Zealot, or Canaanite, was an apostle (Matt. 10:4; Mark 3:18; Luke 6:15; Acts 1:13). **c. Man of Cyrene.** This man was forced to carry Jesus' cross (Matt. 27:32; Mark 15:21; Luke 23:26). **d. Man who was a Pharisee.** This other Simon received Jesus to eat at his table (Luke 7:40, 43, 44). **e. Man who was a magician.** He believed Philip's preaching and was baptized, but offered apostles money, asking for the power to give the Holy Spirit by laying on of hands. Peter rebuked him for his iniquity (Acts 8:9, 13, 18, 24). **f. Man who was a tanner.** He received Peter in his home at Joppa for several days (Acts 9:43; 10:6, 17, 32). **g. One of the brothers of Jesus.** Refs.: Matt. 13:55; Mark 6:3. **h. Leprous man.** Jesus went to his house in Bethany (Matt. 26:6; Mark 14:3). **i. Father of Judas Iscariot.** Refs.: John 6:71; 12:4; 13:2, 26. ¶

SIN (noun) **1.** (*hamartia*; from *hamartanō*: to miss the mark, to go astray, hence: to commit a fault, to sin) **a. The principle of moral evil transmitted to all men from the disobedience of Adam; also, generic manifestation of that principle.** Sin affected the devil before the creation of man (1 John 3:8). It is characterized by insubordination to God's will and word; it leads to a lawless, unbridled walk (1 John 3:4). Sin is made binding by death, its wages (Rom. 5:12; 6:23). Before conversion, people are dead in sins (Eph. 2:1). Sending His own Son, in the likeness of flesh of sin, and for sin, God condemned sin in the flesh (Rom. 8:3). Christ died for our sins (1 Cor. 15:3); He did no sin (1 Pet. 2:22); He knew no sin (2 Cor. 5:21); there is no sin in Him (1 John 3:5). The word is found more than forty times in Romans alone. **b. Offence constituted by disobeying the will and the word of God.** Paul asks if he had committed sin in humbling himself (2 Cor. 11:7). **2.** (*hamartēma*; from *hamartan*: see **1.**) **Act of disobedience to the will of God.** Refs.: Mark 3:28; 4:12; Rom. 3:25; 1 Cor. 6:18. ¶ **3.** (who is without sin: *anamartētos*; from *a*: neg., and *hamartanō*: see **1.**) **Person who has never committed sin, who is without fault.** An accuser without sin might throw the first stone at the adulteress (John 8:7). ¶

SIN (verb) **1.** (*hamartanō*; lit.: to miss the mark) **To disobey the will of God, thus offending Him by such transgression.** A brother might sin against us (Matt. 18:15; Luke 17:3, 4). Judas sinned by betraying Jesus (Matt. 27:4). Jesus told a healed man (John 5:14) and an adulteress (8:11) to sin no more. The prodigal sinned vs. heaven and before his father (Luke 15:18, 21). All who sinned without law will perish without law; all who sinned under law will be judged by the law (Rom. 2:12). All have sinned and come short of the glory of God (Rom. 3:23; 5:12). He who commits sexual immorality sins vs. his own body (1 Cor. 6:18); one who sins vs. the brothers, sins vs. Christ (8:12). "Be angry and do not sin" (Eph. 4:26). God did not spare the angels who sinned (2 Pet. 2:4). If anyone sin, we have an advocate with the Father, Jesus Christ (1 John 2:1). From the beginning the devil sins (1 John 3:8); everyone begotten of God cannot practice sin and does not practice sin (v. 9; 5:18), i.e., his new nature is incapable of sinning. **2.** (to sin before, earlier, in the past, already: *proamartanō*; from *pro*: before, and *hamartanō*: see **1.**) **To sin previously, in the past.** Many sinned before (2 Cor. 12:21; 13:2). ¶

SIN TO DEATH (*hamartia pros thanaton*; sin: *hamartia*; death: *thanatos*) **Very serious sin committed by a believer in particular conditions intensifying his responsibility.** This serious sin (1 John 5:16) prompts God's extreme discipline, removing a believer from earth by death; it contrasts with a sin not leading to death (v. 17). Examples of sin leading to death: Ananias and Sapphira lied to the Holy Spirit (see Acts 5:1–11), believers at Corinth took part in the Lord's Supper unworthily (see 1 Cor. 11:30). Such divine punishment does not affect the believer's salvation by grace; it is related to God's government, reproving a public dishonor.

SINAI (*Sina*) **Mountain in Arabia, where Moses received the law of God (see Ex. 19:20).** The covenant of Mount Sinai inaugurated the dispensation of the law for Israel, God's earthly people. An angel (the Lord Himself) appeared in the wilderness of Mount Sinai (Acts 7:30, 38). Sinai contrasts with Jerusalem above, representing the covenant of grace (Gal. 4:24, 25; see v. 26). ¶

SINNER 1. (*hamartōlos*; from *hamartanō*: to miss the mark, to go astray, hence: to commit a fault) **One who possesses the sinful nature and commits sins; this is the natural state of every man and woman.** Jesus ate with publicly known sinners; He came to call sinners to repentance (Matt. 9:10, 11, 13;

Mark 2:15–17; Luke 5:30, 32; 15:2). People reproached Him for being a friend of sinners (Matt. 11:19; Luke 7:34) and said He Himself was a sinner (John 9:24, 25). He was betrayed into sinners' hands (Matt. 26:45; Mark 14:41; Luke 24:7). There is joy in heaven for one repenting sinner (Luke 15:7, 10). A sinner could not perform the signs done by Jesus (John 9:16). Sometimes the word is used synonymously re Gentiles (Rom. 3:7; Gal. 2:15). While we were still sinners, Christ died for us (Rom. 5:8); by Adam's disobedience, men were constituted sinners (v. 19). The Lord was set apart from sinners (Heb. 7:26) re His nature, exempt from sin and incapable of sinning. He came into the world to save sinners (1 Tim. 1:15). **2.** (*opheiletēs*; from *opheilō*: to owe) **One who owes something, one who is guilty.** Eighteen killed by a fallen tower in Siloam were not worse sinners than others in Jerusalem (Luke 13:4).

SION → ZION

SKULL (*Kranion*; comp. *kara*: head) **Rock near Jerusalem having the form of a skull; in Aram.: *Golgotha*; in Lat.: *Cranium*.** Jesus was crucified at Golgotha: the Place of the Skull (Matt. 27:33; Mark 15:22; Luke 23:33; John 19:17). ¶

SMYRNA 1. (*Smurna*: myrrh) **City of western Asia Minor, north of Ephesus.** It was one of seven churches in Asia (Rev. 1:11; 2:8 in some mss.). ¶ **2.** (of Smyrna: *Smurnaios*; of *Smurna*: see **1.**) **Which is of Smyrna.** The Lord addresses this church (Rev. 2:8 in some mss.), recognizing her tribulation and poverty; He warns of suffering to come (see 2:9, 10). ¶

SODOM (*Sodoma*: burning, in Heb.) **City of the plain of the Jordan River; see GOMORRAH.** Lot went out of there, escaping divine punishment (Luke 17:29; see Gen. 19:15, 16). In the Day of Judgment, the lot of Sodom will be more bearable than that of Capernaum (Matt. 11:23, 24; Luke 10:12). Jerusalem, where the Lord was crucified, is called spiritually Sodom (Rev. 11:8). Other refs.: Matt. 10:15; Rom. 9:29; 2 Pet. 2:6; Jude 7. ¶

SOLOMON (*Solomōn*: peaceful, in Heb.) **Son of David and king of Israel.** He is mentioned in the genealogy of Jesus (Matt. 1:6, 7). He was renowned for his glory (Matt. 6:29; Luke 12:27) and wisdom (Matt. 12:42; Luke 11:31). He built the temple of God (Acts 7:47), which included a porch bearing his name (John 10:23; Acts 3:11; 5:12). ¶

SON 1. (*huios*) **Person of masculine gender, considered in relation to father or mother.** This word signifies the relationship of a descendant with a parent (e.g., John 9:19, 20; Gal. 4:30). It is used to designate **a.** a male descendant (Gal. 4:30), **b.** a legitimate descendant in contrast to an illegitimate one (Heb. 12:8), **c.** descendants, without reference to gender (Rom. 9:27), **d.** friends present at a wedding (Matt. 9:15), **e.** those who enjoy certain privileges (Acts 3:25; Gal. 3:7), **f.** those who do wrong (Matt. 23:3), **g.** those who give evidence of a wicked character (Acts 13:10; Eph. 2:2) or a good character (Luke 6:35; Acts 4:36; Rom. 8:14), **h.** the destiny corresponding to a wicked character (Matt. 23:15; John 17:12; 2 Thes. 2:3) or a good character (Luke 20:36), **i.** the dignity of the relationship with God (Rom. 8:19; Gal. 3:26). (After Walter Biggar Scott.) See **SON OF GOD**. **2.** (*pais*; lit.: child) **Lit.: boy, young man.** A royal official's sick son lived (John 4:51).

SON OF DAY (*huios hēmeras*; son: *huios*; day: *hēmera*) **Christian morally characterized by the light of the word of God.** Sons of day are not of the night (1 Thes. 5:5). ¶

SON OF GOD (Son: *Huios*) **Name of the Lord Jesus.** The Lord Jesus is the Son of God (e.g., Matt. 16:16; John 1:34; Gal. 2:20; 1 John 5:12), the Son of Man (Matt. 8:20; John 3:13), the Son of the Father (1 John 1:3; 2 John 3), the Son of David (Matt. 9:27), the Son of the Most High (Mark 5:7; Luke 1:32), the Son of the Blessed (Mark 14. 61). He who has the Son of God has life; he who does not have the Son of God does not have life (1 John 5:12).

SON OF HELL (*huios geennēs*; son: *huios*; hell: *geenna*; see **HELL**) **Person who is morally characterized by the sphere of eternal torment.** The scribes and the Pharisees made a convert twice as much a son of hell as they were (Matt. 23:15). ¶

SON OF LIGHT (*huios tou phōtos*; son: *huios*; light: *phōs*) **Christian morally characterized by the light of the word of God.** The sons of this world are shrewder than the sons of light (Luke 16:8). We become sons of light by believing in Jesus, the light (John 12:36). Christians are sons of light (1 Thes. 5:5). ¶

SON OF PERDITION (*huios tēs apōleias*; son: *huios*; perdition: *apōleia*; from *apollumi*: to completely destroy, which is from *apo*: intens., and *ollumi*: to destroy) **One who is doomed to eternal perdition.** This expr. is used re Judas, the apostle who betrayed Jesus (John 17:12). It is a syn. for the man of lawlessness (2 Thes. 2:3). ¶

SON OF THE BRIDECHAMBER (*huios tou numphōnos*; son: *huios*; bridechamber: *numphōn*; from *numphē*: bride) **Companion of him who is getting married; also transl.: friend, attendant, guest of the bridegroom, child of the bridechamber.** This expr. is used re the disciples (Matt. 9:15; Mark 2:19; Luke 5:34) in relation to Jesus, who is figur. the bridegroom. ¶

SON OF THIS AGE, SON OF THIS WORLD (*huios tou aiōnos*; son: *huios*; age, world: *aiōn*) **Person who belongs to this world and is not saved.** They are contrasted with the sons of light (Luke 16:8); they marry and are given in marriage (20:34). ¶

SOPATER (*Sōpatros*: safe father) **Christian man of Berea, son of Pyrrhus.** He accompanied Paul to Asia (Acts 20:4). ¶

SORCERY 1. (*mageia*; from *magos*: wise man, magician) **Occult practice by which one pretends to produce, using supernatural means, surprising and marvelous effects.** Simon astonished Samaritans with his sorceries (Acts

8:11). ¶ **2.** (to practice sorcery, to use sorcery: *mageuō*; from *magos*: wise man, magician) **To practice magic; see defin. of 1.** Simon practiced sorcery (Acts 8:9). ¶ **3.** (*pharmakeia*; from *pharmakon*: drug (to cure or to poison), potion) **Witchcraft which calls on the use of drugs.** Sorcery is one of the works of the flesh (Gal. 5:20). In Rev. 9:21, men did not repent of their sorceries (*pharmakon* in some mss.). In Rev. 18:23, all nations were deceived by Babylon's sorcery. ¶ See also **MAGIC**.

SOSIPATER (*Sōsipatros*: preserved father) **Relative of Paul.** He sent greetings to Christians in Rome (Rom. 16:21). ¶

SOSTHENES (*Sōsthenēs*: of sound strength; *sōs*: sound, and *sthenos*: strength) **Ruler of the synagogue of Corinth.** He was beaten before Gallio's judgment seat (Acts 18:17). Associated with Paul, he addressed a letter to the Corinthians (1 Cor. 1:1). ¶

SOUL 1. (*psuchē*; from *psuchō*: to breathe, to blow) **a. One of the three components of a person, the seat of emotions; the soul and the spirit constitute the immaterial part of a human being.** The soul is the natural life in us (e.g., Acts 20:10). The word is often transl. "life" (e.g., John 10:15: Jesus laid down His life for the sheep). Spirit, body, and soul constitute the person (1 Thes. 5:23). The spirit and the soul are immaterial and invisible (e.g., Matt. 10:28). The soul is the seat of emotions and feelings (Luke 1:46) whereas the spirit is the seat of intelligence and conscience. The word is used to designate living persons (Acts 2:41, 43; Rom. 2:9; et al.) or deceased persons who live separated from their bodies (Rev. 6:9; 20:4). The spirit is the principle of life given by God to men; the soul is the life that results from it in the individual (see Gen. 2:7); the body is the material organism animated by the spirit. It is not easy to differentiate between the spirit and the soul (Heb. 4:12); they are similar in their nature and activities. **b. Person.** There were 276 souls in a ship (Acts 27:37). Eight souls were saved in the ark (1 Pet. 3:20). **2.** (joined in soul: *sumpsuchos*; from *sun*:

together, and *psuchē*: soul) **Agreeing, being in harmony; also transl.: being of one accord, being one in spirit, united in spirit.** The Philippians were to be joined in soul (Phil. 2:2). ¶

SPAIN (*Spania*) **Country of southwest Europe.** Paul proposed to go there (Rom. 15:24). ¶

SPIRIT (*pneuma*; from *pneō*: to breathe) **Immaterial part of a person where the intellectual and moral power resides; it is the principle of life in the human being.** Although the demarcation of spirit and soul is fine, God's word distinguishes them (Heb. 4:12). This invisible, immaterial part of the person leaves the body at death (Luke 8:55). Jesus committed His spirit into His Father's hands (Matt. 27:50; Luke 23:46; John 19:30). This word is used to designate God the Holy Spirit (e.g., Matt. 4:1; Luke 4:18); see **HOLY SPIRIT**. It also designates demons (e.g., Matt. 8:16) and angels (e.g., Heb. 1:14).

SPRINKLING 1. (*proschusis*; from *proscheō*: to pour upon, which is from *pros*: upon, and *chuō*: to pour) **Action of scattering a liquid (blood or water for purification), to attribute its value to a person or an object.** Moses kept the sprinkling of blood (Heb. 11:28). ¶ **2.** (*rhantismos*; from *rhantizō*: to sprinkle) **See defin. of 1.** This word is used figur. re Jesus' blood (Heb. 12:24; 1 Pet. 1:2). ¶

STACHYS (*Stachus*: ear of corn) **Christian man of Rome.** Paul sent him greetings (Rom. 16:9). ¶

STADION (*stadion*; from *histēmi*: to stand) **Measure of distance of about 600 feet (183 meters); also transl.: furlong, mile.** Emmaus was about 60 stadia (i.e., about seven miles or 11 kilometers) from Jerusalem (Luke 24:13).

STATER (*statēr*; from *histēmi*: to stand) **Piece of money worth two didrachmas.** Peter would find a stater in a fish's mouth (Matt. 17:27). ¶

STEPHANAS (*Stephanas*: crown) **Christian man of Corinth.** Paul baptized his household (1 Cor. 1:16); they were among the first converts of Achaia and devoted to serving the saints (16:15); he visited Paul, refreshing his spirit (v. 17). ¶

STEPHEN (*Stephanos*: crown) **First Christian martyr.** He was full of faith and of the Holy Spirit, of grace and power (Acts 6:5, 8). He was chosen to serve tables (Acts 6:2–6). Men from the Freedmen's Synagogue disputed with him (Acts 6:9). At his martyrdom, he saw the heavens opened and the Son of Man, the Lord Jesus, standing at God's right hand (see Acts 7:55, 56). He was stoned (Acts 7:59) and devout men carried his body to burial (8:2); then persecution arose in connection with him, scattering Christians (11:19). Approving his martyrdom, Paul kept the clothes of those who killed him (Acts 22:20). ¶

STOIC (*Stoikos*) **For the Stoic philosophers, happiness lay in virtue and in indifference regarding that which affects one's person.** Stoic philosophers disputed with Paul (Acts 17:18). ¶

STONE 1. (*lithazō*; from *lithos*: a stone) **To put a person or animal to death by throwing stones at them.** O.T. people of faith were stoned (Heb. 11:37). Jews wanted to stone Jesus (John 10:31–33; 11:8). Paul was stoned once (Acts 14:19; 2 Cor. 11:25). Other ref.: Acts 5:26. ¶ **2.** (*katalithazō*; *kata*: intens., and *lithazō*: to stone) **See defin. of 1.** Religious leaders feared the people would stone them if they denied John's prophetic authority (Luke 20:6). ¶ **3.** (*lithoboleō*; from *lithos*: a stone, and *ballō*: to throw) **See defin. of 1.** It was the method prescribed by God for putting the wicked to death (see Lev. 20:2, 27; Deut. 21:18–21; Josh. 7:25). In a parable, vinedressers (Jews) stoned the landowner's (God's) servants (prophets) (Matt. 21:35); Jerusalem stoned those sent to her (Matt. 23:37; Luke 13:34). Stephen was stoned (Acts 7:58, 59). When the law was given, any beast that touched Mount Sinai was to be stoned (Heb. 12:20; see Ex. 19:12, 13). Other refs.: Mark 12:4 in some mss.; John 8:5; Acts 14:5. ¶

STONING → STONE

STUMBLING BLOCK 1. (*proskomma*; from *proskoptō*: to trip, which is from *pros*: against, and *koptō*: to strike) **Obstacle against which one falls carelessly; that which causes harm to another and may lead to a fall.** Jesus Christ is a stone (*lithos*) of stumbling (*proskomma*) for unbelieving Jews (Rom. 9:32, 33) and the disobedient (1 Pet. 2:8). We should not put a stumbling block before our brother (Rom. 14:13) and take care that one's liberty does not become a stumbling block for the weak (1 Cor. 8:9). Other ref.: Rom. 14:20. ¶ **2.** (*proskopē*; from *proskoptō*: see **1.**) **Scandal, occasion of falling.** We should not put a stumbling block in anyone's way (2 Cor. 6:3). ¶ **3.** (*skandalon*; lit.: hook to trigger a trap) **Occasion, means of falling or stumbling for another; also transl.: obstacle, occasion of stumbling, occasion to fall, cause to fall, fall-trap, hindrance, offence, scandal, thing that causes sin, thing that offends.** This word is used figur. re unbelievers (Matt. 13:41), Satan (16:23), professing disciples (Luke 17:1). It is also used re the cross (Gal. 5:11), that which Balak put before Israel (Rev. 2:14; see Num. 25:1–3).

SUBSTITUTION This term is not found per se in the Bible, but it describes the act by which Jesus Christ, the only righteous One, took sinful man's place on the cross. He bore the sins of many (see Heb. 9:28; 1 Pet. 2:24) and died for our sins (see 1 Cor. 15:3). God made Him "sin" and condemned sin in the flesh, so that believers in Him might become God's righteousness in Him (see Rom. 8:3; 2 Cor. 5:21).

SUN OF RIGHTEOUSNESS This O.T. expr. (Mal. 4:2) characterizes the Lord Jesus Christ at His coming to judge and reign. Prophetically, the Sun of righteousness appears after the Morning Star, another figure of Christ.

SUPPER (*deipnon*) **a. Evening meal, banquet, feast.** Scribes and Pharisees loved first places at suppers (Matt. 23:6; Mark 12:39; Luke 20:46). Herod made a supper on his birthday (Mark 6:21). When making a dinner (*ariston*) or supper (*deipnon*), one should call the disadvantaged (Luke 14:12); in a parable, a man made a great supper (vv. 16, 17, 24). The family at Bethany made Jesus a supper (John 12:2). He partook of the last supper with His disciples before He suffered (John 13:2, 4; 21:20). Birds are to assemble for God's great supper (Rev. 19:17). **b. Lord's Supper.** The Lord Jesus instituted the Lord's Supper (1 Cor. 11:20) the night He was betrayed. In Israel, it was customary to break bread and drink the cup of consolation for the dead (see Jer. 16:7). Bread represents the unity of the church, Christ's body; the broken bread speaks of the body in which Jesus suffered on the cross. The cup recalls His blood, shed to purify Christians from all sins and introduce them into heavenly blessings. The Lord desires that this memorial in remembrance of Him be perpetuated until His return. Read 1 Cor. 10:14–22 and 11:20–34. Apparently, early Christians customarily broke bread on the first day of the week (see Acts 20:7). Disorderly conduct is contrary to the Lord's Supper (1 Cor. 11:21). **c. Supper of the Lamb.** Blessed are those called to the marriage supper of the Lamb (Rev. 19:9.). ¶

SUSANNA (*Sousanna*: lily) **Christian woman of the N.T.** She ministered to Jesus and His disciples (Luke 8:3). ¶

SYCAMINE TREE (*sukaminos*; from *sukon*: fig) **Black tree producing edible fruit and measuring between 20 and 30 feet (6 and 9 meters).** A sycamine tree would obey the command of faith (Luke 17:6). ¶

SYCAMORE (*sukomorea*; from *sukon*: fig) **Tall fig tree having a thick trunk and leaves which are downy on the underside; the fruit is edible; also transl.: sycamore.** Zaccheus climbed up into a sycamore to see Jesus (Luke 19:4). ¶

SYCHAR (*Suchar*; site of Shechem: shoulder, in Heb.; see Gen. 12:6; 33:18; Judg. 9:1) **City of Samaria.** Jesus came there and met a woman at Jacob's well, offering her living water (John 4:5); read vv. 1–30. ¶

SYCHEM → SHECHEM

SYCOMORE → SYCAMORE

SYNAGOGUE 1. (*sunagōgē*; from *sunagō*: to assemble, which is from *sun*: together, and *agō*: to lead) **Religious assembly of the Jews.** This word is used, e.g., in Acts 9:2; 13:14, 43; 14:1. A synagogue was identified with the place where it was convened; meetings were held mainly on the Sabbath day (Mark 1:21; Luke 4:16). Jesus, Paul, Barnabas, and Apollos preached there (e.g., Matt. 4:23; Acts 9:20; 13:5; 18:26). The expr. "synagogue of Satan" is used re religious groups under Satan's influence; such groups oppose the faithful, represented by two churches: Smyrna and Philadelphia (Rev. 2:9; 3:9). **2.** (ruler of the synagogue: *archisunagōgos*; from *archō*: to begin, to command, which is from *archē*: beginning, ruling, and *sunagōgē*: see **1.**) **Person in authority in a synagogue; also transl.: leader, chief ruler of the synagogue.** Crispus (Acts 18:8) and Sosthenes (v. 17) were rulers of a synagogue. Other refs.: Mark 5:22, 35, 36, 38; Luke 8:49; 13:14; Acts 13:15. ¶

SYNTYCHE (*Suntuchē*: fortunate) **Christian woman of Philippi.** Paul urges Euodia and Syntyche, who had both labored with him in the gospel, to be of the same mind in the Lord (Phil. 4:2, see v. 3). ¶

SYRACUSE (*Surakousai*) **Capital of Sicily, in the southeast part of the island.** Paul stayed there for three days (Acts 28:12). ¶

SYRIA (*Suria*) **Region north of Israel.** Quirinius was its governor when Jesus was born (Luke 2:2). Jesus' fame went throughout all Syria (Matt. 4:24). Paul, Barnabas, Silas, and Luke traveled there (Acts 15:23, 41; 18:18; 20:3; 21:3; Gal. 1:21). ¶

SYRIAN (*Suros*) **Inhabitant of Syria.** Naaman, the leper, was a Syrian (Luke 4:27). ¶

SYROPHOENICIAN (*Surophoinikissa*) **Phoenician woman who was a native of Phoenicia in Syria.** This name is used re the mother of a demon-possessed daughter healed by Jesus (Mark 7:26). ¶

SYRTIS (*Surtis*; from *surō*: to draw) **Region of northern Africa (coasts of Cyrenaica and Tripolitania).** Its sandbanks menaced seafarers (Acts 27:17).

T

TABERNACLE 1. (*skēnē*) **a. Term designating the tent constructed to be God's habitation in the desert among the Israelites.** Moses was to make a tabernacle per the pattern shown by God (Heb. 8:5). It consisted of a holy place (containing the showbread table, a lampstand, and the incense altar) and, on the other side of the veil, the Most Holy Place, or Holy of holies (containing the ark of the covenant). Only the high priest could enter the Most Holy Place once a year, with incense and the blood of a sacrifice: see Lev. 16. God's presence was visible upon it, in the form of the cloud by day and fire by night. In front of it was an altar for offering sacrifices and a brass laver for purifying priests. Its court was enclosed by curtains of fine linen. Other refs.: Heb. 9:1 (in some mss.), 2, 3, 6, 8, 21; 13:10 and the expr. "tabernacle of testimony": Acts 7:44, Rev. 15:5. See **SANCTUARY. b. Dwelling.** The expr. "eternal tabernacles" means "eternal dwellings" in Luke 16:9. **c. Habitation or tent of Moloch, a pagan god.** The house of Israel was guilty of having carried it (Acts 7:43). **d. Other ref.:** Acts 15:16. **e. Heavenly habitation.** Elsewhere the term corresponds to the heavenly places (Heb. 8:2; 9:11; Rev. 15:5). **2.** (*skēnōma*; from *skēnoō*: to pitch a tent, which is from *skēnos*: tent) **Tent considered as the habitation of God or as the body of the Christian.** David asked to find a tabernacle for God (Acts 7:46). Other refs.: 2 Pet. 1:13, 14. ¶ See also **TENT.**

TABERNACLES (FEAST OF) (*Skēnopēgia*; from *skēnē*: tent, habitation, and *pēgnumi*: to fix, to pitch) **Seventh and last annual feast in Israel, celebrated for seven days starting from the fifteenth day of the seventh month (our month of October), at the end of the harvest.** The Jews' Feast of Tabernacles was celebrated in the Lord's time (John 7:2; see v. 37), reminding the Jews that their fathers lived in tents after leaving Egypt, before entering the promised land. On the eighth day of this feast, there was a holy convocation before the Lord. See Lev. 23:39–44; Deut. 16:13; Zech. 14:16, 18, 19. ¶

TABITHA (*Tabitha*: gazelle, in Aram.) **Name of a woman who was a disciple.** Refs.: Acts 9:36, 40. See **DORCAS.** ¶

TALENT 1. (*talanton*; from *tlaō*: to bear; lit.: scale of a balance) **Unit of weight, also used as a denomination for money; it is estimated that the talent was worth at least one thousand dollars.** A servant owed his king the fabulous sum of 10,000 talents (Matt. 18:24). The parable of the talents (Matt. 25:15, 16, 20, 22, 24, 25, 28) illustrates abilities entrusted to the Lord's servants, for which they are accountable. ¶ **2.** (the weight of a talent, as the weight of a talent: *talantiaios*; from *talanton*: see **1.**) **Which weighs one talent.** Hail about the weight of a talent (Rev. 16:21; see 8:7) represents sudden, terrifying judgment, of heavenly origin. ¶

TALITHA KOUMI (young girl: *talitha*; lit.: the fresh (fem.); to arise: *koumi*) **Aram. words which mean "young girl" and "arise".** Jesus said to a young girl who was dead (Mark 5:41): "Talitha koumi,", which means "Young girl, arise". ¶

TAMAR (*Thamar*: palm tree, in Heb.) **Wife successively of two sons of Judah, Er and Onan.** She is one of four women, in addition to Mary, mentioned in Jesus' genealogy (Matt. 1:3). ¶

TARSUS 1. (*Tarsos*; maybe: flat basket) **Capital of Cilicia in Asia Minor.** Brothers sent Paul there after his conversion (Acts 9:30); Barnabas went there to seek him (11:25); Paul was born there (22:3). ¶ **2.** (of Tarsus: *Tarseus*) **Inhabitant of Tarsus.** Saul, later known as the apostle Paul, was a native of Tarsus (Acts 9:11); he was a Jew, of Tarsus (21:39). ¶

TEACHER 1. (*didaskalos*; from *didaskō*: to teach, to instruct, which is from *daō*: to know, to teach; *disco*, in Lat.: to learn) **Person who helps another to learn; more specifically in the N.T., one who teaches the commandments of God and the responsibilities of man; also transl.: master.** Believers in Christ should not be called teachers, for He alone is their Teacher (Matt. 23:8: *kathēgētēs* in some mss.; cf. v. 10: *kathēgētēs*). This word is used re the Lord Jesus (Matt. 8:19; Luke 6:40; John 1:38; 3:2; etc.), teachers in Israel (Luke 2:46), John the Baptist (3:12), Nicodemus (John 3:10), teachers in the church of Antioch (Acts 13:1), a Jewish teacher (Rom. 2:20), teachers of God's word in the church (1 Cor. 12:28, 29; Eph. 4:11; Jas. 3:1). Paul was appointed a teacher of the Gentiles (1 Tim. 2:7; 2 Tim. 1:11). The Hebrews should have been teachers (Heb. 5:12), i.e., advanced in the knowledge of God's word. Men will accumulate for themselves teachers to suit their own desires (2 Tim. 4:3). **2.** (teacher of good things, of what is right: *kalodidaskalos*; from *kalos*: good, and *didaskalos*: see **1.**) **Person who helps another learn good things.** Older women are to be teachers of good things (Titus 2:3). ¶ **3.** (*kathēgētēs*; from *kathēgeomai*: to lead, which is from *kata*: in front, before, and *hēgeomai*: to lead, to give direction) **Guide, conductor, instructor; in the N.T., the word also means: leader.** Refs.: Matt. 23:8 in some mss., v. 10. ¶

TEACHER OF THE LAW (*nomodidaskalos*; from *nomos*: law, and *didaskalos*: see **TEACHER 1.**) **Scribe specialized in the teaching of the law, and Scriptures in general; also transl.: doctor of the law.** Teachers of the law sat nearby when Jesus taught (Luke 5:17). Gamaliel was a teacher of the law (Acts 5:34) and some who turned aside (1 Tim. 1:7). ¶

TEMPLE 1. (*hieron*; from *hieros*: holy, sacred) **Building where worship is rendered; courts and sacred building considered as a whole.** This word is used re a place dedicated to the worship of God (e.g., Matt. 21:12) or of a pagan divinity (e.g., Diana in Acts 19:27). God's temple at Jerusalem included the Holy Place containing the table of consecrated bread, the candlestick, and the altar of incense; the Most Holy Place contained the ark covered by the mercy seat. In all ages, the temple remains the sole and unique physical house of God on earth. **2.** (*naos*; from *naiō*: to dwell) **Sanctuary itself within the precinct of the temple grounds, i.e., the holy place where the priests might enter; this holy place also includes the most holy place where the high priest alone might enter once a year.** This word is used re Jesus' body (John 2:19, 21). Christians are the holy temple of the living God (1 Cor. 3:16, 17; 2 Cor. 6:16), the temple of the Holy Spirit, who dwells in them (1 Cor. 6:19), a holy temple in the Lord (Eph. 2:21). The antichrist shall sit down in the temple of God (2 Thes. 2:4). It is also used re the dwelling of false gods (Acts 17:24; 19:24). **3.** (robber of temples: *hierosulos*; from *hieron*: temple, and *sulaō*: to spoil, to steal) **One who steals the goods of a temple, a sacrilegious person.** Paul's companions were not robbers of temples (Acts 19:37). ¶

TEMPTER (to tempt: *peirazō*; from *peira*: attempt, trial) **To examine, to test.** After Jesus fasted forty days, He was approached by the tempter (lit.: the one who tempts (Matt. 4:3), i.e.: the devil (see v. 5). Paul's work among the Thessalonians might have been rendered useless by the tempter (1 Thes. 3:5).

TERAH (*Thara*: loiterer, in Heb.; see Terah in Gen. 11:24–26, 31, 32) **Father of Abraham; also transl.: Thara.** He is mentioned in the genealogy of Jesus (Luke 3:34). He took Abraham and Lot to go to the land of Canaan. He died in Haran. ¶

TERTIUS (*Tertios*: third, in Lat.) **Christian man to whom Paul dictated his letter to the Christians of Rome.** Tertius greets them in the Lord (Rom. 16:22). ¶

TERTULLUS (*Tertullos*; dimin. of Tertius: third, in Lat.) **Roman orator.** He informed the governor Felix vs. Paul (Acts 24:1, 2). ¶

TEST (noun and verb) **1.** (test: *dokimē*; to test: *dokimazō*; from *dokimos*: approved, tested; comp. *dechomai*: to accept, to receive) **a. A test is what acts**

upon a person to demonstrate the reality of certain qualities; also transl.: proof, trial, to prove, to examine, to try. These qualities may be obedience (2 Cor. 2:9), liberality (2 Cor. 8:2), sincerity of love (v. 8), diligence (v. 22), faith (13:5), faithfulness (Phil. 2:22), hearts (1 Thes. 2:4), and personal life (1 Tim. 3:10). The Christian must test himself and thus remember the Lord (1 Cor. 11:28); he must prove his own work (Gal. 6:4), all things (1 Thes. 5:21), the spirits of the prophets (1 John 4:1), and what is acceptable to the Lord (Eph. 5:10, "find out", lit.: test, discern). Fire will test the quality of each one's works (1 Cor. 3:13) at the tribunal of Christ. **b. To try.** A man was going to test the oxen (Luke 14:19). Other refs.: Heb. 3:9; see **2.**; 1 Pet. 1:7. **2.** (to test: *peirazō*; from *peira*: experience, trial) **To tempt; to prove, to examine; also transl.: to try, to put to the test.** Pharisees and Sadducees, seeking to find fault, frequently tested Jesus (Matt. 16:1; 19:3; 22:35; Mark 8:11; 10:2; Luke 11:16; John 8:6). Israelites tried (*peirazō*) God by testing (*dokimazō*) Him in the desert (Heb. 3:9); tested, Abraham offered up Isaac (11:17). Jesus tested Philip's faith (John 6:6). Ephesus tested self-proclaimed apostles (Rev. 2:2); some in Smyrna would be tested by being thrown into prison (v. 10). **3.** (to test, to put to the test: *ekpeirazō*; from *ek*: intens., and *peirazō*: see **2.**) **To tempt, to prove.** A certain lawyer tested Jesus (Luke 10:25). Other refs.: Matt. 4:7; Luke 4:12; 1 Cor. 10:9. ¶

TETRARCH 1. (*tetrarchēs*; from *tetra*: four, and *archō*: to rule, which is from *archē*: beginning, authority, rule) **Governor of the fourth part of a country; this title also designated a governor subordinated to an ethnarch or a king.** Herod was a tetrarch (Matt. 14:1; Luke 3:19; 9:7; Acts 13:1). ¶ **2.** (to rule as tetrarch: *tetrarcheō*; from *tetrarchēs*: see **1.**) **Who rules as tetrarch.** This verb is used re Herod, Philip, and Lysanias (Luke 3:1; lit.: who rules as tetrarch). ¶

THADDAEUS (*Thaddaios*) **One of the twelve apostles of Jesus.** It was the surname of Lebbaeus, James' brother (Matt. 10:3). This is prob. Jude, author of the epistle of the same name (Mark 3:18; see Acts 1:13). ¶

THEATRE (*theatre*; from *theaomai*: to behold) **Public building used for theatrical performances, public speeches, public meetings; theatres were open air structures.** The theater at Ephesus (Acts 19:29, 31) could accommodate up to 24,500 spectators. Other ref.: 1 Cor. 4:9. ¶

THEOPHILUS (*Theophilos*: friend of God) **Man to whom Luke addresses his Gospel and the book of Acts.** He is called "most excellent" in Luke's Gospel (1:3) and simply by his name in Acts 1:1. ¶

THESSALONIAN (*Thessalonikeus*) **Inhabitant of the city of Thessalonica in Macedonia; also transl.: from Thessalonica.** Aristarchus and Secundus were Thessalonians (Acts 20:4; 27:2). Paul wrote two letters to the church of the Thessalonians (1 Thes. 1:1; 2 Thes. 1:1). ¶

THESSALONICA (*Thessalonikē*) **City in northern Greece, which was the most populous at the time of the apostle Paul; it was named in honor of Thessalonica, the sister of Alexander the Great.** It was one of the starting points for preaching the gospel in Europe (Acts 17:1, 11, 13). Philippians sent Paul a gift during his stay there (Phil. 4:16). Demas abandoned Paul and went to Thessalonica (2 Tim. 4:10). Paul wrote two letters to Christians there (see 1 Thes. 1:1; 2 Thes. 1:1). ¶

THEUDAS (*Theudas*: thanksgiving) **Israelite man.** He stirred up four hundred men, was slain, and his followers were dispersed (Acts 5:36). ¶

THOMAS (*Thōmas*: twin, in Aram.) **One of the twelve apostles of Jesus Christ.** His Greek name was Didymus or Twin (John 11:16; 20:24; 21:2). He said he was ready to die with Jesus (John 11:16) but did not understand that Jesus would suffer and die (14:5). He was not present when Jesus appeared to the other disciples on the resurrection evening; he refused to believe that Jesus was risen (John 20:24); he was present on the following first day of the week when Jesus appeared again to His disciples (v. 26); Jesus reproached him for his unbelief (v. 27); then Thomas, believing, exclaimed "My Lord and my God" (v. 28). Later he went fishing with Peter, and Jesus again manifested Himself to him and other disciples (John 21:2, see vv. 3, 4). Other refs.: Matt. 10:3; Mark 3:18; Luke 6:15; Acts 1:13. ¶

THORN 1. (thorn: *akantha*; of thorns: *akanthinos*; from *akē*: point) **Bush with sharp, pointed spines on its flexible branches; the sharp, prickly, pointed spines growing on such a bush.** Many plants in Israel have thorns. The Lord's crown of thorns was plaited with twisted thorns from a flexible bush, plentiful on hills around Jerusalem (Matt. 27:29; Mark 15:17; John 19:2). Jesus came out, wearing the crown of thorns (John 19:5): a derisive version of Roman emperors' crowns. In a parable, some seed fell among thorns (Matt. 13:7, 22; Mark 4:7, 18; Luke 8:7, 14). Neither grapes (Matt. 7:16) nor figs (Luke 6:44) are gathered from thorns. If ground bears thorns, it is rejected (Heb. 6:8). ¶ **2.** (*skolops*) **Object with a sharp point which pierces like a thorn or a stake; something that keeps troubling or irritating.** A thorn in the flesh (a painful bodily infirmity) was given to Paul (2 Cor. 12:7) so that the Lord's strength would be made perfect in weakness (see v. 8, 9) ¶

THREE INNS (*Treis Tabernai*; *taberna*, in Lat.: inn) **Name of a place south of Rome.** Brothers from Rome came there to meet Paul (Acts 28:15). ¶

THYATIRA (*Thuateira*) **City of Lydia in Asia Minor.** Lydia, a seller of purple, was of this city (Acts 16:14). The Lord addresses the church of Thyatira (Rev. 1:11), recognizing her works, love, faith, service, and patience, but reproaching her for tolerating Jezebel who calls herself a prophetess (Rev. 2:18, 24; see v. 20). ¶

TIBERIAS (*Tiberias*: from the name of Tiberius, a Roman emperor) **a. Other name of the Sea of Galilee.** Jesus went to the other side of this sea (John

6:1). Risen, He manifested Himself to disciples at this sea (John 21:1). **b. City southwest of the Sea of Tiberias.** Little boats came from there (John 6:23). ❡

TIBERIUS (*Tiberios*: which relates to the Tiber, the main river of Rome) **Second emperor of Rome, known as Tiberius Caesar.** During his reign, God's word came to John (Luke 3:1). ❡

TIMAEUS (*Timaios*: honorable, from *timē*: honor, respect) **Father of Bartimaeus.** Jesus healed his son who was blind (Mark 10:46). ❡

TIMON (*Timōn*: who honors; from *timē*: honor, respect) **Christian man of the N.T.** He was one of seven men chosen to serve in the church of Jerusalem (Acts 6:5). ❡

TIMOTHY (*Timotheos*: who honors God; from *timē*: honor, respect, and *Theos*: God) **Christian man of the N.T. to whom Paul addresses two letters.** He was a disciple with a good testimony among brothers at Lystra; he was the son of a believing Jewish woman and a Greek father (Acts 16:1). Paul took him for the ministry. Timothy remained with Silas at Berea (Acts 17:14, 15) and met Paul at Corinth (18:5). He ministered to Paul (Acts 19:22) and accompanied him to Asia (20:4). Paul associates Timothy with himself in addressing various Christian gatherings (2 Cor. 1:1; Phil. 1:1; Col. 1:1; 1 Thes. 1:1; 3:2, 6; 2 Thes. 1:1; Phm. 1). He calls him his fellow worker (Rom. 16:21) and his child in the faith (1 Cor. 4:17; 1 Tim. 1:2, 18; 2 Tim. 1:2). Timothy worked the work of the Lord, as Paul did (1 Cor. 16:10). Paul, Timothy, and Silvanus preached the Son of God among the Corinthians (2 Cor. 1:19). Paul hoped to send him to the Philippians (Phil. 2:19). He urged Timothy to keep that which had been committed to him (1 Tim. 6:20). Paul wrote two letters to Timothy (1 Tim. 1:2; 2 Tim. 1:2). Timothy was imprisoned, then released (Heb. 13:23). ❡

TITHE (noun and verb) **1.** (tenth, tenth part, tenth portion: *dekatē*; to receive tithe, to tithe, to give a tenth: *dekatoō*; from *deka*: ten) **Tenth part of an**

income; to give this part. The tithe was given to the Lord under the law; it was holy (see Lev. 27:30–32). Tithing was practiced before the law: Abraham gave a tenth part of all to Melchizedek (Heb. 7:2, 4, 6, 8, 9). ¶ **2.** (to tithe; to pay, take, give tithes; to give a tenth: *apodekatoō*; from *apo*: from, and *dekatoō*: see **1.**) **To give the tenth part of one's income.** Scribes and Pharisees tithed herbs (Matt. 23:23; Luke 11:42; other mss.: *apodekateuō*). In a parable, a Pharisee gave tithes of all he acquired (Luke 18:12). Levi's sons received tithes from the people (Heb. 7:5). ¶

TONGUE 1. (*glōssa*) **a. The organ of speech found in the mouth.** The tongue may cause much evil (Jas. 1:26; 3:5, 6, 8). Other ref.: 1 Cor. 14:9. **b. A particular language spoken by a group of people.** The Lamb redeemed saints out of every tongue (Rev. 5:9); a multitude of diverse tongues stood before the Lamb's throne (7:9; 10:11). Other refs.: Rev. 11:9; 13:7; 14:6; 17:15. **c. The gift of tongues consists in speaking another language without having learned it.** In Acts, those speaking in tongues announced God's wonderful works and were understood by listeners in their own languages (Acts 2:4, 11; 10:46; 19:6): this was predicted as a sign accompanying those who believed (Mark 16:17). Paul discusses this gift (1 Cor. 12:10, 28, 30; 13:1); the gift of tongues was to cease (13:8). Paul regulates the exercise of this gift (1 Cor. 14:2, 4-6, 13, 14, 18, 19, 21–23, 26, 27, 39). ¶ **2.** (other tongue, strange tongue: *heteroglōssos*; from *heteros*: another, and *glōssa*: see **1.**) **Different language.** The Lord would speak to Israel by people of other tongues (1 Cor. 14:21). ¶ **3.** (*dialektos*; from *dialegomai*: to deliberate by reflection or discussion) **The whole body of words in use in a particular community; also transl.: language, dialect.** The Hebrew tongue is mentioned (Acts 21:40; 22:2; 26:14). Other refs.: Acts 1:19; 2:6, 8. ¶

TOPAZ (*topazion*) **Transparent yellow precious stone.** It adorns the ninth foundation of heavenly Jerusalem's wall (Rev. 21:20). ¶

TORTURER (*basanistēs*; from *basanizō*: to agitate, to torture, which is from *basanos*: torture, interrogation) **Individual inflicting severe pains to obtain**

information, to force confession, to have a debt paid. The master delivered his wicked servant to torturers (Matt. 18:34). ¶

TRACHONITUS (*Trachōnitis*: rough or rugged; from *trachus*: rough) **Region northeast of Israel.** Philip was its tetrarch (Luke 3:1). ¶

TRAMPLE → TREAD

TRANSFIGURE (*metamorphoō*; from *meta*: indicating change, and *morphoō*: to form, which is from *morphē*: form, shape) **To transform the appearance, referring to a change which is related to the inward reality.** Jesus was transfigured before three disciples: His face shone like the sun, and His clothes became white as snow, as white as the light (Matt. 17:2; Mark 9:2). The Christian is to be "transformed" by the renewing of his mind (Rom. 12:2); he is "transformed" by contemplating the glory of the Lord (2 Cor. 3:18). ¶

TRANSFORM (*metaschēmatizō*; from *meta*: indicating change, and *schēmatizō*: to form, which is from *schēma*: figure; lit.: to transfigure) **a. To take another form, to disguise oneself, referring to a superficial, outward change which does not correspond to inner reality.** Satan transforms himself into an angel of light; false apostles and deceitful workers transform themselves as servants of righteousness (2 Cor. 11:13–15). **b. To change the form (from a transient condition).** The Lord will transform the bodies of Christians into conformity to His glorious body (Phil. 3:21). Other ref.: 1 Cor. 4:6. ¶ See also **TRANSFIGURE**.

TRANSLATION (*metathesis*; from *metatithēmi*: to transfer, which is from *meta*: prep. indicating a change, and *tithēmi*: to put) **Action of removing from one place and bringing into another.** Before his translation, Enoch had this testimony: that he pleased God (Heb. 11:5). Enoch's translation prefigures the translation of Christians who will be caught up to meet the Lord (see 1 Thes. 4:17). Other refs.: Heb. 7:12; 12:27. ¶

TREAD 1. (to tread out the grain, to tread out the corn: *aloaō*; comp. *alōē*: threshing floor) **Action of an ox trampling heads of wheat to separate the grain of wheat from its chaff; also transl.: to thresh.** The ox treading out grain was not to be muzzled (1 Cor. 9:9; 1 Tim. 5:18): it is an image of God's servant (1 Cor. 9:10). ¶ **2.** (to tread, to tread down, to tread underfoot: *pateō*; from *patos*: path) **To trample (e.g., grapes), to bring (people) into subjection.** Jerusalem would be trodden down by Gentiles (Luke 21:24), predicting its destruction in 70 A.D.; also, in the future (Rev. 11:2); treading the wine press symbolizes judgment of apostasy on earth (14:20) and destruction of enemies (19:15; see Is. 63:1–6). Other ref.: Luke 10:19. ¶ **3.** (to tread, to tread underfoot: *katapateō*; from *kata*: intens., and *pateō*: see **2.**) **a. To trample, to step on.** If salt loses its flavor, it is fit only to be trampled down (Matt. 5:13). This verb is used re that which is holy and pearls (Matt. 7:6), seed (Luke 8:5), myriads of people (Luke 12:1). **b. To despise.** One who has trodden underfoot the Son of God shall be judged worthy of a more severe punishment (Heb. 10:29). ¶

TREE 1. (*dendron*) **Tall woody plant with branches.** The axe is laid to the root of the trees; every tree that does not produce good fruit is cut down (Matt. 3:10; 7:17-19; 12:33; Luke 3:9; 6:43, 44). A grain of mustard becomes a tree (Matt. 13:32; Luke 13:19). The formerly blind man saw men like trees, walking (Mark 8:24). Branches from trees were cut down and spread on the road before Jesus (Matt. 21:8; Mark 11:8). Jesus told a parable re the fig tree (*sukē*) and all the trees (*dendron*) (Luke 21:29). Evil people are like late autumn trees without fruit (Jude 12). Other refs.: Rev. 7:1, 3; 8:7; 9:4). ¶ **2.** (*xulon*; from *xuō*: to scrape, to plane) **a. The wooden cross on which Jesus was crucified; also transl.: cross.** Everyone who hangs on a tree is cursed (Gal. 3:13). Other refs.: Acts 5:30; 10:39; 13:29; 1 Pet. 2:24. **b. Term designating Christ.** He is the "green tree", spiritually alive and unjustly condemned, in contrast to Israel, "the dry" (Luke 23:31). **c. Tree of life.** The tree of life (Rev. 2:7; 22:2, 14, 19 in some mss.) will provide eternal enjoyment of fruits of divine life, Christ being the source.

TRIBULATION (*thlipsis*; from *thlibō*: to compress, to oppress) **Physical or moral trial provoking great suffering; also transl.: affliction, distress, hardship, persecution, suffering, trial, trouble.** Believers have tribulation in the world (John 16:33). We must enter the kingdom of God with much tribulation (Acts 14:22). Paul boasted in tribulations, knowing that tribulation produces perseverance (Rom. 5:3; 12:12; 2 Cor. 6:4). God comforted Paul in all his tribulation that he might be able to comfort those who were in any tribulation (2 Cor. 1:4); Paul was exceeding joyful in all his tribulation (7:4). He did not want the Ephesians to lose heart over his tribulations for them (Eph. 3:13). The Thessalonians received God's word in much tribulation (1 Thes. 1:6). See **GREAT TRIBULATION**.

TRIBUNAL → JUDGMENT SEAT

TRIBUTE 1. (*kēnsos*; from Lat. *census*: census, counting of people) **Personal or property tax; also transl.: tax, taxes, poll-tax.** Refs.: Matt. 17:25; 22:17, 19; Mark 12:14 (*epikephalaion* in some mss.). ¶ **2.** (*phoros*; from *pherō*: to bring) **Tax imposed upon people annually; also transl.: tax, taxes.** Jews had to pay tribute to Caesar (Luke 20:22; 23:2). Christians must pay tribute to authorities (Rom. 13:6, 7). ¶

TROAS (*Trōas*) **Region of northwest Asia Minor.** Paul came there during his second missionary journey (Acts 16:8, 11) and stayed there seven days during his third journey (20:5, 6; 2 Cor. 2:12). He left a cloak there (2 Tim. 4:13). ¶

TROGYLLIUM (*Trōgullion*) **City of western Asia Minor, southwest of Ephesus.** Paul stayed there during his third missionary journey (Acts 20:15 in some mss.). ¶

TROPHIMUS (*Trophimos*: adopted child; from *trophē*: nourishment) **Christian man originally from Ephesus.** He accompanied Paul into Asia (Acts

20:4) and, at the end of this journey, to Jerusalem (21:29). Paul had to leave him sick at Miletus (2 Tim. 4:20). ¶

TRUMPET 1. (*salpinx*) **Wind instrument which produces a blasting sound; also transl.: bugle, trump.** The sound of the trumpet accompanies divine interventions. After the great tribulation, the elect shall be assembled with a great sound of trumpet (Matt. 24:31). The trumpet calling to battle should not give an unclear sound (1 Cor. 14:8); at the last trumpet (15:52), the Lord will descend with the trumpet of God (1 Thes. 4:16). Hebrew Christians had not come to the sound of a trumpet (Heb. 12:19). John heard a great voice, as of a trumpet (Rev. 1:10; 4:1). Trumpets precede divine judgments in Rev. 8:2, 6, 13; 9:14. ¶ **2.** (to sound a trumpet: *salpizō*; from *salpinx*: see **1.**) **To produce a sound with a trumpet.** Hypocrites sound a trumpet before themselves when giving to the poor (Matt. 6:2). The trumpet will sound, and the Christian dead shall be resurrected incorruptible, and the living shall be changed (1 Cor. 15:52). Seven angels sound seven trumpets to announce divine judgment (Rev. 8:6–8, 10, 12, 13; 9:1, 13; 10:7; 11:15). ¶

TRYPHAENA (*Truphaina*: refined; from *truphē*: luxury) **Christian woman of Rome; also spelled Tryphena.** Paul sends her greetings; she labored in the Lord (Rom. 16:12). Her and Tryphosa were perhaps twin sisters. ¶

TRYPHENA → TRYPHAENA

TRYPHOSA (*Truphōsa*: delicate; from *truphaō*: to be delicate) **Christian woman of Rome.** Paul sends her greetings. Her and Tryphaena labored in the Lord (Rom. 16:12). ¶

TWIN GODS (*Dioskouroi*; sons of Zeus) **Name of two demigods of the Greeks and Romans, Castor and Pollux; actually, they were both sons of Jupiter (or Zeus for the Greeks) but of different mothers according to mythology; also transl.: Castor and Pollux, Dioscuri.** Paul sailed on an

Alexandrian ship with the twin gods for its figurehead (Acts 28:11); they were supposed to protect vessels from shipwrecks. ¶

TYCHICUS (*Tuchikos*: fortuitous; close to *tunchanō*: to obtain) **Christian man of Asia.** Tychicus accompanied Paul into Asia (Acts 20:4). Paul charged this beloved brother and faithful servant in the Lord to bring his news to the Ephesians (Eph. 6:21) and to the Colossians (Col. 4:7). Paul sent him to Ephesus (2 Tim. 4:12) and proposed to send him to Titus (Titus 3:12). ¶

TYPE (*tupos*; from *tuptō*: to strike, as in using a stamp) **Figure, representation of a reality; also transl.: example, form, idol, image, pattern.** Israelites made forms of foreign gods (Acts 7:43). O.T. types have their actual correspondence in N.T. teaching (1 Cor. 10:6 and 11: *tupikōs* in some mss., i.e., serving for admonition). Adam is a type of Christ, the second man (Rom. 5:14).

TYRANNUS (*Turannos*: ruler, tyrant) **Man of Ephesus.** Paul reasoned daily in the school of Tyrannus for two years (Acts 19:9). ¶

TYRE (*Turos*: rock, in Heb.) **Port city of Phoenicia on the Mediterranean Sea, south of Sidon.** For seven days, Paul stayed there (where his ship had landed on his return from his third missionary journey) (Acts 21:3, 7). See **SIDON**.

TYRIAN (*Turios:* rock) **Inhabitant of Tyre.** Herod was very displeased with them (Acts 12:20). ¶

U

UNBELIEF (*apistia*; from *apistos*: faithless, unfaithful, which is from *a*: neg., and *pistos*: believing, faithful) **Lack of confidence, lack of faith; also transl.: little faith, littleness of faith, unfaithfulness.** The term is used re the unbelief of the Jews (Matt. 13:58), of Jesus' disciples (17:20 (other mss.: *oligopistia*: small faith); Mark 16:14), of those in Jesus' own country (Mark 6:6), of the father of a possessed child (9:24). The unbelief of those who have not believed does not nullify the faithfulness of God (Rom. 3:3); Abraham did not hesitate through unbelief (4:20). Other refs.: Rom. 11:20, 23; 1 Tim. 1:13; Heb. 3:12, 19. ¶

UNBELIEVER (*apistos*; from *a*: neg., and *pistos*: believing, faithful) **Person without faith, incredulous individual.** The lord of an unfaithful servant would appoint his portion with unbelievers (Luke 12:46).

UNBELIEVING 1. (*apistos*; from *a*: neg., and *pistos*: believing, faithful) **Who does not believe, unfaithful; also transl.: doubting, faithless, infidel, unbeliever, who is not a Christian.** The unbelieving does not trust in God and His word; thus, he has no relationship with God. Jesus used this term re His contemporaries (Matt. 17:17; Mark 9:19; Luke 9:41). He told Thomas not to be unbelieving (John 20:27). Christians are not to be unequally yoked with unbelievers (2 Cor. 6:14). The portion of the unbelieving will be in the lake of fire (Rev. 21:8). Other refs.: Luke 12:46; Acts 26:8; 1 Cor. 6:6; 7:12-15; 10:27;

14:22-24; 2 Cor. 4:4; 6:15; 1 Tim. 5:8; Titus 1:15. ¶ **2.** (to believe not: *apeitheō*; from *apeithēs*: disobedient, which is from *a*: neg., and *peithō*: to believe, to have confidence) **To not have confidence.** Unbelieving Jews stirred up Gentiles vs. the brothers (Acts 14:2). Rahab did not perish with the unbelieving (Heb. 11:31).

UNCIRCUMCISION (*akrobustia*; from *akron*: extremity, and *buō*: to cover; this word designates the foreskin) **State of a man who has not been circumcised; the word is often transl. "uncircumcised".** This term is used lit.: Acts 11:3; Rom. 2:25, 26, 27; 4:9, 10-12; 1 Cor. 7:18, 19; Gal. 5:6; 6:15; Col. 2:13; 3:11. Jews call the nations "uncircumcision" (Rom. 3:30; Eph. 2:11). The gospel of the uncircumcision was entrusted to Paul (Gal. 2:7), i.e., he was responsible for preaching the gospel to the nations. ¶

UNCTION (*chrisma*; from *chriō*: to anoint) **Preparation of oil and aromatic herbs; the word applies to the Holy Spirit; also transl.: anointing.** Christians have the unction from the Holy One (1 John 2:20); this unction abides in them and teaches them all things (v. 27). ¶

UNLEAVENED BREAD (*azumos*; from *a*: neg., and *zumē*: leaven) **Bread without yeast.** Leaven, in Scripture, is a figure of evil. Only unleavened bread, prefiguring Jesus Christ as the sinless man, might be offered to the Lord in the O.T. (see Ex. 29:2, 23–25; Num. 6:15; Jug. 6:19–21). Exceptionally, two wave-loaves baked with leaven were to be offered at Pentecost (Lev. 23:15–17), representing the church (Jews and Gentiles); see Eph. 2:11–18; Gal. 3:28. Christians, termed "unleavened", are to keep the feast with the unleavened bread of sincerity and truth (1 Cor. 5:7, 8).

URBANUS (*Ourbanos*: polite, refined, in Lat.) **Paul's fellow-worker at Rome.** Paul sends him greetings (Rom. 16:9). ¶

URIAH (*Ourias*: Jehovah is my light, in Heb.) **Man of the O.T.** His wife, Bathsheba, was Solomon's mother (Matt. 1:6). David had Uriah killed and took Bathsheba as his wife (see 2 Sam. 11:14–17; 12:9). ¶

UZZIAH (*Ozias*: might of Jehovah, in Heb.) **King of Judah, also called Azariah.** See 2 Kgs. 15:1, 2; 2 Chr. 26:1, 3. He is mentioned in Jesus' genealogy (Matt. 1:8, 9). ¶

V

VINE (*ampelos*) **Woody climbing plant producing clusters of grapes; the vine is cultivated only for its fruit.** The Lord will drink of the fruit of the vine in His Father's kingdom (Matt. 26:29; Mark 14:25; Luke 22:18). The true vine (i.e., the main stem of the vine) is an image of the Lord (John 15:1, 4, 5). A vine cannot produce figs (Jas. 3:12). The vine of the earth (Rev. 14:18, 19) represents apostates. ¶

VINE-GROWER → VINEDRESSER

VINEDRESSER (*geōrgos*; from *gē*: earth, and *ergon*: work) **Person who cultivates the soil, wine grower; also transl.: vine-grower, farmer, husbandman, tenant.** In a parable, a landowner leased his vineyard to vinedressers (Matt. 21:33–35, 38, 40, 41; Mark 12:1, 2, 7, 9; Luke 20:9, 10, 14, 16). Jesus' Father is the vinedresser (John 15:1). Other refs.: 2 Tim. 2:6; Jas. 5:7. ¶

VINEGAR (*oxos*; from *oxus*: sharp) **Sour wine used as drink in the Roman army; also transl.: sour wine, wine.** At the crucifixion, the Lord would not drink a mixture of vinegar and gall to alleviate His sufferings (Matt. 27:34); later, He received vinegar presented on a sponge (v. 48; Mark 15:36; Luke 23:36; John 19:29, 30), fulfilling Scripture (see Ps. 69:21; John 19:28). ¶

VIPER (*echidna*) **Venomous serpent.** "Brood of vipers" is an expr. used by John the Baptist re scribes, Pharisees, and the crowd (Matt. 3:7; Luke 3:7) and by Jesus re scribes and Pharisees (Matt. 12:34; 23:33). At the island of Malta, a viper fastened itself on Paul's hand (Acts 28:3; comp. Mark 16:18). ¶

VISITATION (*episkopē*; from *episkopeō*: to look after, which is from *epi*: upon, and *skopeō*: to watch, to give attention, which is from *skopos*: goal, mark) **Intervention of God, whether in grace or in judgment.** Israel did not know the time of her visitation (Luke 19:44; see 1:68, 78). On the day of God's visitation, unrepentant slanderers will acknowledge that Christians' good works were done to God's glory (1 Pet. 2:12; see Is. 26:21). Other refs.: Acts 1:20; 1 Tim. 3:1. ¶

VOW (*euchē*; from *euchomai*: to wish, to pray) **Commitment, pledge made before God to fulfill a promise.** The Nazirite vow, practiced by Israelites (see Num. 6), was a sign of separation and consecration to the Lord. Paul shaved his head in Cenchrea, for he had made a vow (Acts 18:18); four men at Jerusalem took a similar vow (21:23, see v. 24). Other ref.: Jas. 5:15. ¶

WATER POT (*hudria*; from *hudōr*: water) **Vessel to hold water, jar; also transl.: water jar, water-vessel.** Jesus said to fill six stone water pots (John 2:6, 7); after meeting Jesus, the woman at the well of Sychar left her water pot (4:28). ¶

WEAKNESS 1. (*astheneia*; from *asthenēs*: see **3.**) **Helplessness, infirmity, fragility; also transl.: bodily illness, disease, illness, physical infirmity, sickness.** Jesus healed many people of weaknesses (Luke 5:15; 8:2; 13:11, 12). The Spirit helps in the Christian's weakness (Rom. 8:26); the Lord sympathizes with such weaknesses (Heb. 4:15). Paul speaks of the weakness of the flesh (Rom. 6:19; Gal. 4:13) and of his weaknesses (2 Cor. 11:30; 12:5, 9, 10). Paul was present in weakness (1 Cor. 2:3). The Christian's body is sown in weakness but raised in power (1 Cor. 15:43). Christ was crucified in weakness (2 Cor. 13:4). The high priest was subject to weakness (Heb. 5:2); O.T. people of faith from weakness were made strong (11:34). **2.** (*asthenēma*; from *astheneō*: to be weak, to lack strength, which is from *asthenēs*: see **3.**) **Infirmity, scruple of conscience.** Strong Christians are to bear the weaknesses of the weak (Rom. 15:1). ¶ **3.** (*asthenēs*; from *a*: neg., and *sthenos*: strength, physical vigor; lit.: without strength) **Powerless, without vigor, helpless.** God's weakness is stronger than men (1 Cor. 1:25). The former commandment is set aside because of its weakness (Heb. 7:18).

WINEPRESS (*lēnos*) **Place where grapes were pressed under a turning millstone or crushed underfoot.** In a parable, a landowner dug a winepress (Matt.

21:33). Other refs.: Rev. 14:19, 20; 19:15: this winepress of God's wrath refers to the execution of God's judgment on the wicked before the millennium. ¶

WINESKIN (*askos*; comp. *skeuos*: vessel) **Container used to transport and store liquids, wine in this case; it was made of animal skin.** New wine would burst old wineskins, so it is put in new wineskins (Matt. 9:17; Mark 2:22; Luke 5:37, 38). New wine (i.e., wine of the current year) corresponds to a new order of grace, presented by the Lord, that could not be received by those who remained under the principle of the law and old religious forms. ¶

WINNOWING FAN (*ptuon*; from *ptuō*: to spit) **Sort of basket, which is flat at the front, used to toss beaten grain in the air, so that the wind may carry away the chaff and thus separate it from the kernel of wheat; possibly a shovel to throw grain against the wind; also transl.: fan, winnowing fork.** The winnowing fan is in the Lord's hand (Matt. 3:12; Luke 3:17): used figur. re the exercise of God's judgment by Christ. ¶

WINNOWING FORK → WINNOWING FAN

WISE MAN (*magos*) **Member of a caste of priests and astrologers.** This is the name given to learned men (unspecified in number or by name) of sound judgment who came from the East to worship the young Child (Matt. 2:1, 7, 16). Other refs.: Acts 13:6, 8. ¶

WOLF (*lukos*) **Wild carnivorous mammal which resembles a dog; also used figur.** False prophets are compared to ravenous wolves (Matt. 7:15); Jesus sent out His disciples as lambs in the midst of wolves (Matt. 10:16; Luke 10:3). The wolf comes to catch and scatter the sheep (John 10:12). Savage wolves, not sparing the flock, would come into the church (Acts 20:29). ¶

WORMWOOD (*apsinthos*) **Bitter aromatic plant; also: absinthe, the noxious spirit extracted from this plant.** A star named "Wormwood" fell from heaven; a third of the waters became wormwood (Rev. 8:11), suggesting bitterness (see Lam. 3:15) and unrighteousness (see Amos 5:7; 6:12) that poison the moral life of men and lead them to spiritual death: a terrible judgment of God on rebellious nations before Christ's millennial reign. ¶

WORTHLESS 1. (*adokimos*; from *a*: neg., and *dokimos*: approved, tested; comp. *dechomai*: to accept, to receive) **Set aside, rejected; also transl.: debased, depraved, disqualified, reprobate, unapproved, unfit.** God gave up godless men to a depraved mind (Rom. 1:28). Ground producing thorns and briars is worthless (Heb. 6:8), as is one professing to be Christian who is in fact lifeless (2 Cor. 13:5). The word is also used re Christian service (1 Cor. 9:27), faith (2 Cor. 13:5–7; 2 Tim. 3:8), and good works (Titus 1:16). ¶ **2.** (*achreios*; from *a*: neg., and *chreia*: necessity, utility) **Which is not useful, which is profitless.** The worthless servant was to be thrown out into outer darkness (Matt. 25:30). Other ref.: Luke 17:10. ¶

Y

YOKE 1. (*zeugos*; from *zeugnumi*: to join) **Pair.** A man bought five yokes of oxen (Luke 14:19). Other ref.: Luke 2:24. ¶ **2.** (*zugos*; from *zeugnumi*: to join) **Piece of wood used for harnessing draft animals.** The term is used figur. re subjection, constraint (1 Tim. 6:1). It is also used figur. re the Lord's authority, which is easy to bear, over the believer (Matt. 11:29, 30). O.T. law was a yoke of bondage (from which the Lord has set Christians free) for the Israelites (Acts 15:10; Gal. 5:1). Other ref. (balance): Rev. 6:5. ¶

YOKED (BE) (to be yoked, to be diversely (unequally) yoked: *heterozugeō*; from *heteros*: other, strange, and *zugos*: yoke) **To form a discordant, improper association.** Christians are not to be unequally yoked with unbelievers, e.g.: in marriage (2 Cor. 6:14). ¶

YOKEFELLOW (*suzugos*; from *suzeugnumi*: to join together, which is from *sun*: together, and *zugos*: yoke) **Collaborator, associate in the work of the Lord.** A true yokefellow of Paul is addressed, but not named (Phil. 4:3). ¶

Z

ZABULON → ZEBULUN

ZACCHEUS (*Zakchaios*: pure, in Heb.) **Man of the N.T.** He was a rich chief tax collector (Luke 19:2) who climbed up into a sycamore tree to see Jesus; Jesus told him to come down for He must stay in his house (v. 5), where Zaccheus received Jesus with joy (see v. 6). He told the Lord that he was giving half of his goods to the poor and that he would restore four times the amount if he had taken anything by false accusation (Luke 19:8). Jesus told him: "Today salvation is come to this house" (see Luke 19:9). ❡

ZACHARIAS (*Zacharias*: Jehovah remembers, in Heb.; also transl.: Zechariah) **a. Priest of the O.T.** He was stoned in the temple court (Matt. 23:35; Luke 11:51; see 2 Chr. 24:20–22). **b. Priest of the N.T.** This Zacharias was a priest of the order of Abijah (Luke 1:5) and father of John the Baptist. He saw an angel who told him that his wife would bear a son to be named John (Luke 1:12, 13). Neighbors and relatives wanted to call his son after his own name (Luke 1:59), which Zacharias opposed. He was mute until after John's birth (Luke 1:18, 21, see vv. 20, 22); having recovered speech, he was filled with the Holy Spirit and prophesied (v. 67, see v. 64). Mary, the mother of Jesus, came to visit her cousin Elizabeth, wife of Zacharias, when the women were each expecting a child (Luke 1:40). God's word came to John, son of Zacharias, in the wilderness (Luke 3:2). ❡

ZADOK (*Sadōk*: just, in Heb.) **Man of the O.T.** He is mentioned in Jesus' genealogy (Matt. 1:14). ¶

ZARA → ZERAH

ZAREPHATH (*Sarepta*: smelting house, in Heb.) **City of Phoenicia between Tyre and Sidon on the coast of the Mediterranean Sea; also transl.: Sarepta.** Elijah was sent to a widow of Zarephath during a great famine (Luke 4:26; see 1 Kgs. 17:9). ¶

ZEALOT (*Zēlōtēs*: zealous) **Member of an extremist faction of the Pharisees, very zealous for the law and tradition; surname of Simon, one of the twelve apostles.** The name Zealot is used in Luke 6:15; Acts 1:13. See **SIMON (b)**. The Zealots were Jewish militants who hated the Roman occupiers and who fought them fiercely. ¶

ZEBEDEE (*Zebedaios*: gift of Jehovah) **Father of James and John, two of the Lord's disciples.** He was a fisherman (Matt. 4:21, see v. 22; 10:2; 20:20, see v. 21; 26:37; 27:56; Mark 1:19, 20; 3:17; 10:35, see vv. 36–38; Luke 5:10; John 21:2). ¶

ZEBULUN (*Zaboulōn*: habitation, in Heb.; see Gen. 30:20) **Son of Jacob and name of one of the twelve tribes descended from him.** Capernaum is in the borders of Zebulun and Naphtali (Matt. 4:13, 15). Jesus began to preach repentance there (see Matt. 4:16, 17). Twelve thousand out of the tribe of Zebulun will be sealed (Rev. 7:8). ¶

ZELOTES → ZEALOT

ZENAS (*Zēnas*) **Jewish doctor of the law.** He was to be diligently brought on his journey (Tit. 3:13). ¶

ZERAH (*Zara*: dawn, in Heb.; Zerah or Zarah in Gen. 38:30) **Man of the O.T., son of Judah and Tamar.** He is mentioned in Jesus' genealogy, although not in the line of descent (Matt. 1:3). ¶

ZERUBBABEL (*Zorobabel*: begotten in Babylon, in Heb.) **Descendant of David; also transl.: Zorobabel.** He was governor of Judah at the return from captivity (see Ezra 2:2; Hag. 1:1; 2:21, 23) and is mentioned in Jesus' genealogies (Matt. 1:12, 13; Luke 3:27). ¶

ZEUS (*Zeus*) **Supreme divinity of the Greeks.** He is identified as Jupiter among the Romans; also transl.: Jupiter. After a lame man was healed at Lystra, the crowds called Barnabas by the name of Zeus (Acts 14:12, 13). ¶

ZION (*Siōn*: sunny, in Heb.) **One of the hills of Jerusalem (see Ps. 48:2; 78:68, 69); Zion also designated the city of Jerusalem (see 1 Kgs. 8:1).** Zion symbolizes the future messianic reign on earth (Matt. 21:5; John 12:15; Rom. 9:33; 11:26). Mount Zion represents the heavenly Jerusalem, i.e., the blessing of believers in the Lord under grace (Heb. 12:22; 1 Pet. 2:6; Rev. 14:1). ¶

ZOROBABEL → ZERUBBABEL

Bibliography

Comprehensive Dictionary of New Testament Words, E. Richard Pigeon. AMG Publishers, Chattanooga (Tennessee), USA, 2014.

Handbook of the New Testament, Walter Biggar Scott. Books for Christians, Charlotte (North Carolina), USA, reprint 1977.

Strong's Exhaustive Concordance, James Strong. Crusade Bible Publishers, Nashville (Tennessee), USA.

The Complete Word Study New Testament, Spiros Zodhiates. AMG Publishers, Chattanooga (Tennessee), USA, 1992.

Vine's Expository Dictionary of New Testament Words, W. E. Vine. Macdonald Publishing Company, McLean (Virginia), USA.

Other Works of the Author

Comprehensive Dictionary of New Testament Words. AMG Publishers, Chattanooga (Tennessee), USA, 2014.

Comprehensive Dictionary of Old Testament Words. AMG Publishers, Chattanooga (Tennessee), USA, 2016.

Dictionnaire du Nouveau Testament. Bibles et Publications Chrétiennes, Valence, France, 2008, 2024.

Dictionnaire de l'Ancien Testament. Bibles et Publications Chrétiennes, Valence France, 2022.

Le due lettere di Paolo ai Tessalonicesi – Commentario. Il Messaggero Cristiano, Valenza (AL), Italia, 2009.

Pequeño Diccionario de las Palabras del Nuevo Testamento. AMG Publishers, Chattanooga (Tennessee), USA, 2015.

Petit dictionnaire du Nouveau Testament. Bibles et Publications Chrétiennes, Valence (France), 1994.

Première Épître aux Thessaloniciens – Commentaires sur une lettre d'encouragement. Le Messager Chrétien, Gatineau (Québec), Canada, 1987.

Seconde Épître aux Thessaloniciens – Commentaires sur une lettre d'encouragement. Le Messager Chrétien, Gatineau (Québec), Canada, 1988.

Words of Encouragement While Awaiting the Lord's Return. WestBow Press, USA, 2021.